WONDER WOMAN
DESTINY CALLING

Dan DiDio Senior VP-Executive Editor
Karen Berger Editor-original series
Art Young Assistant Editor-original series
Anton Kawasaki Editor-collected edition
Robbin Brosterman Senior Art Director
Paul Levitz President & Publisher
Georg Brewer VP-Design & DC Direct Creative
Richard Bruning Senior VP-Creative Director
Patrick Caldon Executive VP-Finance & Operations
Chris Caramalis VP-Finance
John Cunningham VP-Marketing
Terri Cunningham VP-Managing Editor
Stephanie Fierman Senior VP-Sales & MArketing
Alison Gill VP-Manufacturing
Rich Johnson VP-Book Trade Sales
Hank Kanalz VP-General Manager, WildStorm
Lillian Laserson Senior VP & General Counsel
Jim Lee Editorial Director-WildStorm
Paula Lowitt Senior VP-Business & Legal Affairs
David McKillips VP-Advertising & Custom Publishing
John Nee VP-Business Development
Gregory Noveck Senior VP-Creative Affairs
Cheryl Rubin Senior VP-Brand Management
Jeff Trojan VP-Business Development, DC Direct
Bob Wayne VP-Sales

WONDER WOMAN: DESTINY CALLING

Published by DC Comics. Cover, introductiion and compilation copyright © 2006 DC Comics. All Rights Reserved.

Originally published in single magazine form in WONDER WOMAN #20-24 and WONDER WOMAN ANNUAL #1. Copyright © 1988 DC Comics. All Rights Reserved. All characters, their distinctive likenesses and related elements featured in this publication are trademarks of DC Comics. The stories, characters and incidents featured in this publication are entirely fictional. DC Comics does not read or accept unsolicited submissions of ideas, stories or artwork.

DC Comics, 1700 Broadway, New York, NY 10019
A Warner Bros. Entertainment Company
Printed in Canada
First Printing
ISBN: 1-4012-0943-2
ISBN 13: 978-1-4012-0943-8

"Who Killed Myndi Mayer?" based on an idea by Carol Flynn
Black and white reconstruction on selected pages by Dale Crain

WONDER WOMAN
DESTINY CALLING

GEORGE PÉREZ Writer & Penciller

ART ADAMS JOHN BOLTON JOSÉ LUIS GARCÍA-LÓPEZ
CURT SWAN CHRIS MARRINAN BRIAN BOLLAND Additional Pencillers

BOB McLEOD WILL BLYBERG GEORGE PÉREZ ART ADAMS
JOHN BOLTON JOSÉ LUIS GARCÍA-LÓPEZ MARK FARMER Inkers

CARL GAFFORD Colorist

JOHN COSTANZA TODD KLEIN Letterers

GEORGE PÉREZ Original Series Covers

Heroic Age Color reconstruction and enhancement

Wonder Woman created by William Moulton Marston

Over three thousand years ago, the goddess Artemis proposed to the Olympian gods that a new race of mortal human beings be created, which she would call Amazons — a female race that would set an example for the rest of humanity and promote equality between the sexes. Artemis, along with Athena, Aphrodite, Demeter and Hestia, created the Amazons from the souls of women who were killed before their time due to violence by men. The first to be reborn, Hippolyte, was designated as the queen.

The Amazons founded a city-state called Themyscira, where compassion and justice would reign. But the war god Ares found the Amazons an obstacle to his quest for absolute power, and so had a pawn taunt the demigod Heracles with false reports that Hippolyte was besmirching his reputation. Heracles tricked the Amazons into a celebratory gathering with his warriors. When the Amazons were caught off guard, Heracles and his men treacherously attacked, defeated, and enslaved them.

Hippolyte prayed to the goddesses for forgiveness. Athena appeared to her and said she would be free if she rededicated herself to her ideals. Hippolyte escaped her cell, freed the other Amazons, and led them in defeating their captors.

The goddesses decreed that Hippolyte and her Amazons do penance for failing to lead humanity to establish new ways of justice and equality. Therefore, the goddesses sent Hippolyte's Amazons to a distant island, beneath which lay a source of great evil. As long as Amazons served to keep that evil from menacing humanity, the Amazons would be immortal.

Hippolyte's Amazons established a new city-state on Paradise Island, and the Amazons renewed their sense of purpose and self-discipline as the centuries passed. Various Amazons were killed over the years in carrying out the difficult task of keeping the great evil confined underground. During all this time, the Amazons of Paradise Island had no contact with the outside world.

Hippolyte had been the only one of the Amazons who was pregnant when she was killed in her previous incarnation, and the soul of Hippolyte's unborn daughter was still waiting to be reborn. On Artemis' instructions, Hippolyte formed the image of a baby from the clay of Paradise Island. The five goddesses who were the Amazons' patrons, along with the god Hermes, endowed the unborn soul with various gifts, including super-human strength and speed and the power of flight. Then the unborn soul entered the clay form, which came to life as a real baby. The child was named Diana, after a revered warrior who had died to save the Amazon race.

After Hippolyte's daughter had grown to adulthood, the gods revealed to the Amazons that Ares had gone insane and might destroy the Earth with a terrible source of power. The gods decreed that the Amazons choose through a tournament a champion who could confront Ares in the world outside Paradise Island.

Diana asked to participate in the tournament but was forbidden to do so by Hippolyte. Nonetheless, urged on by Athena, a disguised Diana entered the contest and won. Unable to defy the gods' will, Hippolyte agreed to let Diana be the champion to be sent against Ares. Diana was given a costume bearing the standard of her deceased namesake.

Hermes transported Diana to Boston, Massachusetts, where she met a professor of classical Greek history named Julia Kapatelis, who taught her how to speak English and serves as her guide to contemporary civilization. Diana presented herself as an ambassador from Paradise Island to the rest of society, here to teach the ways of her just and peaceful civilization to a violent world.

Diana ultimately accomplished the mission for which she was sent to Man's World, defeating Ares before the god could bring about a third World War. The media dubbed her "Wonder Woman," and she became an overnight sensation — while reluctantly gaining a publicist in the eccentric and power-hungry Myndi Mayer. Myndi made the most of the public's newfound fascination for Wonder Woman, and soon Diana's image and message was everywhere. Myndi's intentions were good (even though she mostly had dollar signs in her eyes), but the over-exposure made Diana uncomfortable.

Julia and her daughter, Vanessa, took Diana into their home, but soon the Princess was summoned to face a challenge from Zeus to prove the Amazons' worth. Diana encountered obstacle after obstacle while uncovering the truth about the mysterious heroine for whom she was named — which turned out to be the mother of pilot Steve Trevor. Plus, Diana learned of the terrible evil that lies beneath Paradise Island, which her fellow Amazons were charged with keeping contained for all time.

After an adventure in Greece — where Wonder Woman faced the witch Circe for the first time — the Amazon was prepared to come back to the States, but she was shocked to discover the front page of an American newspaper that bore the headline "Star Publicist Found Slain," showing a picture of Myndi Mayer...

WHO KILLED MYNDI MAYER?

MURDERED 'STAR PUBLICIST' HAD MANY ENEMIES

TON—Police investigating the brutal death of contro-
al publicist Myndi Mayer have found no shortage of
ects among her clientele and acquaintances, according
Detectives Ed Indelicato and *(Continued on Page 2)*

photos by George Perez

Happier times: the late Myndi Mayer at a 1986 function.

ess Diana, Boston's "Wonder Woman," is escorted by her companion Julia
elis and police detectives after learning of the apparent murder of her
r publicist. The Princess was in Greece at the time.

TUESDAY 'BOARD MEETING MASSACRE' NETS MAIN SUSPECT—*Story on page 3*

A FACE OF A KILLER?

Suspects: Art Director Steve London, Secretary Christine Fenton, PR Manager Mike "Skeeter" Boyd, Art Asst. Deni Hayes.

WONDER WOMAN

CHAPTER ONE

BOSTON AT NIGHT.

THE COMBAT ZONE.

⟨ HEY, C'MON, GUYS. SLOW DOWN! I GOTTA CATCH MY BREATH! ⟩ *

⟨ KEEP RUNNIN', PUKEBRAIN! OR I'LL KILL YA MYSELF! ⟩

* Translated from Chinese.

⟨ OH YEAH? WHAT DIFFERENCE WOULD IT MAKE? ⟩

⟨ WE'RE ALL DEAD, ANYWAY! ⟩

⟨ SHUT UP! OR I SWEAR... ⟩

BLAM! BLAM! BLAM!

PTNNGG

PTNNGG

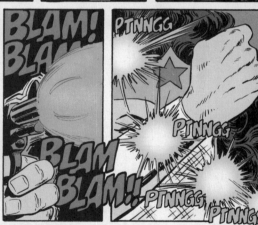

BLAM! BLAM!

BLAM BLAM!!

PTNNGG

PTNNGG

PTNNGG

PTNNGG

KRRRASHH!

7

FEEEEEYAAA!

UUHHGK!

NO! PLEASE DON'T HURT ME! I'LL TALK!

I'LL TELL YA WHATEVER Y'WANNA KNOW!

PLEASE...

WHADDYA WANT?

ANSWERS.

Tales From the Front Lines

by Edward Indelicato

Chapter 8:

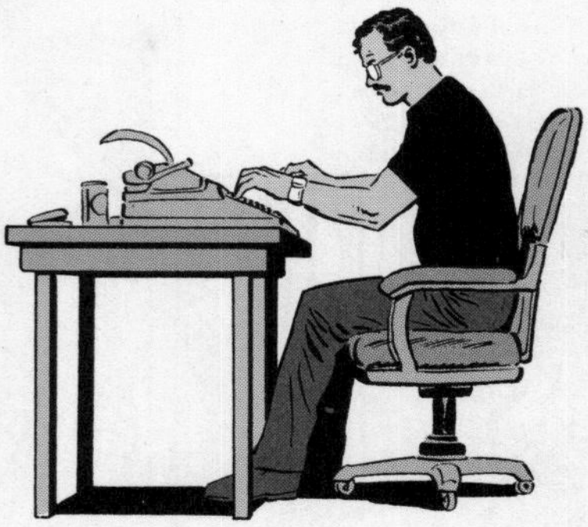

"Who Killed Myndi Mayer?"

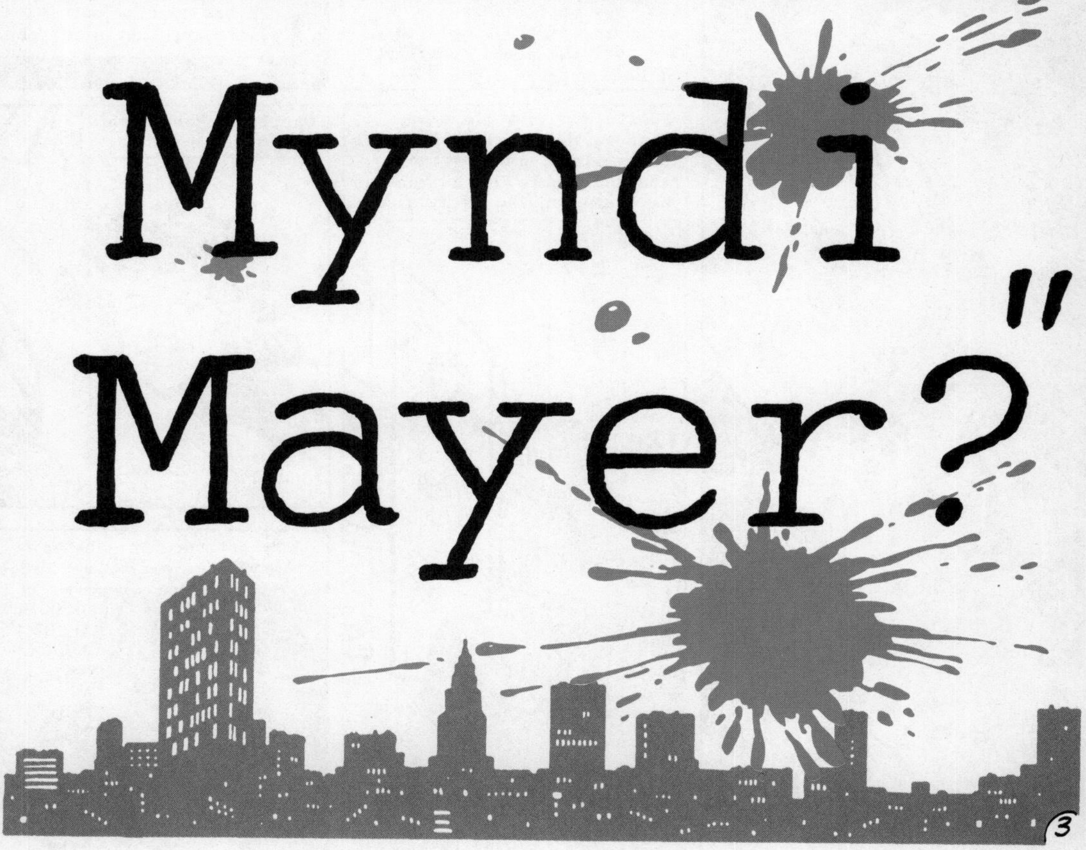

She had been dead a few hours. The cleaning lady who found her obviously knew the ropes. Nothing had been touched. When we got there, Myndi Mayer, the controversial "Publicist of the Stars," was just lying there--a shattered porcelain doll in an Evan Picone suit, the scent of fancy perfume still traceable through the smell of spilt booze and smothered cigarettes.

You could tell that the girl had class, and the money to pay for it. She had the pampered body of a showgirl. Even the coroner's tape outline flattered her.

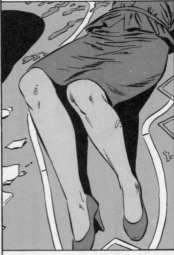

I'd seen photos of her. She was about forty but still a looker, in a plastic sort of way. Now that classy, expensive face was splattered all over the room, courtesy of some nutcase's gun.

Positioned in a place of honor on that Wall of Fame was the familiar, unforgettable face and figure of the babe in the star-spangled bathing suit.

Boston used to be such a normal city, bigger than some, smaller than some, yet with that comforting New England style of predictability.

Staring down at her were the faces of her celebrity clients, all framed and mounted on shiny pink walls. I began to wonder if one of those glossy, capped smiles could be covering the snarl of a vicious killer.

I had to find out. I'm a cop. That's my job.

Until "Wonder Woman" came into town.

My partner, Lt. Shands, snapped me out of my trance.

OKAY, GUYS. WHAT'VE WE GOT?

WELL, LIEUTENANT. LOOKS LIKE SHE DIDN'T GO WITHOUT A *FIGHT.* SHE HAD THIS BLOODY *LETTER-OPENER* IN HER HAND.

WE'RE RUNNING IT OVER TO THE LAB.

HER PURSE WAS NEXT TO THE BODY. IT'S BEEN *EMPTIED.*

ROBBERY? A LITTLE *EXTREME,* DON'T YA THINK?

I MEAN, BLOWIN' UP A GAL'S *KISSER* FOR A COUPLE OF *BUCKS?*

MAYBE THERE WAS *MORE* TO IT THAN THAT, INSPECTOR.

WE ALSO FOUND TRACES OF *WHITE POWDER* ON HER DESK.

I'VE BEEN IN THE BUSINESS LONG ENOUGH TO KNOW *COCAINE* WHEN I SEE IT.

WHAT A *SHAME.* A FINE-LOOKIN' BABE LIKE *THAT.*

A CRYIN' SHAME.

SERGEANT, WHERE'S THE CLEANING LADY WHO CALLED THIS IN?

The charwoman claimed she saw a short, stocky, bearded white man entering the building after hours. He wore a jacket with the words "Common Sense" written on the back.

She said, "He looked very upset."

After the coroner carted off the body, Lt. Shands and I paid a visit to Mayer's secretary, Christine Fenton.

When we told her about her boss' murder, she didn't even look surprised.

NO, INSPECTOR. I'M *NOT.* IT WAS ONLY A MATTER OF *TIME.*

I *WARNED* HER ABOUT HIM. BUT THEN, I'M *ONLY* HER SECRETARY.

She was as cold as a Boston winter.

But we were in for a quick thaw.

THIS SKETCH WAS MADE FROM AN EYEWITNESS' DESCRIPTION.

IS *THIS* THE MAN?

WHAT!? OH MY GOD!

YOU *RECOGNIZE* HIM?

NO... I MEAN, YES, I *RECOGNIZE* HIM. BUT IT CAN'T BE. IT *CAN'T!*

WHAT'S HIS *NAME,* MISS?

STEVE... STEVE LONDON, OUR ART DIRECTOR.

I MEAN *EX-*DIRECTOR. HE WAS *FIRED* LAST WEEK.

5

Finding Steve London was almost too easy. His wife had taken him to St. Eligius to be treated for a knife wound--or, to be precise, a letter-wound. He was still wearing the bloody jacket with the name of his rock group on it

Against his lawyer's advice, London decided to speak to us. It didn't look good for him.

ARE YOU TRYING TO TELL US YOU DON'T *REMEMBER* KILLING MYNDI MAYER?

OR EVEN GETTING *STABBED*?

YES--I MEAN... I DON'T *KNOW*.

I DON'T KNOW *WHAT* HAPPENED.

He was also stinking of beer and gin. We took him in for questioning

I WAS *DRUNK*... AND *ANGRY*.

I JUST HAD TO *TALK* TO HER.

SO YOU WENT IN, HAD YOUR TALK AND *SHOT* HER, IS *THAT* IT?

NO! I DON'T EVEN *OWN* A GUN.

WHY WOULD I KILL HER?

IT WOULDN'T GET ME MY *JOB* BACK.

At this point, he began to tell us his version of the "Tuesday Massacre." Although Miss Fenton had provided us with the official minutes of that board meeting called by Myndi Mayer, London's rendition was a lot more meaty.

"We were all called in," he said. "All the department heads.

"Myndi--Ms. Mayer was sitting in her usual seat. You could smell the liquor in her coffee cup.

"Her eyes were dark and puffy and even makeup couldn't hide that red nose of hers.

HER SKIN USED TO BE SO *SMOOTH, SO CLEAN.* WITHOUT A LINE ON IT. NOW.... SHE LOOKED SO...*BURNT OUT.*

CHRISSIE SAT AT HER LEFT.

THE *SLEAZE BAG* WAS ON HER RIGHT.

"He just sat there. Grinnin'. Like the Cheshire Cat. I could tell who was in control now. We all could tell.

"'Skeeter' La Rue. Sounds like a cartoon, doesn't it?
"Well, he wasn't a cartoon.

"He was a goddamn monster movie."

"After torturing us with silence, Ms. Mayer finally began."

OKAY, DARLINGS, WHAT THE HELL IS GOING ON!?

IN THE PAST SIX MONTHS, WE HAVE LOST SEVEN *CORPORATE* AND FIFTEEN *INDIVIDUAL* ACCOUNTS.

MY LAWYERS, BLESS 'EM, INFORM ME THAT NO LESS THAN 153 LAWSUITS HAVE BEEN FILED AGAINST US.

ONE HUNDRED AND FIFTY-THREE!

ATTEMPT TO DEFRAUD.

BREACH OF CONTRACT.

EMBEZZLEMENT.

OH, HERE'S A *GREAT* ONE: *RECKLESS ENDANGERMENT!*

SWEETHEARTS, EVERY ONE OF THESE LITTLE LOVE NOTES HAS THE NAME OF *YOURS TRULY* WRITTEN IN *BIG, OFFICIAL LETTERS.* ISN'T THAT JUST *DANDY?*

WELL, DARLINGS, *NO ONE* MAKES A *FOOL* OF MYNDI MAYER.

I DO *NOT* FORGIVE AND FORGET...

I LOP *HEADS!*

"'Finally,' I thought,'La Rue was gonna get it!' Man, was I wrong. He just kept smiling as she started to rattle off the names."

"When she read out mine, I felt the blood just rush outta my face."

"After all those years, after all we..." London's voice ebbed for a moment.

"She fired me."

THOSE LAST DAYS I WAS JUST A *ZOMBIE.*

ALTHOUGH I THINK *DENI* TOOK IT WORSE THAN *I* DID.

WHO'S DENI?

"Deni Hayes," he answered. "My ex-assistant. Nice kid, but a little high-strung. She definitely didn't like Skeeter, or Myndi.

"Last night we decided to hit the bars and get good 'n' **ripped.**"

AND, MAN, DID WE *EVER.*

IT'S ALL A *BLUR* AFTER THAT.

I JUST REMEMBER DENI SAYING... SOMETHING... ABOUT SKEETER AND MYNDI...

SOMETHING THAT MADE ME *FURIOUS...*

OH GOD! I COULDN'T HAVE!

I COULDN'T HAVE KILLED HER!

I COULDN'T...

7

CHINATOWN AT NIGHT.
TO-CHOI INDUSTRIES.
SO, YOUR HIGHNESS. I'M TOLD YOU HAVE BEEN LOOKING FOR ME.
HOW MAY I SERVE YOU?
PLEASE, MR. CHOI. I AM LOOKING FOR LA RUE.
SKEETER LA RUE.
HE WORKS FOR YOU.
DOES HE?
I KNOW OF NO SUCH PERSON IN MY EMPLOY.
YOU MUST HAVE BEEN MISINFORMED.
NO, MR. CHOI. THAT'S IMPOSSI
MAYBE HE'S NOT ON YOUR RECORDS, BUT HE HAS WORKED FOR YOU.
I MUST FIND HIM.
I'M SORRY, PRINCESS. I CANNOT HELP YOU.
NOW, IF YOU DON'T MIND, I SUGGEST YOU LEAVE MY OFFICE.
I WOULDN'T WANT TO HAVE YOU ARRESTED FOR TRESPASSING.
PLEASE, MR. CHOI. IN THE NAME OF THEMIS, I BESEECH YOU TO TELL ME WHERE SKEETER LA RUE IS.
YOU HEARD THE MAN, QUEENIE. GET YOUR SEXY LITTLE BUTT OUTTA HERE!
PLEASE...
DON'T.
8

UUGNF!!

I WARNED YOU, PRINCESS!

WE'LL SEE HOW MUCH OF A "WONDER WOMAN" YOU ARE BEHIND BARS!

PUT DOWN THE PHONE, MR. CHOI.

I ONLY WANT THE TRUTH. SINCE YOU WON'T GIVE IT VOLUNTARILY, MY MAGIC LASSO WILL COMPEL YOU TO DO SO.

PLEASE. I MUST KNOW.

WHERE IS SKEETER LA RUE?

I-IN... A SMALL WAREHOUSE... IN BEDFORD...

TH-THIS IS THE ADDRESS...

THANK YOU, MR. CHOI.

NOW, DON'T BE AFRAID... I'M NOT GOING TO HURT YOU...

...I'M JUST GOING TO PUT YOU TO SLEEP.

AS THE ORIENTAL BUSINESSMAN FALLS INTO THE ARMS OF MORPHEUS...

...THE PRINCESS OF PARADISE DIVES BACK INTO THE MOONLESS SKY. 9

The public defender finally got London to keep quiet, but the damage was already done. London had practically placed the noose around his own neck. The noose tightened around his windpipe when the shotgun was found in the building's dumpster--with his fingerprints all over it. When Ballistics confirmed it as the murder weapon, it was just the ribbon Capt. Ablamsky needed to tie up this neat little package.

Yeah, nice and neat. I've been a cop long enough to know that nothing's ever that neat.

Although Deni Hayes didn't do much to rumple the package any.

NOW, TAKE IT EASY, MISS HAYES.

WE'RE JUST LOOKING FOR SOME *ANSWERS*.

DO YOU REMEMBER GOING TO THE BAR WITH STEVE LONDON THE NIGHT OF MYNDI MAYER'S MURDER?

UH-HUH. I REMEMBER.

I NEEDED A STIFF DRINK... SO I COULD TELL STEVE... WHAT I FOUND OUT...

...ABOUT MAYER AND THE *SLEAZE BAG*.

"'Skeeter La Rue'?" I asked knowingly.

"Yeah, that's him. I guess his reputation gets around, huh?"

"What did you tell London?" the lieutenant queried.

"Nothing he wanted to hear. I told him I broke into Skeeter's office and went through his files."

"I found records of strange transactions with merchandise measured in kilos.

"A little more snooping gave me the answer."

STEVE, SKEETER IS A *DRUG DEALER!* HE PEDDLES *COCAINE!*

HE'S BEEN USING THE COMPANY'S *CLIENT LIST* TO MAKE SCORES, SUPPLYING TO A LOT OF *BIG* PEOPLE.

INCLUDING MYNDI MAYER!

DIDN'T YOU EVER *WONDER* HOW A *COUNTRY HICK* LIKE SKEETER MANAGED TO CLIMB UP THE LADDER SO *FAST?*

I-I JUST *FIGURED*... IT WAS *SEX*.

UH-UH. AIN'T NO ONE *THAT GOOD.*

THAT SLEAZE BAG'S BEEN USING *COCAINE* TO *TAKE OVER* MAYER PUBLICISTS!

10

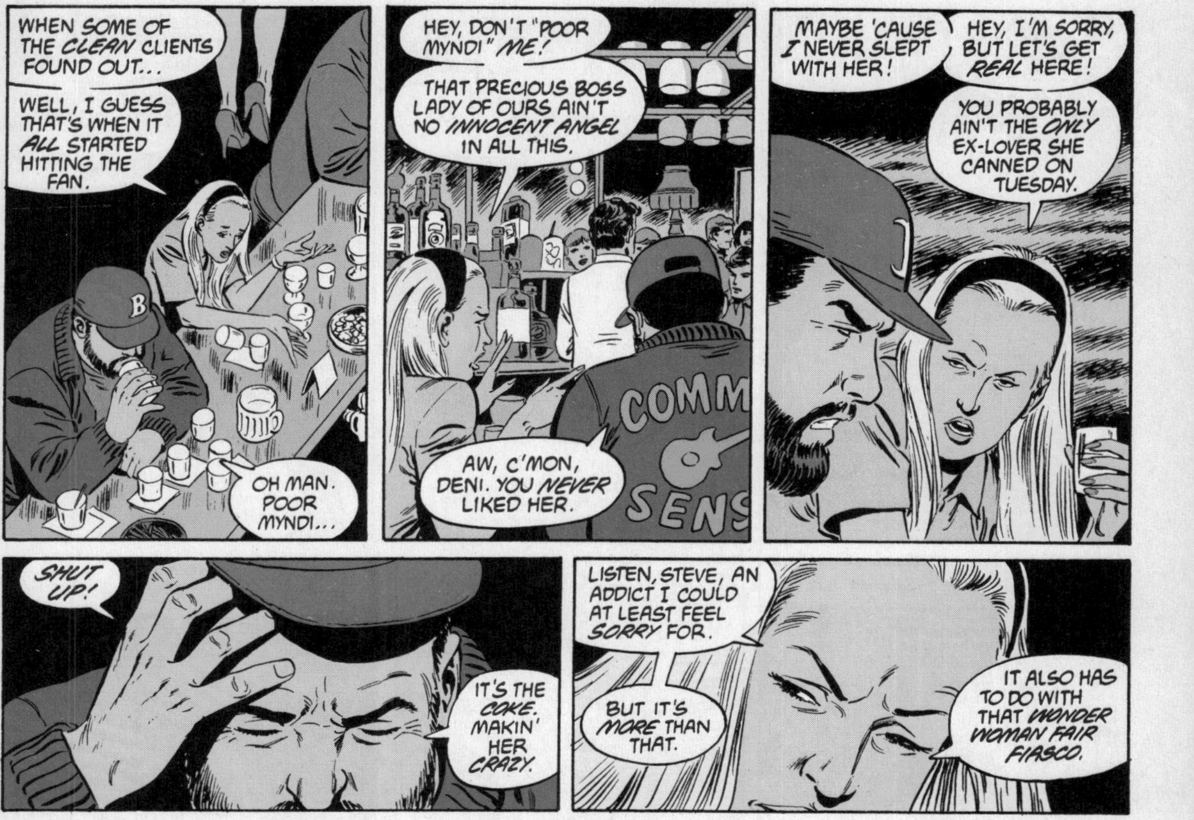
WHEN SOME OF THE CLEAN CLIENTS FOUND OUT...
WELL, I GUESS THAT'S WHEN IT ALL STARTED HITTING THE FAN.
OH MAN. POOR MYNDI...
HEY, DON'T "POOR MYNDI" ME!
THAT PRECIOUS BOSS LADY OF OURS AIN'T NO INNOCENT ANGEL IN ALL THIS.
AW, C'MON, DENI. YOU NEVER LIKED HER.
COMM
SENS
MAYBE 'CAUSE I NEVER SLEPT WITH HER!
HEY, I'M SORRY, BUT LET'S GET REAL HERE!
YOU PROBABLY AIN'T THE ONLY EX-LOVER SHE CANNED ON TUESDAY.
SHUT UP!
IT'S THE COKE. MAKIN' HER CRAZY.
LISTEN, STEVE, AN ADDICT I COULD AT LEAST FEEL SORRY FOR.
BUT IT'S MORE THAN THAT.
IT ALSO HAS TO DO WITH THAT WONDER WOMAN FAIR FIASCO.

It was a bit embarrassing to learn the facts about the Wonder Woman/Silver Swan case from a mousey little amateur. Ever since our one real lead, Solomon Buchman, escaped custody, we'd been hitting nothing but dead ends. The masked crooks we had apprehended were simply hired talent who were to keep the stolen monies as long as the Silver Swan got the specially marked sack from the cashier's office. We never did recover that sack or ever found out what it contained.

Until now, that is.

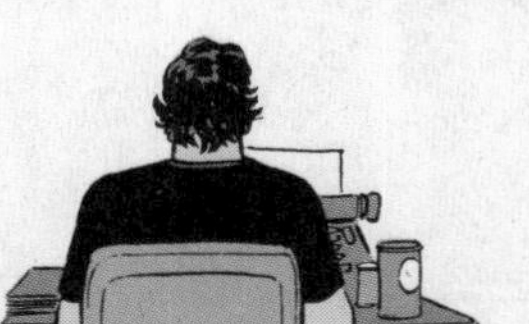

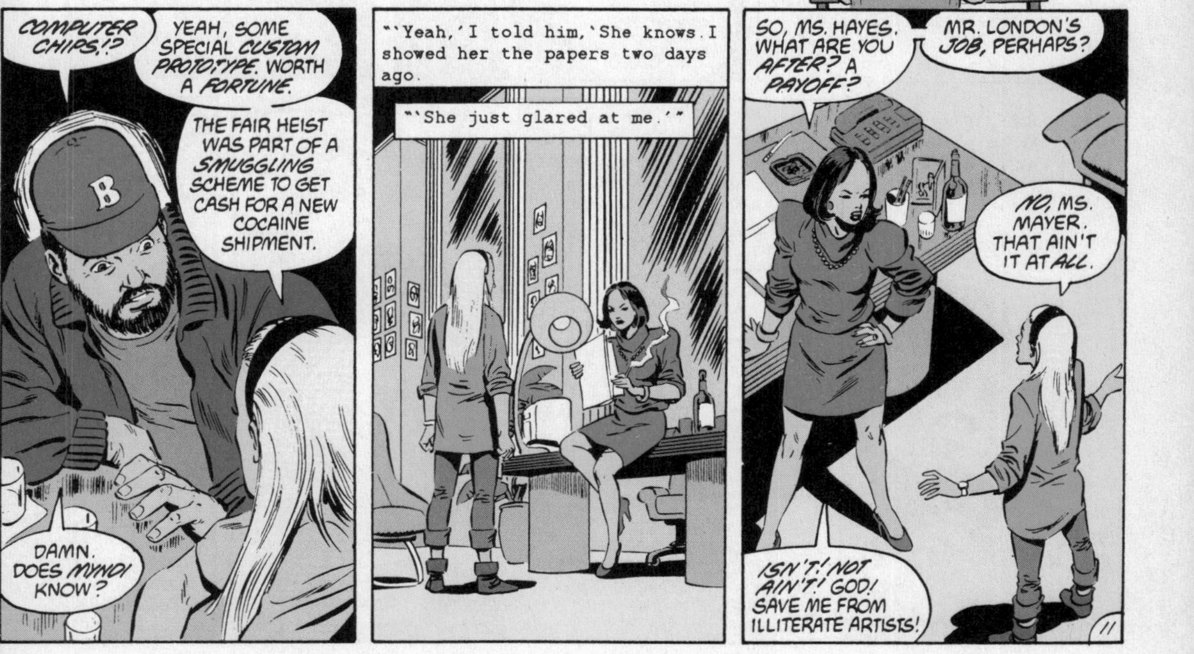
COMPUTER CHIPS!?
YEAH, SOME SPECIAL CUSTOM PROTOTYPE. WORTH A FORTUNE.
THE FAIR HEIST WAS PART OF A SMUGGLING SCHEME TO GET CASH FOR A NEW COCAINE SHIPMENT.
DAMN. DOES MYNDI KNOW?
"'Yeah,' I told him, 'She knows. I showed her the papers two days ago.
"'She just glared at me.'"
SO, MS. HAYES. WHAT ARE YOU AFTER? A PAYOFF?
MR. LONDON'S JOB, PERHAPS?
NO, MS. MAYER. THAT AIN'T IT AT ALL.
ISN'T! NOT AIN'T! GOD! SAVE ME FROM ILLITERATE ARTISTS!
11

MS. MAYER, YOU *GOTTA* GIVE STEVE HIS JOB BACK.

THESE *PAPERS.* YOU *CAN'T...*

I CAN'T *WHAT?*

LISTEN, YOU LITTLE *SIMP!* LOSING *YOUR* JOB WILL ONLY BE THE *LEAST* OF YOUR TROUBLES IF YOU *DARE* LET ANY OF THIS GET OUT!

I STILL HAVE A LOT OF *POWER* IN THIS TOWN. YOU DON'T KNOW WHAT *HELL* IS UNTIL YOU'VE MESSED WITH *ME!*

SHE SAID SHE'D GIVE YOU A *GOOD RECOMMENDATION.* FOR *OLD TIMES'* SAKE.

SHE KEPT THE FILES AND THREW ME OUT.

YOUR *PRECIOUS MYNDI* WAS *LAUGHING.*

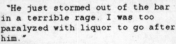

"I never saw Steve so mad.

"He just stormed out of the bar in a terrible rage. I was too paralyzed with liquor to go after him."

I DIDN'T *MEAN* TO SAY THOSE THINGS. MAYER *WASN'T* LAUGHING!

I JUST *SAID* THAT TO SNAP HIM *OUT...*

I WAS *DRUNK!* I DIDN'T MEAN...

MS. HAYES, WHERE WERE *YOU* AT THE TIME OF THE MURDER?

STILL IN THE BAR--*SICK.* I-I *THREW UP* ON THE BARTENDER.

OH DEAR GOD. WHAT HAVE I *DONE?*

What she had done was spring the trap door on the scaffold. She'd just hanged Steve London.

Capt. Ablamsky was sold, but some pieces in this jigsaw seemed to be missing. Shands and I decided to do a little computer check on the ever-popular 'Skeeter' La Rue.

MAN, THEY WERE *RIGHT.* THE GUY *IS* A SLEAZE BAG.

REAL NAME: MICHAEL BOYD. FORMER JUVENILE OFFENDER GRADUATED TO THE BIG TIME. ARMED ROBBERY, CAR THEFT, PIMPING. THE LIST GOES ON AND ON.

AND GET *THIS.* HE'S NOT EVEN *SOUTHERN.*

THAT *HICK* IS FROM *JERSEY!*

WHAT YOU *THINK, BOSS?*

I THINK HE RATES A *VISIT,* DON'T YOU?

12

INSPECTOR, SOMEONE'S HERE TO SEE YOU ABOUT THE MAYER CASE.

RECORDS AUTHORIZED PERSONNEL ONLY

I'LL HEAD OVER TO BOYD'S PLACE WHILE YOU TAKE CARE OF JOHN Q. PUBLIC.

YEAH, RIGHT. JUST BE *CAREFUL*, OKAY? TAKE SOME *BACK UP*.

YES, MOTHER.

AWRIGHT, WHAT IS IT *THIS TIME*? WITNESS, PRESS OR *CRACKPOT*?

PUT IT *THIS WAY*, INSPECTOR...

YOU'RE *NOT* GOING TO *BELIEVE* IT.

She was right.

She was a goddess, or what a goddess ought to look like. Firm, round curves packed into a tiny, tight, armor-plated American flag. Her hair was a cascade of lustrous black curls bouncing gently off her smooth, tanned shoulders down to the small of her bare, muscular back. Her eyes were shimmering blue pools that you ached to dive into. From her moist, shiny lips came a gentle, sultry voice, flavored with an accent both exotic and musical

INSPECTOR INDELICATO?

It was like hearing my name for the first time.
"Eddie," I thought, "you are definitely having the best dream of your life."

DAILY TIMES
SHOWBIZ SHOCKER
STAR PUBLICIST FOUND SLAIN
MYNDI MAYER
BODY FOUND SHOT IN BOSTON OFFICE

Unfortunately, it was time to wake up.

BEDFORD AT NIGHT.

WARNING! ELECTRICALLY CHARGED FENCE NO TRESPASSING HIGH VOLTAGE

DRAKE WAREHOUSE.

HEY, LISTEN! DID YOU *HEAR* THAT?

HEAR *WHAT*?

THERE'S *SOMEONE* IN THE WAREHOUSE!

BOYD, Y'BEEN SAYIN' THAT *ALL NIGHT.* THERE AIN'T *NOTHIN'* OUT THERE. WE *CHECKED.*

THEN CHECK IT *AGAIN.* CHOI ORDERED YOU TO *PROTECT* ME.

D-DO IT!

AWRIGHT, BOYD. BUT I SURE AIN'T GONNA BE *SAD* TO SEE YOUR CHICKEN BUTT ON THAT *PLANE* TOMORROW.

C'MON, GUYS.

AW, *MAN!* CAN'T WE EVEN FINISH THIS *HAND?*

OH HEAVENS NO! WE *MUST* PROTECT *FROSTY THE SNOWMAN!*

"HEY, I *LIKE* THAT! HOW DOES THAT SONG GO *AGAIN?*"

♪ "Frosty the snowman was a very jolly soul..."

♪ "With a corncob pipe, and a button nose..."

♪ "And two eyes made outta coal!..."

♪ "Frosty the sn...♪"

"HEY, LARRY. WHAT HAPPENED? FORGET THE REST OF IT?"

"LARRY?"

"LARRY!"

RATATATAT! PTNNGPTNNGPTNN TATATATA!! PTNNGPTNNGPTNN

RATATATAT PTNNGPTNNGPTNN TATATATAT (14)

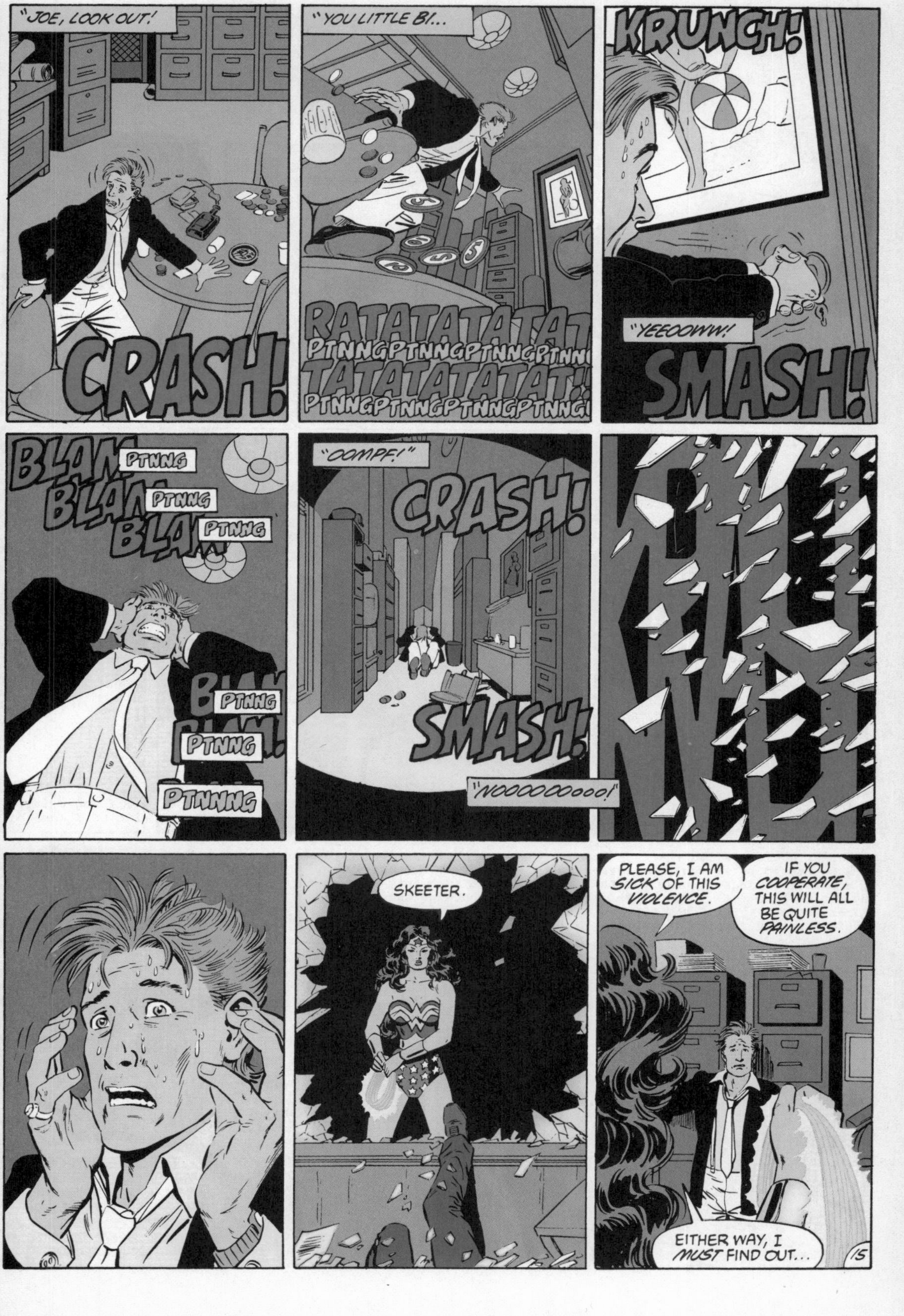
"JOE, LOOK OUT!
CRASH!
"YOU LITTLE BI...
RATATATATATAT
PTNNGPTNNGPTNNGPTNNG
TATATATATATAT!!
PTNNGPTNNGPTNNGPTNNG!
KRUNCH!
"YEEOOWW!
SMASH!
PTNNG
PTNNG
PTNNG
PTNNG
PTNNG
PTNNNG
"OOMPF!"
CRASH!
SMASH!
"NOOOOOOOOOO!"
SKEETER.
PLEASE, I AM SICK OF THIS VIOLENCE.
IF YOU COOPERATE, THIS WILL ALL BE QUITE PAINLESS.
EITHER WAY, I MUST FIND OUT...
15

WHO KILLED MYNDI MAYER?

The Princess' eyes pleaded for answers. She and her companion, Prof. Julia Kapatelis, had been in Greece at the time of the murder. Trying to maintain an air of professionalism despite my ogling, I proceeded to tell her the facts of the case. Don't know why, really. I just couldn't say "no" to her.

Her blue eyes welled up with iridescent tears, the first genuine sign of sadness over Mayer's death that I had seen so far.

Christine Fenton, on the other hand, was not as demure in her reaction.

YOU INCOMPETENT, SIMPLE-MINDED *IDIOTS!*

MYNDI MAYER MAY HAVE BEEN MANY THINGS, BUT SHE WAS *NOT* A SMUGGLER!

THAT'S AS LUDICROUS AS THE IDEA OF STEVE KILLING HER!

INSPECTOR, *YOU* DON'T BELIEVE STEVE IS GUILTY *EITHER,* DO YOU?

PRINCESS, MY *CAPTAIN* BELIEVES IT AND THE *D.A.* BELIEVES IT. BEYOND THAT, *MY* OPINION MEANS *SQUAT.*

WHAT IF PRINCESS DIANA CAN *PROVE* MR. LONDON'S INNOCENCE?

YEAH? HOW?

WITH *THIS.*

Her magic lasso. I'd read about it.

The Princess claimed that the lasso was the reforged girdle of the earth-goddess Gaea and anyone snared by it would be forced to tell the truth. Supposedly the "Fires of Hestia" (the goddess who allegedly gave her the lariat) would burn away even insanity-- and most likely alcoholic blackout--to reveal the truth, without harming the subject.
That was something I had to see.
Unfortunately, Capt. Ablamsky didn't share my driving curiosity.

ARE YOU *NUTS,!?* ARE YOU FREAKIN' *NUTS,!?*

CAP'N, LISTEN...

I *AM* LISTENING! AND A *BIGGER* CROCK OF *BULL* I *NEVER* HEARD!

NO *OFFENSE,* LADIES.

OFFENSE *TAKEN,* CAPTAIN. I DON'T APPRECIATE DIANA, *OR MYSELF,* BEING LABELED AS *CRACKPOTS.*

THE QUESTION OF A MAN'S GUILT OR INNOCENCE IS NOT SOMETHING WE *DISMISS* SO *CAVALIERLY* AS YOU SEEM TO. NO *OFFENSE.*

16

PLEASE, CAPT. ABLAMSKY. YOU *MUST* LET ME HELP.

MYNDI WAS NOT A *CLOSE* FRIEND. BUT I *CARED* FOR HER.

WHETHER SHE *WAS* OR *WASN'T* WHAT THEY *SAID* SHE WAS, SHE DID NOT *DESERVE* TO BE *MURDERED.*

NO ONE DESERVES THAT.

PLEASE, ALL I WANT IS TO LEARN THE *TRUTH.*

WITH *THAT* LASSO?

YES.

ON STEVE LONDON?

YES.

AND WHEN YOU BRING THE *SLEAZE BAG* IN, THEN YOU'LL HAVE THE *REAL* KILLER!

SLEAZE BAG?

MICHAEL BOYD. THE REPORT'S ON YOUR DESK.

CAPTAIN, I AM A PROFESSOR OF *HISTORY* AND *ARCHAEOLOGY.* I CAN *ATTEST* TO THE LASSO'S *AUTHENTICITY.*

C'MON, CAP'N, IT'S WORTH A *TRY.*

OH, *SURE.* I CAN JUST SEE THE LAWYERS HAVING A *FIELD DAY* WITH *THIS* ONE.

LET'S ASSUME FOR A MOMENT THAT THE ROPE *DOES* WORK.

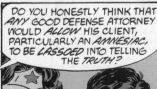

DO YOU HONESTLY THINK THAT *ANY* GOOD DEFENSE ATTORNEY WOULD *ALLOW* HIS CLIENT, PARTICULARLY AN *AMNESIAC,* TO BE *LASSOED* INTO TELLING THE *TRUTH?*

WHAT IF HE *IS* GUILTY?

ON THE *OTHER* HAND, WHAT IF LONDON SAYS HE *DIDN'T* KILL THE GIRL?

THE D.A. WILL INSIST THAT HE WAS TRYING TO SAVE HIS OWN NECK BY USING THE LASSO AS A *RUSE* TO LEND *CREDIBILITY* TO HIS NEWLY ACQUIRED "*RECOLLECTIONS.*"

YEP, I CAN SEE IT ALL NOW.

CAPTAIN, PLEASE. AT LEAST LET *STEVE LONDON* MAKE THE DECISION.

I IMPLORE YOU IN THE NAME OF *JUSTICE.*

PRINCESS, WE'RE *NOT* TALKING ABOUT *JUSTICE.*

WE'RE TALKING ABOUT THE *LAW.*

17

The Princess' tenacity paid off. Even a curmudgeon like Ablamsky couldn't turn down those eyes. I took Diana and her friends where London was being held.

His wife, the public defender and Deni Hayes were already with him.

At first, London seemed willing but I wasn't going to get the chance to see the lariat in action after all. Ivy London and the P.D. talked him out of it. Just like the captain predicted.

Diana pleaded her case again, but Mrs. London wouldn't back down. I guess I couldn't blame her.

After all, she'd already learned that her husband was a cheat. She was too afraid to find out that he may also be a murderer.

Those luminous blue orbs turned to me for assistance, but there was nothing I could do. My big chance, and I blew it.

I stood there like a bag of dirty laundry as that gorgeous Amazon walked toward the exit. Deni Hayes had gotten her attention with something.

I couldn't hear her, and I didn't care. This case wasn't finished yet. I still had one more suspect to grill.

Unfortunately, when Lt. Shands returned, it was without the infamous sleaze bag. The Boyd had flown the coop.

Boyd's disappearance added some new twists to this maze. Although not as many as the coroner's rep

BZZZZ

HUH?

BZZZZZ

AW, DAMN.

YEAH, HELLO?

EDDIE, IT'S MIKE. I'M AT THE DRAKE WAREHOUSE IN BEDFORD.

I THINK YOU BETTER GET OVER HERE.

BEDFORD? WHAT ARE YOU DOIN' OVER THERE?

WE FOUND BOYD.

HE'S DEAD.

BEDFORD AT DAWN.

WARNING!
ELECTRICALLY CHARGED FENCE
NO TRESPASSING

HIGH VOLTAGE

THE END OF THE SEARCH.

WE GOT A CALL ABOUT A *DISTURBANCE.* WE FOUND THIS GUY PROPPED UP THERE LIKE A CHICKEN ON A GRILL.

YEP, THAT'S *SKEETER.*

WHERE'S THE *PRINCESS?*

NING!
RICALLY
RGED
NCE
SPASSING

"WONDER WOMAN? IN THE WAREHOUSE WITH LT. SHANDS."

HOW DID YOU *FIND* HIM?

DENI HAYES REMEMBERED SOME *NAMES* FROM SKEETER'S FILES. PEOPLE INVOLVED IN THE *FAIR ROBBERY.* I TRACKED THEM DOWN.

MY SEARCH LED ME *HERE*, TO *SKEETER.*

"WHERE I FINALLY FOUND THE TRUTH."

YEAH! I DID IT. I HAD TO!

THAT *TRAMP* WAS GONNA SPOIL EVERY-THING!

YOU SLIMY CRUD! HOW *DARE* YOU USE MY AGENCY AS A *FRONT?*

WHOA THEAH, SWEET HIPS. Y'ALL'S GONNA *BUST* OUTTA YO' SEAMS IF YOU DON'T *EASE UP* SOME.

Y'ALL BEEN AT THE *HOOCH* AGAIN?

OH, SPARE ME THE *JETHRO BODINE* CRAP! THE *CHARADE* IS OVER.

I'VE *READ* YOUR *FILES.*

HUH? WHERE'D YOU GET THOSE?

NEVER MIND. I'M NOT *PROUD* OF WHAT I HAD TO DO TO GUARANTEE THAT THIS *SCANDAL* WOULDN'T BE MADE *PUBLIC.*

BUT, THIS IS *MY* AGENCY... MY *LIFE*... AND...

DAMN IT! YOU *USED* ME. AFTER ALL I *DID* FOR YOU. HELL, SKEETER... I *LOVED* YOU.

MAYER

NO, SWEETHEART. YOU LOVED *THIS.*

THIS IS WHY YOU *WON'T* TURN ME IN.

19

HERE. YOUR *NOSE* IS SHINY. *POWDER* IT.

NO!

NO MORE! GET OUT! IF YOU *EVER* COME BACK... I *SWEAR* I'LL TAKE YOU DOWN!

I'LL MAKE YOU *PAY* FOR WHAT YOU'VE DONE TO ME!

YOU DID IT TO *YERSELF*, BABE. YOU *DEMANDED* IT. I *SUPPLIED* IT.

GET OUT!

SHE WAS *BLUFFING!* I *KNEW* IT! THAT *LUSH!* THAT *JUNKIE.* SHE *NEEDED* ME!

BUT *CHOI*, HE DIDN'T *TRUST* HER. SHE WAS TOO *DANGEROUS*, HE SAID. TOO *UNPRE-DICTABLE.*

"IT WAS EITHER HER OR ME. THEY GAVE ME THE *SHOTGUN* AND WAITED WHILE I WENT BACK INTO THE BUILDING."

"I *MADE* SURE NOBODY WAS AROUND. I *OPENED* THE DOOR TO HER OFFICE.

"SHE JUST SAT THERE. STARING. SHE DIDN'T THINK I WOULD DO IT.

"BUT I HAD TO. I WAS *DEAD* OTHERWISE.

"THE LAST THING I SAW WAS HER EYES, ALL RED AND GLASSY."

THEN I *BLEW* HER HEAD APART.

SKEETER *PANICKED.* HE *RANSACKED* THE OFFICE TO MAKE IT LOOK LIKE A *ROBBERY.*

THAT'S WHEN STEVE LONDON STORMED IN.

IT WAS *DARK.* HE COULDN'T *SEE* ME. I- I REACHED FOR THE *LETTER OPENER.*

"I *STABBED* HIM, BUT THAT GUY WAS *STRONG.* WE FOUGHT FOR WHAT FELT LIKE *FOREVER.*

"FINALLY, HE WENT *DOWN.* I THOUGHT HE WAS *DEAD.* HE *WASN'T.*"

HOLD IT. LET ME *GUESS* THE REST.

BOYD FIGURED HE NOW HAD THE *PERFECT PATSY.*

"HE WIPED HIS FINGERPRINTS FROM THE LETTER OPENER AND PLACED IT IN MAYER'S HAND.

"THEN HE DID THE *SAME* THING WITH THE RIFLE AND PUT *LONDON'S* PRINTS ON IT."

20

HE THREW THE GUN IN THE DUMPSTER AND WAS BROUGHT HERE. PRESUMABLY TO BE FLOWN TO SOMEWHERE SAFE.

OR *ELIMINATED.* NOT BAD FOR AN IMPROMPTU PLAN.

BUT WHAT ABOUT *BOYD?* I KNOW YOU WELL ENOUGH TO KNOW *YOU* DIDN'T *THROW* HIM INTO THE ELECTRIFIED FENCE. *DID* YOU?

NO. I WAS *UPSET.* I LET MY GUARD DOWN.

"AS I WAS UNTYING SKEETER, TWO OF THE GUNMEN MANAGED TO GET TO THEIR WEAPONS."

RATATATATATATA

PTNNG PTNNG PTNNG PTNNG

"I THANK ARTEMIS THAT MY REFLEXES WERE STILL SHARP."

"AS I FOUGHT THE GUNMEN, SKEETER RAN OFF, FRIGHTENED BEYOND REASON."

"I ENDED THE BATTLE QUICKLY AND WENT AFTER HIM."

SKEETER!

SURRENDER, SKEETER! YOU CAN'T...

YYYEEEEAAHH!

SKEETER WAS *DEAD* WHEN I REACHED HIM.

21

STEVE DID *NOT* KILL MYNDI.

HE WAS *USED.* AS *MYNDI* WAS USED.

AS WE WERE *ALL* USED.

MYNDI WAS *SCARED.* BUT, IN THE END, SHE FOUGHT BACK.

SHE WAS GOING TO BEAT HER ADDICTION. I *KNOW* IT.

BUT SKEETER *SNUFFED OUT* THAT LAST CHANCE.

AW, JEEZ.

WHAT? WHAT IS IT?

PRINC...*ER...DIANA,* YOU GOTTA KNOW THAT I'D RATHER GIVE UP MY *PENSION* THAN HAVE TO TELL YOU THIS...

BUT IT'LL ALL BE IN THE *NEWS* TOMORROW, ANYWAY.

TELL ME *WHAT?*

SKEETER *DIDN'T* KILL MYNDI. NOT *REALLY.*

BUT MY *LASSO.* BY THE GODS, I THOUGHT AT LEAST *YOU* BELIEVED ME.

I *DO,* DIANA, REALLY, I *DO.* IT'S THAT...

DAMMIT, MIKE. *TELL* HER!

OKAY, EDDIE. BUT YOU'LL OWE ME A *PENSION.*

YOUR HIGHNESS, WE RECEIVED THE *AUTOPSY REPORT* ON MISS MAYER.

THE REPORT CONCLUDED THAT SHE HAD HAD A MASSIVE *CEREBRAL HEMORRHAGE...*

...*BEFORE* THE ASSAULT WITH THE RIFLE.

THE CORONER ATTRIBUTED IT TO EXCESSIVE *ALCOHOL* AND *COCAINE* IN HER SYSTEM.

WHEN MICHAEL BOYD *FIRED* THAT SHOTGUN, MYNDI MAYER WAS *ALREADY DEAD.*

THAT PACKET OF COKE ON HER DESK MUST'VE BEEN *TOO MUCH* OF A TEMPTATION.

I GUESS SHE JUST WASN'T *STRONG* ENOUGH.

OH, DEAR GAEA, *WHY?* SHE WAS SO *YOUNG,* SO *VITAL.*

WHY?

There were no easy answers to give her. We'd solved the mystery of who killed Myndi Mayer and learned that it was Mayer herself. The idea of a suicide, even accidental, would never have occurred to an innocent like the Princess. At least the hoods she caught might help in springing Steve London, but that seemed almost trivial now.

As she soared away into the dawn, I couldn't help but hope that we'd meet again. Someplace where there was no need for guns and badges.

As I closed the folder on this case, I stared at the photos of Diana, and of Myndi Mayer, another beautiful bird who just wanted to keep flying higher.

Until she ran out of sky.

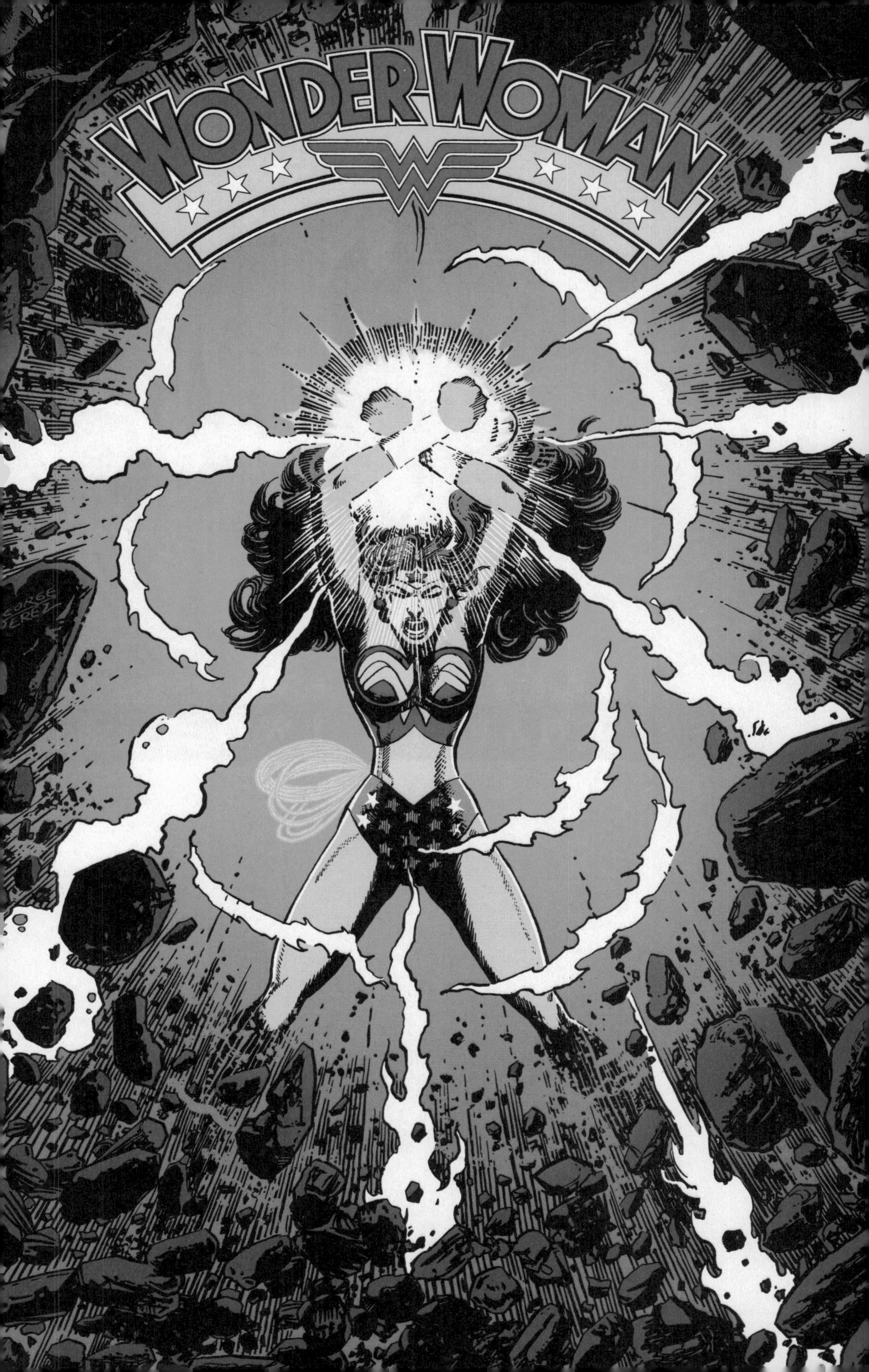
WONDER WOMAN
GEORGE PEREZ

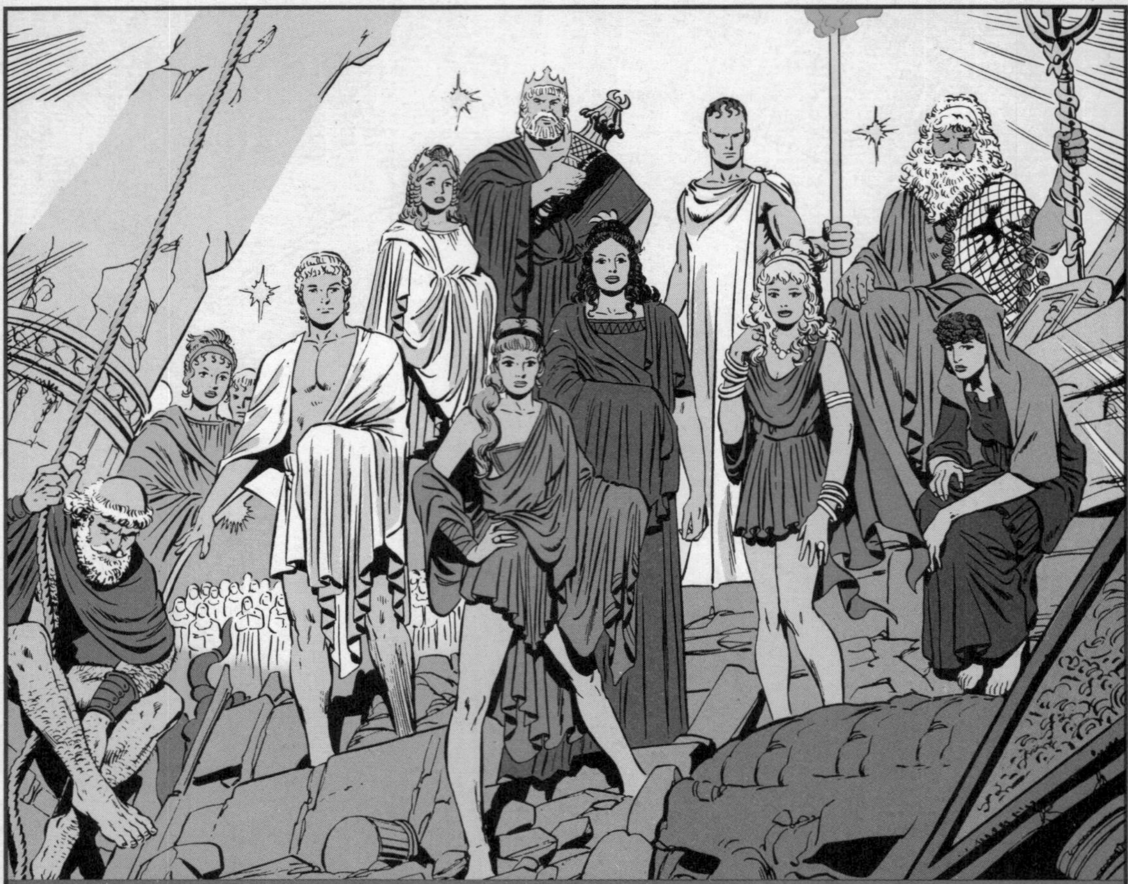

WONDER WOMAN

CHAPTER TWO

"IT IS SO PEACEFUL TONIGHT. THEMYSCIRA RESTS SERENELY UNDER THE LIGHT OF ARTEMIS' MOON."

"SEE? HOW SOFTLY THEY SLEEP HOW DEEP IN REVERIE. MUST YOU INFRINGE UPON THAT VISTA NOW?"

"YES, MORPHEUS. IT IS THE WILL OF OLYMPUS. OPEN YOUR PORTAL, SO THAT I MAY ENTER HER DREAMSCAPE."

"AS YOU WISH, APOLLO. IT IS DONE."

"MENALIPPE. HEAR ME. YOU MUST HEAR ME.

"MENALIPPE..."

‹GODS!›

The COSMIC MIGRATION

WAKEFIELD, MASSACHUSETTS.

WE'RE HOME.

THANK GOD! I'M GOIN' UP TO MY ROOM.

WOULD YOU LIKE ME TO MAKE YOU SOME LUNCH?

NO THANKS, MOM.

I'M NOT VERY HUNGRY RIGHT NOW.

NESSIE IS TAKING MYNDI'S DEATH MUCH HARDER THAN I WOULD HAVE THOUGHT.

SHE *LIKED* MYNDI. SHE *ADMIRED* HER.

SHE WAS RICH, SUCCESSFUL, BEAUTIFUL. EVERTHING THAT A LITTLE GIRL COULD WANT.

UNTIL ALL THOSE DRUGS AND LIQUOR *DESTROYED* HER.

THESE ARE DIFFICULT TIMES FOR A CHILD TO GROW UP IN. YOU HAVE TO PREPARE THEM *SO YOUNG.*

AND *PRAY* THAT YOU'VE *TAUGHT* THEM ENOUGH SO THAT THEY CAN *RECOGNIZE* THE 'SKEETER LaRUES" OF THIS WORLD.

HOW ABOUT *YOU?* YOU'VE BARELY SPOKEN THE ENTIRE DRIVE BACK FROM THE MEMORIAL SERVICE.

I DON'T KNOW, JULIA. THESE PAST WEEKS IT SEEMS LIKE MY *WHOLE* WORLD IS FALLING IN ON ME.

I CAN'T HELP FEELING PARTIALLY *RESPONSIBLE* FOR MYNDI'S DEATH.

2

IF I HADN'T BEEN SO *BLINDED* BY THE CELEBRITY OF BEING *WONDER WOMAN*, MAYBE I WOULD HAVE SEEN THE CORRUPTION AROUND ME.

MAYBE I COULD HAVE *WARNED* HER.

THEY SAID MYNDI MAYER WAS A SLAVE TO HER *AMBITION.* WAS *I* ANY *BETTER?*

EVEN *SUPERMAN.* I HAD TO *IMPLORE* HIM TO CALL ME *DIANA.*

DIANA HAD GOTTEN *LOST.* ONLY THE *FACADE* CALLED *WONDER WOMAN* REMAINED.

I WENT TO GREECE, HOPING TO *CLEANSE* MYSELF. SO THAT MY LIFE'S *PURPOSE* WOULD BE *CLEAR* AGAIN.

WHY DIDN'T THE GODS WARN ME ABOUT HER? WHY DO SO MANY HAVE TO *DIE* SIMPLY BECAUSE THEY BELIEVE IN *ME?*

WHEN I PRAY FOR GUIDANCE, THE GODS FEEL SO *ALOOF.* AS IF THEY'VE *ABANDONED* ME.

OH, JULIA, HAVE I *FAILED* THE GODS SO MISERABLY?

AT THE FAIR, THE *SILVER SWAN* ATTACKED NOT *ME*, BUT *WONDER WOMAN*, THAT *ICON* TO AN UNATTAINABLE *IDEAL* OF FEMININE BEAUTY. A PRINCESS OF *VANITY.*

I DOUBT IF SHE EVEN KNEW WHO DIANA WAS. WHAT HER *MISSION* WAS.

BUT THEN, I MET *CIRCE.*

COULD IT BE THAT THIS MISSION IS JUST *TOO MUCH* FOR ME?

SWEETIE, AS LONG AS YOU POSSESS THE *GREAT POWER* YOUR GODS BESTOWED UPON YOU, THEY SHALL ALWAYS BE *WITHIN* YOU.

IT'S *NORMAL* FOR AN *APOSTLE* TO EXPERIENCE A *CRISIS OF FAITH* AT ONE TIME OR ANOTHER.

I *KNOW* YOU'RE RIGHT, JULIA. I JUST WISH THEY WOULD SEND ME SOME... *SIGN.*

POK POK POK

EH?

POK POK POK POK

"SOMEONE'S AT THE DOOR."

POK POK POK

POK POK POK

WHAT'S *WRONG* WITH THAT PERSON?

POK POK

YES?

DON'T *BLAME* YOURSELF FOR GETTING CAUGHT UP IN THE WONDER WOMAN WHIRLWIND. YOU'RE ONLY HUMAN. *REMEMBER* THAT.

YES, YES, I'M COMING.

DOESN'T HE KNOW HOW TO UTILIZE A *DOORBELL?*

3

GOOD LORD.

TINY ONE!

WHAT ARE *YOU* DOING HERE?

IS THAT THE *MESSENGER PIGEON* FROM *THEMYSCIRA?*

YES. IT BEARS ANOTHER NOTE FROM MY *MOTHER.*

DEAR HERMES, I PRAY THAT EVERYTHING IS *ALL RIGHT.*

MOM! MOM! DIANA'S PIGEON'S OUTSIDE!

YES, BABY, I LET IT IN. DIANA'S READING THE MESSAGE NOW.

IT'S NOT *BAD NEWS,* IS IT?

DIANA? *IS* EVERYTHING OKAY?

YES.

BUT I MUST GO *BACK HOME.* I'M *NEEDED* THERE.

NO! PLEASE, DIANA, *DON'T GO!* EVERYTIME YOU GO, SOMETHIN' *BAD* ALWAYS HAPPENS!

DON'T WORRY, NESSIE. THERE'S NOTHING TO *FEAR.*

THE *PICTOGRAM* INDICATES *URGENCY,* NOT *DANGER.*

TRUST ME. I *WILL* COME BACK.

PROMISE?

PROMISE.

SWEAR?

YES, DARLING, I *SWEAR.*

CROSS YOUR HEART AND HOPE TO DIE?

EXCUSE ME?

A HALF HOUR LATER...

"DO YOU THINK YOU'RE BEING CALLED BACK FOR THE ELECTION?"

I DON'T KNOW, JULIA. MOTHER'S MESSAGE WAS VERY *BRIEF*. BUT SHE *DID* SAY THAT I AM CALLED TO THE *GODS'* SERVICE. MAYBE...

I *UNDERSTAND*, SWEETIE. YOU JUST HAVE A *SAFE* TRIP.

SAY "*HI*" TO YOUR MOM FOR ME, OKAY?

AND...UM... MAY THE GLORY OF GAEA BE WITH YOU.

THANK YOU, NESSIE. AND ALSO WITH YOU.

HOPEFULLY, YOU'LL SOON BE ABLE TO SAY "*HI*" TO MY MOTHER *PERSONALLY*.

FAREWELL... FOR *NOW*.

"FAREWELL, DIANA. I HOPE YOUR RETURN HOME HELPS ASSUAGE THE BURDEN IN YOUR HEART."

"HUH?"

NEVER MIND, BABY. I'LL EXPLAIN IT TO YOU *LATER*.

"MOM, D'YA REALLY THINK SHE'S COMING BACK?"

"YES, BABY, I DO."

OH, MOM... I-I DON'T WANNA LOSE *HER*, TOO.

LIKE MYNDI?

...YEAH...

DO YOU WANT TO TALK ABOUT IT NOW?

"WE CAN SIT BY THE FIREPLACE. MAYBE MAKE SOME POPCORN? HOW DOES *THAT* SOUND?"

"OKAY, I GUESS..."

"*MOMMY?*"

"YES, MY ANGEL?"

"CAN I SLEEP IN YOUR ROOM TONIGHT?"

5

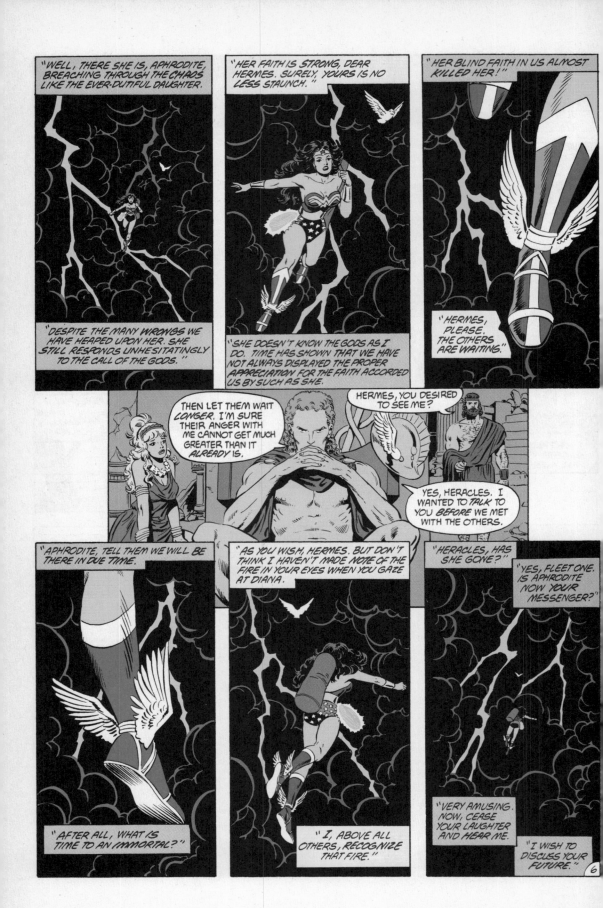

"WELL, THERE SHE IS, APHRODITE, BREACHING THROUGH THE CHAOS LIKE THE EVER-DUTIFUL DAUGHTER.

"DESPITE THE MANY WRONGS WE HAVE HEAPED UPON HER. SHE STILL RESPONDS UNHESITATINGLY TO THE CALL OF THE GODS."

"HER FAITH IS STRONG, DEAR HERMES. SURELY, YOURS IS NO LESS STAUNCH."

"SHE DOESN'T KNOW THE GODS AS I DO. TIME HAS SHOWN THAT WE HAVE NOT ALWAYS DISPLAYED THE PROPER APPRECIATION FOR THE FAITH ACCORDED US BY SUCH AS SHE.

"HER BLIND FAITH IN US ALMOST KILLED HER!"

"HERMES, PLEASE. THE OTHERS ARE WAITING."

THEN LET THEM WAIT LONGER. I'M SURE THEIR ANGER WITH ME CANNOT GET MUCH GREATER THAN IT ALREADY IS.

HERMES, YOU DESIRED TO SEE ME?

YES, HERACLES. I WANTED TO TALK TO YOU BEFORE WE MET WITH THE OTHERS.

"APHRODITE, TELL THEM WE WILL BE THERE IN DUE TIME.

"AFTER ALL, WHAT IS TIME TO AN IMMORTAL?"

"AS YOU WISH, HERMES. BUT DON'T THINK I HAVEN'T MADE NOTE OF THE FIRE IN YOUR EYES WHEN YOU GAZE AT DIANA.

"I, ABOVE ALL OTHERS, RECOGNIZE THAT FIRE."

"HERACLES, HAS SHE GONE?"

"YES, FLEET ONE. IS APHRODITE NOW YOUR MESSENGER?"

"VERY AMUSING. NOW, CEASE YOUR LAUGHTER AND HEAR ME.

"I WISH TO DISCUSS YOUR FUTURE."

6

MEANWHILE, IN THE CAPITAL CITY OF THEMYSCIRA...

< YOU LOOK NERVOUS, PENELOPE. > *

* translated from themysciran -- K

< I AM, MY QUEEN. SELDOM HAVE I SEEN THE HIGH PRIESTESS SO EXCITED. >

< WHEN MENALIPPE LEAPT OUT OF BED SHE WAS IN A GREAT FRENZY. >

< SHE WAS ALREADY HALF-WAY TO YOUR BEDCHAMBER BEFORE I GOT TO MY FEET. >

< I'M SORRY SHE WOKE YOU. >

< ONE OF A QUEEN'S DUTIES IS TO BE PREPARED TO LOSE A NIGHT'S SLEEP WHEN HER SUBJECTS NEED HER. >

< I'M JUST GRATEFUL THAT IT WASN'T LIKE THE LAST TIME. >

< YES, I REMEMBER. WHEN SHE SENSED THE COMING OF ARES. >

< MY QUEEN! LOOK! DIANA APPEARS IN THE LIGHT! >

< YES, BOREAS BLOWS THE CLOUDS ASIDE TO WELCOME MY DAUGHTER HOME. >

< PENELOPE, HAVE YOU EVER SEEN ANYTHING SO BEAUTIFUL? >

< OH, DIANA. PRAISE THE GODS THAT YOU HAVE RETURNED. I'VE MISSED YOU SO TERRIBLY. >

< MOTHER, WITH THESE WINGED SANDALS BEQUEATHED ME BY LORD HERMES, WE CAN NEVER BE APART LONG. >

< PRINCESS, DID YOU BRING YOUR PRAYER ROBE? >

< ER...YES. WHY? >

< YOUR SISTERS AWAIT US IN THE ORACLE'S TEMPLE. IT WILL ALL BE EXPLAINED THERE. >

< COME. MENALIPPE SAYS IT WILL BE GLORIOUS! >

< DIANA, WHAT'S WRONG? >

< NOTHING, MOTHER. IT JUST SEEMS IRONIC... >

< THAT I AM NOW TO PARTICIPATE IN SOMETHING GLORIOUS IN THE SAME ROBES THAT I WORE JUST A SHORT WHILE AGO... >

< ...TO MOURN THE DEATH OF A FRIEND. >

7

37

BUT THE STORY OF MYNDI MAYER IS ONE THE QUEEN MUST HEAR AT SOME LATER TIME.

WITH THE ENTIRE POPULATION OF PARADISE ISLAND ASSEMBLED AS COMMUNAL WITNESS, DIANA AND HIPPOLYTE STAND WITH THE ORACLE MENALIPPE AT THE ALTAR OF APOLLO.

THE INCENSE FROM THE CISTERN SNAKES UPWARD TOWARD THE HEAVENS, ITS BOUQUET OFFERED AS STIMULATION FOR THE GODS.

WITH HEARTS FILLED WITH ZEALOUS ANTICIPATION, THE AMAZONS AWAIT THE WORDS OF THE HIGH PRIESTESS THAT WILL BREAK THE HOLY SILENCE.

AND FINALLY, THE WORDS COME.

< SISTERS! FELLOW WORSHIPPERS! AMAZONS! REMEMBER THIS DAY! >

< BECAUSE ON THIS DAY, THE GODS HAVE HONORED US GREATLY! >

< HEEDING THE WORDS OF OUR LORD APOLLO, OUR QUEEN AND PRINCESS JOIN ME AT THE ALTAR FOR THIS BLESSED EVENT. >

< FOR WE THREE HAVE BEEN CALLED TO APPEAR AT THE COURT OF THE GODS THEMSELVES! >

< WE HAVE BEEN SUMMONED TO MOUNT OLYMPUS! >

< AND YOU, DEAR SISTERS, ARE TO BE AUDIENCE TO THIS MILESTONE. >

< NOW, LET US ALL JOIN IN PRAYER, SO THAT WE MAY PREPARE FOR THIS SACRED CONGREGATION. >

< O, MIGHTY OLYMPUS! WE THANK THEE FOR THY FAVOR. GRANT THAT WE SHALL BE WORTHY OF IT. >

< WE WHO HAVE DEDICATED OUR SOULS TO THEE AWAIT THY PLEASURE! >

8

LIGHTNING LEAPS AND TWISTS IN A FURIOUS DANCE AS THE ONCE-QUIET SKY BELLOWS WITH THE ROAR OF ZEUS' LIGHTNING BOLTS.

AMID THE BLARE OF A THUNDEROUS CONCERT, EACH AMAZON SUBMERGES HERSELF IN SILENT MEDITATION...

...PRAYING FOR STRENGTH...

...AND GUIDANCE.

O DEAR GODS OF OLYMPUS! THANK YOU!

THANK YOU FOR *NOT* FORSAKING ME.

IF *THIS* IS THE *SIGN* I HAVE PRAYED FOR, PLEASE, O MOST LEARNED ATHENA, GRANT ME THE *WISDOM* TO *UNDERSTAND* IT.

FROM OLYMPUS THE FRENZIED CONDUCTOR STRIKES ANOTHER FURIOUS DOWNBEAT.

THE COSMIC CRESCENDO REACHES ITS CLIMAX...

9

39

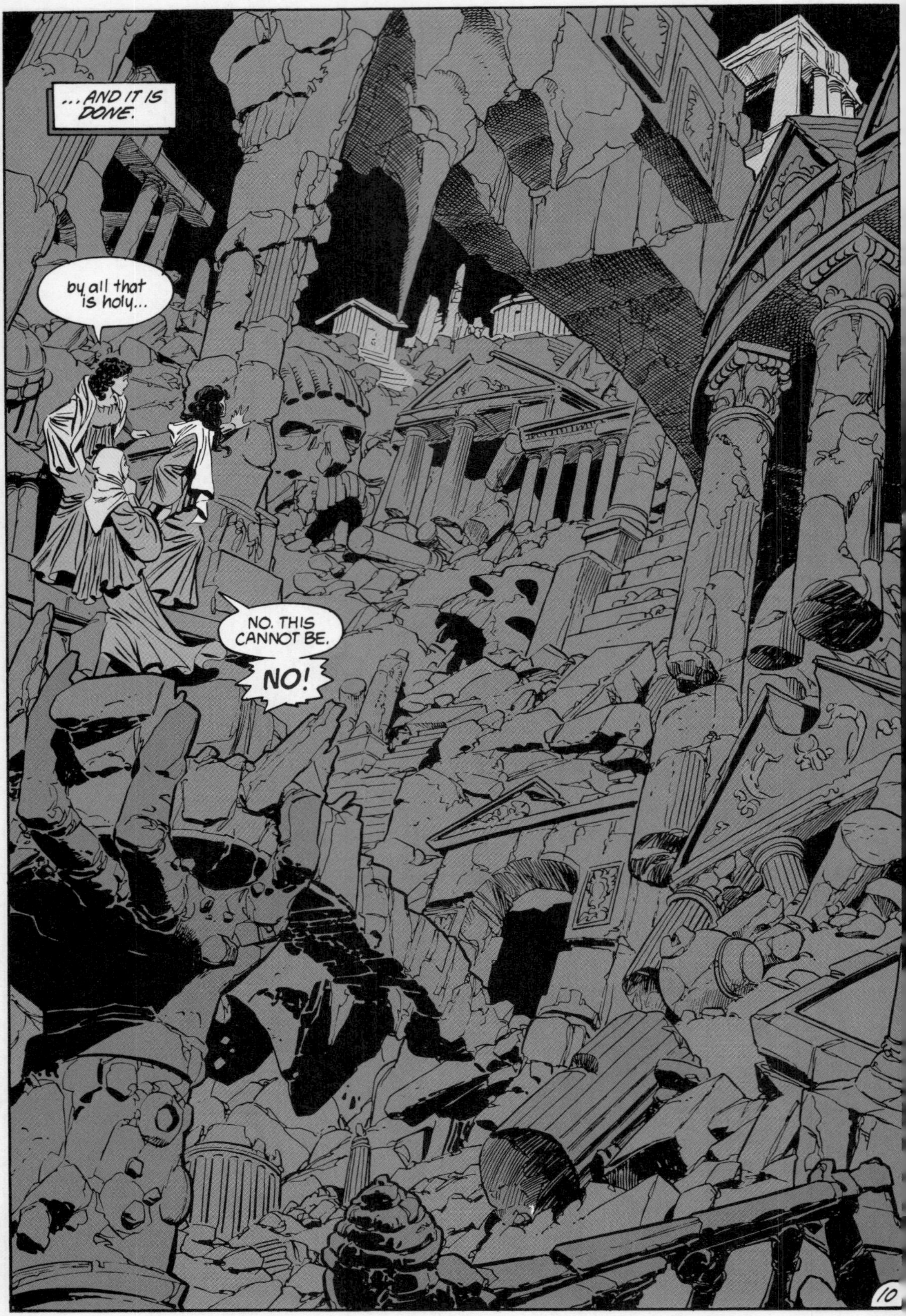
...AND IT IS DONE.
by all that is holy...
NO. THIS CANNOT BE.
NO!
10

OLYMPUS IS A PARADISE, THE IDEAL FOR WHICH WE HAVE DEDICATED OUR LIVES, OUR SOULS.

THIS MUST BE SOME... *MISTAKE.*

DIANA, YOU'VE BEEN CALLED HERE BEFORE. TELL US.

THIS *ISN'T* OLYMPUS. IT *CAN'T* BE.

OH, MOTHER, HOW I WISH IT *WASN'T.*

BUT SEE, IT STILL BEARS THE BRAND OF THE DEMON *DARKSEID* WHO *CORRUPTED* THIS REALM.

I HAD THOUGHT THAT WITH HIS *WITHDRAWAL* THE EVIL SPELL WOULD BE BROKEN...

...BUT IT IS *MORE SEVERE* THAN EVER.

THEN... IS *THIS* WHAT IT HAS ALL COME TO?

IS THIS THE SUM TOTAL OF CENTURIES OF FAITH, HOPE AND SACRIFICE?

IN THE END, IS IT ALL NOTHING BUT A *MOUNTAIN* OF RUBBLE?

PLEASE, MENALIPPE. YOU MUSTN'T LOSE FAITH.

WASN'T IT *YOU* WHO ONCE SAID THAT THE EYES SOMETIMES DO DISSERVICE TO THE SOUL?

DIDN'T YOU TEACH US THAT FAITH IS A PERCEPTION *BEYOND* THE VISION? THAT SOMETIMES WE MUST *CLOSE* OUR EYES TO SEE THE *LIGHT?*

YOU HAVE LEARNED YOUR LESSONS WELL, PRINCESS.

YOU *SHAME* ME.

NO, SISTER. THERE IS NO REASON FOR SHAME. WE HAVE ALL GONE THROUGH OUR MOMENTS OF GREAT DOUBT.

YES. ALL OF US.

HOW CAN YOU HELP BUT BE STRICKEN BY THIS SORRY SPECTACLE?

BUT *I* CAN HARBOR *NO* SUCH SKEPTICISM.

I AM AN *ORACLE.* A HIGH *PRIESTESS.*

AND A *HUMAN,* MENALIPPE.

AS A DEAR, WISE FRIEND REMINDED ME EARLIER...

...WE ARE *ALL* ONLY HUMAN.

SUDDENLY, THE DARK, MUSTY SKY IS SET ABLAZE BY THE GLOW OF A BRILLIANT LIGHT...

...AND THE AMAZONS SENSE THAT THEY ARE NO LONGER ALONE.

11

41

THROUGH SQUINTING LIDS, SHADOWS START TO EMERGE. FORMS TAKE SHAPE AND FINALLY THE FEATURES BECOME CLEAR.

GREETINGS TO YOU, DEAR CHILDREN! WELCOME TO OLYMPUS!

AMID THE SCARRED REMAINS OF A ONCE-MAGNIFICENT EDIFICE, BATHED IN THE SPOTLIGHT OF THEIR OWN LUSTER, STAND THE PROUD RACE OF GODS KNOWN AS THE OLYMPIANS.

WE REGRET NOT WELCOMING YOU IN MORE MAJESTIC SURROUNDINGS.

MIGHTY ONES, PLEASE FORGIVE MY IMPERTINENCE, BUT... WHAT HAS HAPPENED HERE?

ALAS, CHILD, THE WOUNDS INFLICTED BY THAT MALEVOLENT GOD FROM APOKOLIPS HAVE CUT VERY DEEP.

SOME OF THE SCARS MAY NEVER HEAL.

BUT OLYMPUS IS AS IT IS BECAUSE THAT IS HOW WE WISH IT.

IT IS NECESSARY SO THAT WE MAY MAKE READY FOR THE GREAT COSMIC MIGRATION!

12

WE'VE ALSO CONFORMED OURSELVES AND THIS MOUNTAIN TO THE PLANES OF HUMAN PERSPECTIVE SO THAT YOU MAY READILY STAND WITH US IN OUR PREPARATIONS FOR THIS GOLDEN VENTURE.

AS YOUR SISTERS ATTEND FROM BEYOND THE DIMENSIONAL WALLS, YOU *THREE* HAVE BEEN CHOSEN TO *ASSIST* US...

...IN BRINGING ABOUT A *NEW* ORDER!

A NEW ORDER?

ARTEMIS, WHAT DOES APOLLO MEAN?

IS IT NOT *OBVIOUS,* BEAUTIFUL ONE?

DIDN'T YOU YOURSELF SAY THAT YOU'VE FELT A SENSE OF ABANDONMENT FROM THE GODS?

WELL, PRINCESS, YOUR FEARS WERE JUSTIFIED.

TAKE *CARE,* HERMES. THE DECISION HAS BEEN MADE AND YOU WILL ABIDE BY IT.

NO, ZEUS. I WILL PLAY THE *NON-PARTISAN* HERALD NO LONGER.

WHY MUST WE GODS PERSIST IN SPEAKING TO OUR SUBJECTS IN CRYPTIC *VAGARIES?*

TELL THEM! TELL THEM HOW THEIR MILLENNIA OF SELFLESS DEVOTION TO US IS TO BE *REWARDED.*

TELL THEM THAT OLYMPUS IS TO BE *DESTROYED!*

13

DAMN YOU, HERMES. *STOP* IT! YOU'RE FRIGHTENING THEM.

YES, BRAWNY ONE, TELL HER. EXPLAIN TO YOUR *BELOVED* QUEEN HOW YOU INTEND TO BETRAY HER YET *AGAIN.*

HERMES. YOU GO TOO *FAR!*

HERACLES, IS IT *TRUE?* PLEASE *TELL ME.*

HERACLES! NO!

LET THIS *IN-FIGHTING* FINALLY *END.*

AS THE GOD OF MESSENGERS, HERMES *UNDERSTANDS* THE IMPORTANCE OF COMMUNICATION. IT IS TIME WE DID AS WELL.

HERMES IS *RIGHT.* IN OUR *QUEST* FOR A HIGHER PLANE OF *GODLINESS,* WE'VE ALL BUT IGNORED THE VERY SOULS WHO'VE BROUGHT US TO THIS PHASE.

WITH NO EXPLANATION, WE'VE SHUNNED THEIR PLEAS FOR GUIDANCE AND ASSISTANCE.

IF GODS SHOW NO RESPECT FOR THEIR *WORSHIPPERS,* THEN WHAT *NEED* HAVE THOSE WORSHIPPERS FOR GODS?

O DIVINE OLYMPUS. THE AMAZON FAITH IS *STRONG.* ALL WE DESIRE IS THAT YOU HAVE FAITH IN *US.*

AND WHAT SAY *YOU,* DIANA?

THESE ARE THE *SAME* GODS WHO LEFT YOU AT THE MERCY OF *CIRCE.*

YOU CAN *FORGIVE* THAT *INJUSTICE?*

YES, WHATEVER PLANS YOU HOPE TO SET FORTH THIS DAY, WE BELIEVE THAT IT WILL BE FOR THE GOOD OF ALL.

ALL WE ASK IS TO *UNDERSTAND.*

IT'S *YOU* WHO DOES PRINCESS DIANA AN INJUSTICE, HERMES.

AYE. THE REST OF US WERE *CONFIDENT* THAT SHE WOULD TRIUMPH *WITHOUT* YOUR INTERVENTION.

THEN IT WAS *HERMES* WHO...?

YES, DIANA.

AND YOU *DO* DESERVE AN *EXPLANATION.*

14

DIANA, YOUR MANY ADVENTURES ON PATRIARCH'S WORLD MUST HAVE SHOWN YOU HOW SLIM THE LINE IS BETWEEN HUMANITY AND DEITY.

WHILE HUMANS CAN SOMETIMES APPEAR TO BE QUITE GODLIKE, GODS CAN ALSO BE ALL *TOO* HUMAN.

YES, ATHENA.

"THEN REMEMBER THAT, PRINCESS, AND *FORGIVE* US OUR HUMAN FOIBLES.

"AMONG THEM THE FAILURE TO WARN YOU ABOUT CIRCE."

AYE. SO BUSY WERE WE SQUABBLING AMONGST OURSELVES THAT WE SIMPLY *FORGOT* ABOUT THAT SORCERESS.

YET, WHEN WE BECAME AWARE OF HER THREAT TO YOU, WE DARED NOT HELP YOU.

BELIEVE US, DIANA. IT WAS NOT A DECISION WE MADE *LIGHTLY.*

WHAT? YOU CHOSE TO ENDANGER MY DAUGHTER!? WHY?

BECAUSE THE COSMIC MIGRATION MUST COMMAND *ALL* OUR ATTENTION NOW.

UNTIL THE NEW ORDER IS FIRMLY ESTABLISHED, THERE CAN BE *NO* FURTHER CONTACT BETWEEN HUMANS AND GODS.

THEN WHY HAVE YOU CALLED US HERE NOW?

WHY *ELSE,* PRINCESS? THEY NEED YOUR *HELP* TO DESTROY THE MOUNTAIN YOU FOUGHT SO VALIANTLY TO SAVE!

"SO UNPRECEDENTED AND DELICATE IS THIS UNDERTAKING THAT A MISTAKE COULD RUPTURE THE FRAMEWORK OF THE UNIVERSE ITSELF.

"BUT ITS SUCCESS COULD BE THE DAWN OF A NEW GOLDEN AGE."

THEY WANT YOU AMAZONS TO HELP IN THEIR DESERTION OF YOU! I CALL THAT OLYMPIAN *GALL!*

ENOUGH, HERMES. YOU'VE MADE YOUR VIEWS QUITE *CLEAR.*

HIPPOLYTE, YOU ARE THE *QUEEN* OF YOUR NATION. IT MUST BE *YOUR* DECISION.

THIS IS *NOT* A COMMAND. IT IS A HEART-FELT *PLEA.*

"WE REALIZE THAT, OF LATE, WE GODS HAVE DONE LITTLE TO *MERIT* YOUR FAITH...

"...BUT WE *ASK* FOR IT, NEVERTHELESS."

GREAT ARTEMIS, MY BODY AND SOUL ARE THE GODS' TO COMMAND...

...BUT I WILL *NOT* SPEAK FOR MY *SISTERS.*

THIS CHOICE MUST BE *THEIRS* TO MAKE.

15

A SOLEMN SILENCE ECHOES THROUGH THE CRUMBLING HALLS OF OLYMPUS...

...THE ORB FROM WHICH HUNDREDS OF AMAZON FACES, SUSPENDED IN A MYSTIC NEVERLAND, LOOK UP AT THEIR BELOVED QUEEN.

WITHOUT HESITATION, HUNDREDS OF DARK METAL BRACELETS CLINK TOGETHER IN DRAMATIC *UNISON.*

...AS ALL HEADS TURN TOWARD THE CRYSTALLINE ORB OF THE SUN-GOD APOLLO...

HIPPOLYTE NODS HER HEAD, CALLING FOR THEIR VOTE.

GODS OF OLYMPUS, THE SIGN IS *GIVEN.*

WITH GREAT PRIDE AND GREAT HUMILITY, THE AMAZONS, AS ALWAYS, STAND *WITH YOU.*

LATER...

COME, MY QUEEN. THE PREPARATIONS HAVE BEEN ARRANGED.

BUT HERACLES, I'M *STILL* AT A LOSS.

WHY IS MENALIPPE PERCHED SO WITH THE MYSTIC SPHERE?

"SO THAT SHE MAY BEST HARNESS THE *GREATEST* POWER IN ALL OLYMPUS...

"...THE POWER OF *PRAYER.*"

IT IS ALL THAT HAS *SUSTAINED* US FOR YEARS.

EVEN WHEN THE REST OF HUMANITY *RENOUNCED* THE GODS, THE AMAZON FAITH *PERSISTED.*

AND NOW WE ARE CALLED TO PRAY FOR THE *DEATH* OF OLYMPUS.

"NOT OLYMPUS, HIPPOLYTE, MERELY THE MOUNTAIN, A DYING HUSK MADE SQUALID AND VULNERABLE BY THAT WRETCHED DARKSEID.

ONCE THAT IS DONE, WE GODS *SHALL* RETURN TO YOU.

FOR DESPITE HERMES' ACCUSATIONS, I WOULD SOONER HAVE MY EYES PLUCKED FROM THEIR SOCKETS THAN EVER *BETRAY* YOUR TRUST AGAIN.

"HERACLES, I SEE LORD HERMES STANDING *WITH* THE OTHERS. WHY...?"

"ONLY ITS STUBBORN WILL TO SURVIVE SAVED IT. BUT, LIKE A LAME MARE, IT MUST BE PUT OUT OF ITS MISERY.

"AND THE FIRE OF ITS DESTRUCTION SHALL IGNITE THE TORCH OF THE *NEW* OLYMPUS."

I *BELIEVE* YOU, NOBLE HERACLES. WITH ALL MY *HEART.*

"AH, YES. EVEN HE COULD NOT ESCAPE THE FACT THAT HE IS STILL AN *OLYMPIAN.*"

TO HARVEST THE INCREDIBLE ENERGY WE NEED REQUIRES THE AMASSED STRENGTH OF THE *ENTIRE* PANTHEON.

WITH *ARES* ABSENT, HERMES' PARTICIPATION IS *IMPERATIVE.*

THE IMPUDENT LITTLE GOD *BAFFLES* ME. WHEN I WALKED AMONG MORTALS, MY GREAT STRENGTH WAS USED SO OFTEN TO *DESTROY.*

HOW CAN *ANY* BEING PASS UP THE *RAREST* OF OPPORTUNITIES: TO GO FORTH INTO THE UNKNOWN AND *BUILD A NEW WORLD!*

MY MUSCLES *ACHE* WITH *ANTICIPATION* AT THE THOUGHT.

THEN, HERACLES, WHAT WILL *BECOME* OF HERMES AFTER THIS DAY?

AND WHERE IS *DIANA?*

I CANNOT ANSWER ABOUT HERMES...

...BUT AS FOR YOUR DAUGHTER...

"SHE IS WITH LORDS ZEUS, POSEIDON, AND HADES IN THE BELLY OF THE MOUNTAIN. HERS WILL BE THE MOST CRITICAL TASK OF ALL!"

DIANA, THERE IS STILL TIME TO *RECONSIDER.* WE GODS SHALL NOT *OBLIGATE* YOU IN ANY WAY.

I KNOW, MY LORDS, BUT I *WANT* TO HELP.

I JUST HOPE THAT I PROVE *WORTHY.*

47

"FEAR NOT, CHILD. THE BRACELETS YOU WEAR WILL *ASSURE* THAT, FOR THEY ARE THE *KEYS* TO THIS *HOLY ENDEAVOR.*"

MY BRACELETS?

"HAVE YOU NEVER WONDERED ABOUT THE *SOURCE* OF THEIR PROTECTIVE POWER?"

"THOSE TRINKETS WERE ONCE PART OF ZEUS' MIGHTY AEGIS ITSELF...

"THE IMPENETRABLE SHIELD FORMED FROM THE HIDE OF THE GREAT GOAT *AMALTHEIA,* WHO WET-NURSED THE INFANT ZEUS AND THUS PROVIDED THE ENERGY FROM WHICH OLYMPUS SPRUNG."

ONLY *TWO* BEINGS WERE EVER ABLE TO *VIOLATE* THE POWER OF THE AEGIS.

AYE, IT WAS OUR FATHER *CRONUS* WHO *SPLINTERED* THE SHIELD AS HE SMOTE IT WITH HIS FINAL BLOW.

"WHEN I BEQUEATHED THE SHIELD TO MY DAUGHTER *ATHENA*, SHE, UNBEKNOWNST TO ME, HAD HEPHAESTUS REFORGE THE LOOSE FRAGMENTS...

"INTO A GREAT PRIZE TO BE AWARDED TO THE *MIGHTIEST* AND *WORTHIEST* OF ALL HER AMAZONS.

"AND IT WAS *ARES* WHO LONG AGO *DEMOLISHED* THE AEGIS.

"YOUR BRACELETS ARE ALL THAT REMAIN OF IT.

"AMALTHEIA'S POWER FORMED THE CORNER STONE OF THIS *ROYAL MOUNTAIN.* HERS SHALL BE THE POWER THAT *TOPPLES* IT!"

BROTHERS, *LISTEN!* THE CEREMONY OF *SUPPLICATION* HAS *BEGUN!*

"WHAT BEAUTIFUL, GLORIOUS *MUSIC* THEY MAKE!"

THEN LET US BE READY.

"I CAN FEEL THE ELECTRICITY *SURGING!*"

"DIANA, FROM THAT MAW SHALL *CHARGE* A GREAT SURGE OF *COSMIC FORCE,* THE ACCUMULATED ENERGIES OF THE GODS, INTENSIFIED BY AMAZON PRAYER!"

"YOUR DUTY IS TO *DEFLECT* IT WITH YOUR BRACELETS.

"UPON RECEIVING AMALTHEIA'S *KISS,* THE BOLT WILL BE TRANSFORMED INTO A BURST MORE AWESOME THAN BEFORE...

"WHICH MUST THEN BE *DIRECTED* TOWARD THE JUNCTION OF OUR CROSSED *SCEPTERS.*"

18

"AS WE FIRST JOINED OUR STAFFS TO SEAL THE NEW PACT, SO DO WE NOW TO LAUNCH A NEW WORLD!"

"ARE YOU READY, DIANA.?"

YES, LORD ZEUS.

"THERE IS NO WAY TO ASCERTAIN HOW POTENT THE BLAST WILL BE, SO BRACE YOURSELF!"

"FOR THERE CAN BE NO TURNING BACK NOW!"

THE CHORUS OF PRAYER IGNITES THE AIR AROUND THE STUBBORN SHELL OF ONCE-MIGHTY MOUNT OLYMPUS--

POWER THAT PUMPS THROUGH OLYMPIAN VEINS LIKE LIFE'S BLOOD!

POWER SO INTENSE, IT CANNOT BE CONTAINED!

--TORCHING THE HEAVENS WITH THE RAGING FLAMES OF INCENDIARY POWER!

RAW, UNBRIDLED POWER!!

RIPPING THROUGH THE DARK CRAGGY BOWELS OF A PEAK TENACIOUSLY CLINGING TO LIFE.

RACING TO THE MOUNTAIN'S CORE...

WHERE ONLY A TINY, SOLITARY HUMAN STANDS TO MEET IT.

GAEA PROTECT ME.

19

THE FURIOUS FIREBALL SMASHES AGAINST CROSSED BRACELETS BUTTRESSED BY AMAZON MUSCLE...

...TRANSMUTED BY THE TOUCH OF AMALTHEIA'S SKIN...

...AND DEFLECTED TOWARD THE CROSSED SYMBOLS OF THREE ANXIOUS BROTHERS, GODS AND KINGS ALL...

...STRIKING THE AXIS, METAMORPHOSING ONE FINAL TIME...

...INTO A FORCE BEYOND MEASURE!

DESTRUCTION MULTIPLIED TO THE INFINITE POWER!

THE PROUD MOUNTAIN SCREAMS IN AGONY, DEFIANT TO THE LAST.

ITS SKIN BLISTERS AND CRACKS. STREAMS OF DEADLY ENERGY SPOUT FROM OPEN WOUNDS.

UNTIL THE PAIN IS TOO UNBEARABLE. UNTIL THE GREAT PEAK SUCCUMBS.

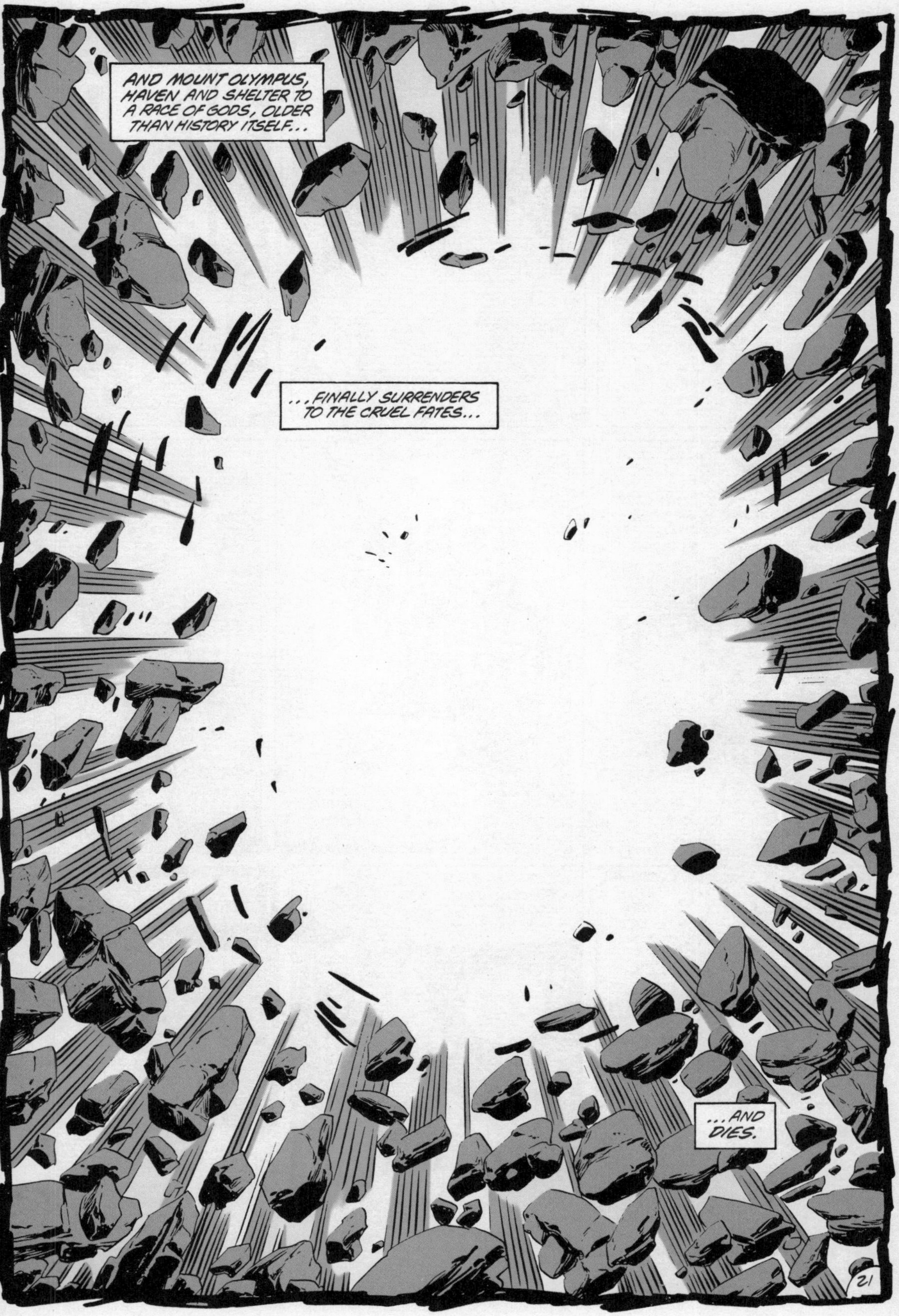
AND MOUNT OLYMPUS, HAVEN AND SHELTER TO A RACE OF GODS, OLDER THAN HISTORY ITSELF...
...FINALLY SURRENDERS TO THE CRUEL FATES...
...AND DIES.
21

‹ DIANA! ARE YOU ALL RIGHT? ›

‹ YES, MOTHER. AND OUR SISTERS? ›

‹ THEY APPEAR UNHURT. A LITTLE SHAKEN, PERHAPS... ›

‹ YES, IT'S JUST... ›

‹ DAUGHTER, ARE YOU CERTAIN YOU'RE WELL? ›

‹ I CAN STILL HEAR OLYMPUS' DEATH SCREAMS ECHOING. ›

‹ OH MOTHER, IT WAS HORRIBLE. DO YOU...›

‹ THEY'RE GONE. ›

‹ THE GODS ARE GONE. ›

‹ I-I DON'T FEEL THEM ANYMORE. ›

‹ MENALIPPE! THE HOLY CISTERN...›

‹ I KNOW, PENELOPE. WE SHAN'T BE NEEDING IT NOW. ›

‹ WE'VE SUCCEEDED. THE GODS GO FORTH NOW TO FIND A NEW HOME. ›

‹ PHILIPPUS, DID YOU HEAR THAT? DO YOU REALLY THINK IT'S TRUE? ›

‹ I DON'T KNOW, PYTHIA. THE LAST THING I REMEMBER IS PRAYING IN SOME STARRY LIMBO...›

‹...AND THEN, THE SOUNDS OF THUNDER. ›

‹ LOOK AT YOUR SISTERS' FACES, DIANA. THE FULL IMPORT OF THIS DAY IS BECOMING CLEAR. ›

‹ TODAY, A NEW PAGE HAS BEEN WRITTEN IN THE TOMES OF AMAZON HISTORY. ›

‹ FROM THIS DAY ON, OUR DESTINIES SHALL BE OURS ALONE TO DETERMINE. ›

‹ IT BRINGS BACK THE WORDS HERACLES SAID TO ME EARLIER, ABOUT FACING THE UNKNOWN AND BUILDING A NEW WORLD. ›

‹ TOMORROW IS THE DAY OF THE GREAT VOTE. ›

‹ TOMORROW WE MUST DECIDE WHETHER OR NOT THEMYSCIRA SHALL ALSO HAVE THE COURAGE TO FACE THE UNKNOWN BEYOND OUR WATERS...›

"‹...TO BUILD A NEW WORLD....›"

"‹...TO FINALLY ALLOW MAN TO SET FOOT ON PARADISE ISLAND! ›"

22

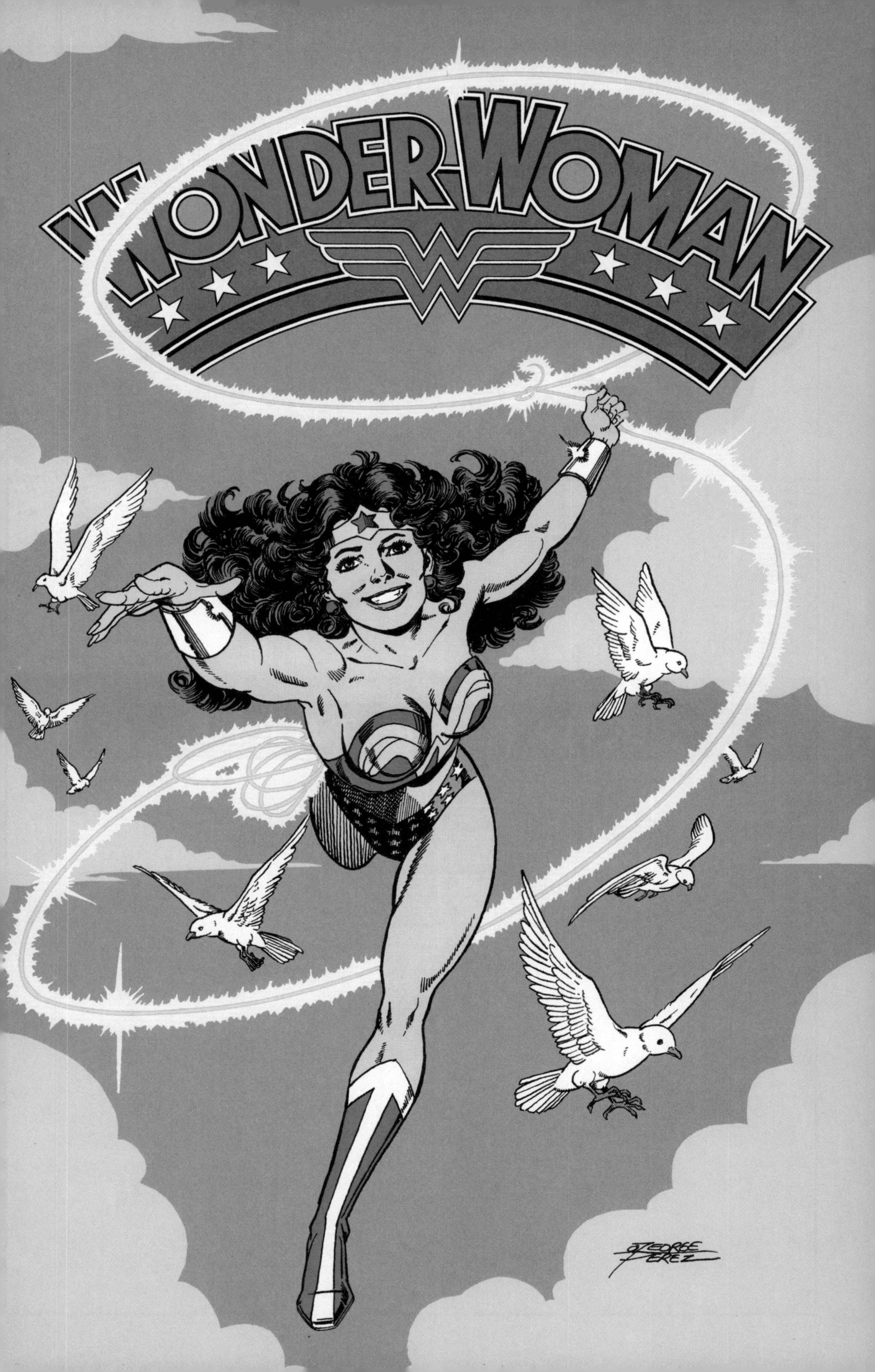
WONDER WOMAN
GEORGE PEREZ

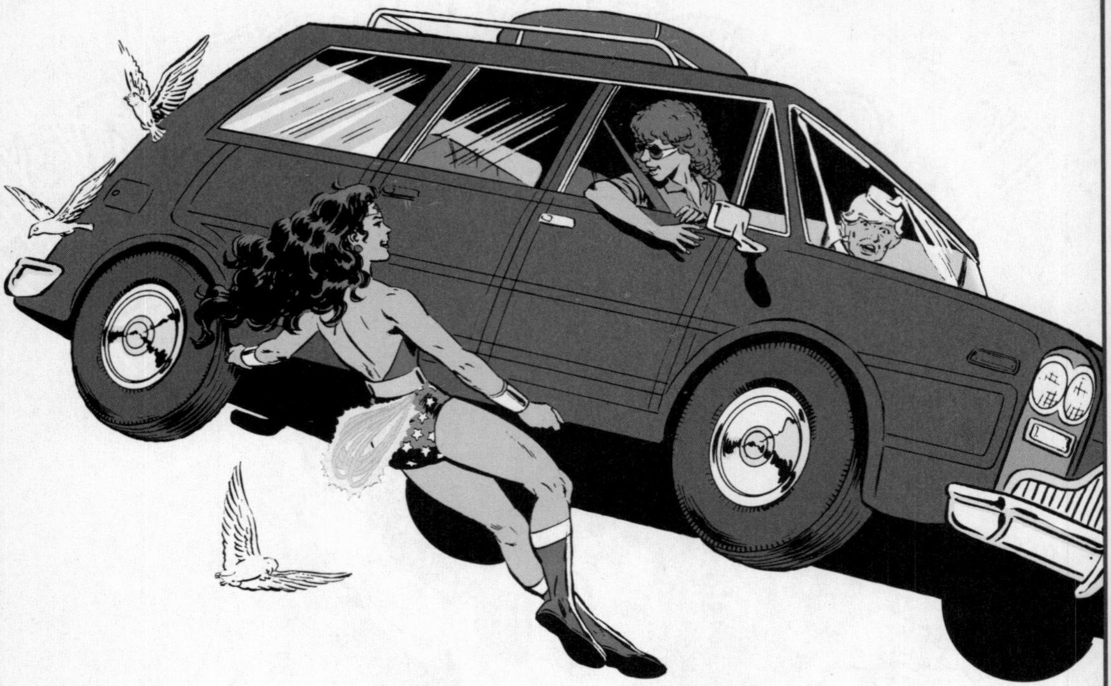

WONDER WOMAN

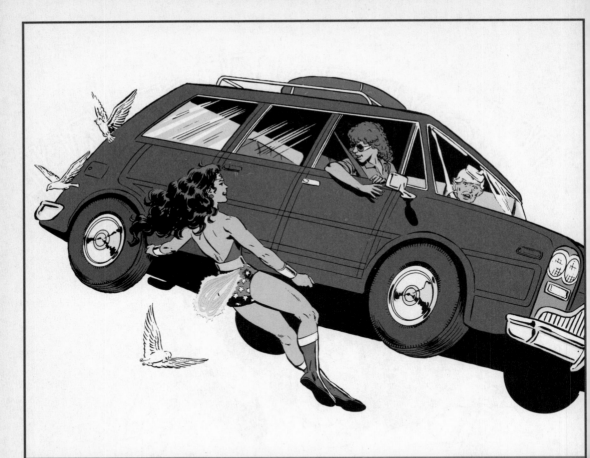

CHAPTER THREE

Through Destiny's Door

BENEATH A SHIMMERING AMBER DAWN, THE RESONANCE OF A BLARING TRUMPET DISPELS THE SILENCE OF MORNING AS DIANA, PRINCESS OF PARADISE, HERALDS THE GREAT NEWS THROUGHOUT THEMYSCIRA.

THE BALLOTS OF THE PREVIOUS DAYS ELECTION HAVE BEEN TALLIED AND THE VERDICT IS IN.

NOW ALL OF PARADISE ISLAND IS CALLED TO SPECIAL AUDIENCE SO THAT THE DECISION MAY BE PROCLAIMED...

...THE DECISION THAT SHALL CHART FOREVER-MORE THE PATH OF AMAZON DESTINY.

WITHIN THE HOUR, THE ENTIRE POPULATION OF THE GREAT GYNOCRACY CONVERGES ON THE COLISEUM, WHERE THE RULING SHALL BE OFFICIALLY ANNOUNCED.

THE HEART OF EACH MEMBER OF THE SISTERHOOD BRIMS WITH BOTH ANTICIPATION AND AMBIVALENCE.

AS THE AMAZONS MAKE THEIR WAY TO MARBLE SEATS, THEIR EYES GLANCE OVER TO THE ROYAL BOX WHERE SITS THEIR BEAUTIFUL, PURPLE-ROBED MATRIARCH.

FLANKED BY HER ORACLE, MENALIPPE, AND THE HEADMISTRESS, MNEMOSYNE, IS HIPPOLYTE, QUEEN OF THE AMAZONS.

KEEN HUNTERS' EYES STRAIN TO READ THE QUEEN'S REGAL FACE, BUT HER COUNTENANCE BETRAYS NOTHING.

IN THE HUSH, ALL AMAZON EYES JOIN THEIR QUEEN'S...

...THE SKY THAT YIELDS TO THEM THEIR PRINCESS.

‹ THE GLORY OF GAEA BE WITH YOU, MY SISTERS! › *

‹ I HAVE BEEN GIVEN THE GLORIOUS HONOR OF PRESENTING THE OFFICIAL TALLY! ›

FROM HER THRONE, THE PATIENT HIPPOLYTE GAZES HEAVENWARD AS THE MURMURS OF THE CROWD FADE RESPECTFULLY INTO SILENCE.

...AND LOOK TO THE SKY...

* Translated from Themysciran.

‹ FOR MANY DAYS HAS THIS QUESTION BEEN DEBATED AND I KNOW, WHATEVER THE OUTCOME, WE SHALL ALL HONOR IT AS THE WILL OF THE MAJORITY! ›

‹ TO THOSE IN DISSENT OF THE POPULAR WILL, I CAN ONLY HOPE THAT YOUR DISAPPOINTMENT WILL BE TEMPERED BY THE KNOWLEDGE THAT THIS JUDGMENT WAS NOT MADE WITHOUT GREAT CARE AND GREAT THOUGHT. ›

2

‹ WELL SAID, MY DAUGHTER. WHATEVER FATES WE ARE TO MEET, WE SHALL FACE THEM TOGETHER... ›

THE APPLAUSE OF THE SISTERHOOD AFFIRMS THE HOPE OF THEIR QUEEN. THE CHEERING CHORUS SINGS OUT IN FERVENT UNISON.

...BREACHED ONLY BY THE CRINKLING OF PARCHMENT.

‹...AS SISTERS...›

‹...AND AMAZONS!›

WITH THE WAVE OF A QUEENLY HAND, THE ARENA RETURNS TO SILENCE...

‹ ATTEND NOW, MY SISTERS!›

‹ ON THE QUESTION OF THEMYSCIRA OPENING HER GATES TO THE WORLD OUTSIDE AND THEREBY SPREADING THE AMAZON AND OLYMPIAN PRINCIPLES THROUGHOUT HUMANITY...›

‹ OF HER CLEARING THE PATH FOR CULTURAL EXCHANGE AND ALLOWING THE WORLD OF MAN TO SET FOOT ON THE SHORES OF PARADISE ISLAND...›

‹ WE AMAZONS, BY MAJORITY VOTE...›

‹...SAY AYE.›

AND SO, IT IS DONE. THE WORD IS GIVEN AND THE NEW PATH CHARTED.

NO FANFARE. NO CHEERS. NO APPLAUSE.

JUST THE SILENCE AGAIN...

...BREACHED ONLY BY THE CRINKLING OF PARCHMENT...

...AS A NEW PAGE IS TURNED IN THE BOOK OF AMAZON HISTORY.

3

SPACE. DEEP, DARK, AND INFINITE.

FROM WITHIN THE VASTNESS OF STAR-CLUSTERED BLACK STREAKS A TINY, GLEAMING PIN POINT...

...HURTLING THROUGH THE VOID FASTER THAN LIGHT...

A SILVERY ORB NO BIGGER THAN A HUMAN FIST...

...BUT PULSING WITH A RAW, BLISTERING ENERGY BEYOND MORTAL MEASURE...

...PROPELLING IT ON ITS LONG, CIRCUITOUS, YET DELIBERATE COURSE...

TIMANDRA SAID SHE SAW HELLENE RIDING TOWARD THE SOUTHERN END OF THE ISLAND.

I HAVE TO SPEAK TO HER.

AH, THERE SHE IS...

JUST WHERE I *THOUGHT* SHE WOULD BE...

LAYING FLOWERS AT THE *SHRINE* WHERE *DOOM'S DOORWAY* ONCE STOOD.

< HELLO, HELLENE. I JUST CAME TO BID YOU FAREWELL BEFORE I LEFT. >

< AND TO SEE IF YOU'RE ALL RIGHT. >

< I AM WELL, PRINCESS. THANK YOU. >

< I PRESUME THEN THAT YOU ARE READY TO RETURN TO THE WORLD OF MAN? >

< OH, YES. I SEE YOU ARE. YOU'RE WEARING YOUR BATTLE ARMOR. >

< PLEASE, HELLENE, I ONLY WEAR IT AS TRIBUTE. >

< TO THE COURAGEOUS WOMAN FROM PATRIARCH'S WORLD WHOSE NAME IS ENGRAVED ALONGSIDE THOSE OF OUR FALLEN SISTERS AT THIS BEAUTIFUL MEMORIAL. >

< YES, IT IS BEAUTIFUL, ISN'T IT? >

< WHEN IPHTHIME SCULPTED IT, SHE WANTED ITS BEAUTY TO OVERWHELM ALL MEMORIES OF THE *HORROR* THAT ONCE DWELT WITHIN THE CAVE. >

< HELLENE, I KNOW HOW MUCH YOU OPPOSED THIS NEW VENTURE, BUT THERE IS SO MUCH *PROMISE* IN THAT WORLD OUTSIDE. WE HAVE A RESPONSIBILITY. >

< YES, PRINCESS. THERE IS GREAT PROMISE AND GREAT SICKNESS OUT THERE. >

< I REMEMBER IT ALL TOO WELL. >

‹I REMEMBER HOW CONTAGIOUS THAT SICKNESS WAS. HOW IT WEAKENED US. CORRUPTED US.›

‹HOW IT CHAINED AND VIOLATED US.›

‹HELLENE... THAT WAS SO LONG AGO.›

‹WHEN HERACLES HUMBLED HIMSELF IN CONTRITION, I ADMIT THAT I, TOO, WAS MOVED.›

‹...AND AS AN AMAZON, I FORGAVE HIM...›

‹...BUT AS A WOMAN...›

‹NOT UNTIL RECENTLY HAVE I HAD TO FACE THESE FEELINGS. FOR CENTURIES, WE HAVE EXTOLLED THE VIRTUES OF HUMANITY, EQUALITY, AND CHARITY...›

‹I GUESS THAT, WHEN ALL IS SAID AND DONE, WHAT I REALLY FEEL IS THAT I MAY NOT BE WORTHY OF BEING AN AMAZON.›

‹PRINCESS, YOU WEREN'T THERE.›

‹IT DIDN'T HAPPEN TO YOU.›

‹YOU COULD NEVER TRULY UNDERSTAND.›

‹...BUT NOW, WHEN WE'RE ALL CALLED TO THE TEST...›

‹I CAN'T HELP BUT DREAD THE INTRUSION OF MAN ON OUR SHORES.›

‹HELLENE, NO. AN AMAZON IS NOT A MINDLESS LEMMING WALKING UNQUESTIONINGLY TOWARD ITS DEATH.›

‹YOU HAVE A RIGHT TO YOUR FEARS, AND THE DUTY TO EXPRESS THEM. AND THAT YOU'VE DONE ADMIRABLY.›

‹ALL AMAZONS ARE NOT ALIKE. NOR ARE ALL MEN.›

‹PLEASE, SISTER. ALL I ASK IS THAT YOU GIVE ME THE CHANCE TO PROVE THAT.›

‹PRINCESS, I AM A GOOD ENOUGH AMAZON TO STAND BY THE MAJORITY VOTE.›

‹YOU SHALL HAVE THAT CHANCE.›

‹I'LL RIDE BACK TO THE CAPITAL CITY TO SEE YOU OFF.›

‹HELLENE, MAY I HAVE THE HONOR OF RIDING WITH YOU?›

‹OH. I'M SORRY. I JUST ASSUMED THAT YOU PREFERRED TO FLY.›

‹SWEET SISTER, WHEN I FLY, I FLY ALONE.›

"‹WHEN WE RIDE...›"

"‹... WE RIDE TOGETHER.›"

WHITE MOUNTAIN NATIONAL PARK, NEW HAMPSHIRE. THE CRISP, CLEAN SCENT OF NATURE FLOATS ALONG THE COOL MORNING BREEZE.

THE SERENITY OF THE PASTORAL LANDSCAPE RUSTLED ONLY OCCASIONALLY BY THE SOFT GUTTURAL EXHALATIONS OF A SLUMBERING BACKPACKER.

SUDDENLY, THE NEW ENGLAND AIR IS CHURNED BY A WHISTLING WIND...

... AND TALL LEAFY SPIRES GIVE WAY TO A BLAZING LIGHT...

...BATHING THE WOODLANDS WITH A GOLDEN WASH.

AS THE WEARY HIKER CONFRONTS THE BRILLIANCE WITH SQUINTING EYES, HE BEGINS TO MAKE SOMETHING OUT...

...A SHADOW IN THE LIGHT...

...THE SHADOW OF SOMETHING FAMILIAR...

OH...MY... GOD!

7

"DON'T DO IT, NESSIE. I'M TELLIN' YA, DON'T DO IT!" "SHUT UP, EILEEN!"

I GOTTA TALK TO HIM. IT'S BEEN OVER A WHOLE WEEK!

CAN'T YA SEE HE'S BEEN AVOIDIN' YOU? C'MON, WHERE'S YOUR PRIDE?

EILEEN, HOW COME YOU ALWAYS GOTTA HANG AROUND ME? CAN'T YOU GO BOTHER SOMEBODY ELSE?

I THOUGHT WE WERE FRIENDS.

OH YEAH. THANKS FOR REMINDIN' ME.

I JUST DON'T WANT YOU TO GO 'N' MAKE A FOOL OF YOURSELF.

I'M NOT GONNA... THERE HE IS!

BARRY! BARRY!

AW GEEZ

BARRY, YOU HAVEN'T CALLED IN A WHILE, SO I JUST THOUGHT I'D...

OH.

UHH... HI, VANESSA.

UM... THIS IS LUCY SPEARS. SHE JUST TRANSFERRED OVER FROM EDGARTOWN.

LUCY, THIS IS MY... FRIEND... VANESSA KAPATELIS.

HI, VANESSA.

YEAH. HI.

BARRY'S BEEN SO NICE. HE'S BEEN SHOWING ME ALL AROUND THE SCHOOL.

I NEVER HAD SUCH A CUTE TOUR GUIDE BEFORE.

LUCY...

AW, ISN'T THAT SWEET? HE'S BLUSHING.

YEAH. SWEET.

BARRY, CAN WE TALK FOR A MINUTE?

UH, MAYBE LATER, VANESSA? WE STILL GOT THINGS TO DO. Y'KNOW...

BARRY'S INTRODUCING ME TO THE COACH OF THE CHEERLEADING SQUAD.

HE THINKS I'VE GOT WHAT IT TAKES. HE'S JUST SO SUPPORTIVE.

ARE YOU A CHEERLEADER, VANESSA?

NO.

OH. THAT'S TOO BAD.

8

UM, C'MON, LUCY. THE COACH IS WAITIN'.

HEY, VANESSA. I'LL TALK TO YA LATER, OKAY?

NICE MEETING YOU, VANESSA.

NESSIE?

DON'T SAY IT, EILEEN. D-DON'T SAY ANYTHING.

YEAH, SURE.

ARE YOU OKAY?

Y'MEAN BESIDES FEELIN' LIKE SOMEONE JUST YANKED OUT MY STOMACH?

OH, YEAH! I FEEL JUST GREAT.

DAMMIT! I FEEL LIKE SCH A JERK!

FIRST, I FLUNK GEOMETRY AND NOW LI'L MISS POM POMS TRANSFERS IN.

GOD, WHAT ELSE CAN GO WRONG ON THIS LOUSY DAY?

YO! KAPATELIS! I SAW YER MOM OUTSIDE.

HER AND YER GEOMETRY TEACHER WERE GETTIN' KINDA CHUMMY OUT THERE.

AAARGH!

WELL, MR. WESTLAKE, I WILL TALK TO VANESSA. I'VE BEEN MEANING TO DISCUSS HER STUDY HABITS WITH HER FOR SOME TIME, BUT THE HOURS JUST KEEP RACING BY.

YES, PROFESSOR, I KNOW HOW INCREDIBLY BUSY YOU ARE. I'VE READ ALL THE ARTICLES ABOUT YOU AND WONDER WOMAN.

TELL ME, HOW DO YOU EVER FIND TIME FOR YOURSELF?

OH, I MANAGE SOMEHOW.

WHEN DIANA STAYS WITH US, SHE AND VANESSA STUDY TOGETHER. VANESSA'S GRADES ALWAYS GO UP WHEN DIANA IS AROUND.

I GUESS IT'S THAT MAGIC AMAZON TOUCH.

THAT USUALLY GIVES ME TIME TO READ, WRITE... KNIT A LITTLE.

HOW ABOUT SOCIAL FUNCTIONS? DO YOU... WELL...SOCIALIZE?

MR. WESTLAKE, WHY DO I HAVE THIS STRANGE FEELING THAT WE'RE NO LONGER DISCUSSING MY DAUGHTER'S GEOMETRY EXAM?

9

OH, I'M SORRY. I-I DIDN'T MEAN TO BE *FORWARD*...

PLEASE, MR. WESTLAKE, DON'T APOLOGIZE. IF MY INFERENCE IS CORRECT, I MUST SAY I'M RATHER *FLATTERED*.

ARE YOU ASKING ME IF I... *DATE*?

YES...WELL...I... OH, DRAT. I'M NOT VERY GOOD AT THIS, AM I?

MAYBE YOU SHOULD APPROACH THIS *GEOMETRICALLY*. THE SHORTEST ROUTE BETWEEN TWO POINTS *IS* A STRAIGHT LINE.

YES... QUITE. ≥AHEM≤

PROF, KAPATELIS. I FIND YOU TO BE A MOST REMARKABLE WOMAN, AND I WOULD CONSIDER IT A GREAT HON—

MOM!

VANESSA. I'M READY TO GO HOME NOW, MOM.

BUT, MOM. YOU DON'T WANNA GET CAUGHT IN THE *RUSH HOUR*, DO YA?

VANESSA, MR. WESTLAKE AND I ARE TALKING RIGHT NOW.

WAIT IN THE CAR. PLEASE.

FINE, DEAR. JUST WAIT IN THE CAR AND I'LL BE RIGHT THERE.

MAYBE THIS ISN'T THE PROPER TIME...

MR. WESTLAKE. *DO* YOU WANT TO GO OUT WITH ME, OR *DON'T* YOU?

WHA...? ER...YES... I *DO*.

VERY WELL, THEN. I'M FREE NEXT SATURDAY. IS THAT CONVENIENT?

ARE YOU FAMILIAR WITH *33 DUNSTER STREET*?

FINE. YOU MAKE THE RESERVATIONS. YOU HAVE MY PHONE NUMBER. CALL ME.

Y-YES. I BELIEVE SO.

THE RESTAURANT? YES, I'VE HEARD IT'S QUITE GOOD.

YES, YES, I WILL.

THANK YOU.

MAN, WHAT A LOUSY DAY.

ONE LAST DETAIL, MR. WESTLAKE.

WHAT?

YOUR FIRST NAME?.

OH YES. YES. IT'S *HORACE*. YES. HORACE.

AND I'M...

JULIA. YES, I *KNOW*.

"WELL, THEN. I'LL CALL YOU FOR DIRECTIONS AND TO ARRANGE A TIME."

"FINE, HORACE, I LOOK FORWARD TO IT."

"AND TELL VANESSA SHE MUST STUDY A LITTLE HARDER, EVEN WITHOUT DIANA."

"COUNT ON IT."

WHAT A BIG FAT *LOUSY* DAY.

10

MEANWHILE...

BOSTON, MASSACHUSETTS; ALONG THE NARROW COBBLE-STONE STREETS OF HISTORIC BEACON HILL:

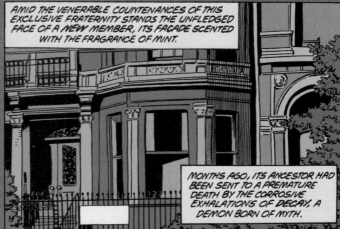

AMID THE VENERABLE COUNTENANCES OF THIS EXCLUSIVE FRATERNITY STANDS THE UNFLEDGED FACE OF A *NEW* MEMBER, ITS FAÇADE SCENTED WITH THE FRAGRANCE OF MINT.

MONTHS AGO, ITS ANCESTOR HAD BEEN SENT TO A PREMATURE DEATH BY THE CORROSIVE EXHALATIONS OF *DECAY*, A DEMON BORN OF MYTH.

NOW, THIS WORTHY DESCENDANT STANDS PROUDLY ON ITS RED-BRICK PEDESTAL TO CONTINUE THE DUTIES OF ITS MARTYRED PREDECESSOR...

THE CONSTRUCTION CREWS ARE GONE NOW AND THE FRESHLY PAINTED WALLS AWAIT THE EVENTUAL RETURN OF THEIR MISTRESSES...

PATIENT. QUIET. DARK.

UNTIL...

BY ALL OF CRONUS! I'VE *DONE* IT!

THIS PLACE. IT ECHOES WITH THE FOOTFALLS OF DIVINE INFLUENCE. *SHE* WAS HERE.

SHE *MUST* HAVE BEEN.

BUT THIS STRUCTURE IS *ABANDONED*. I CAN WASTE NO TIME HERE.

I HAVE TO FIND HER QUICKLY...

OR ELSE WE'RE ALL *DOOMED!*

11

SOMEWHERE ON ROUTE 2:

I *TOLD* YOU WE'D GET CAUGHT IN RUSH-HOUR TRAFFIC!

YES, VANESSA. YOU TOLD ME. IN FACT, THAT'S *ALL* YOU'VE BEEN TELLING ME SINCE I GOT INTO THE CAR.

WHAT'S WRONG? DOES MY SEEING MR. WESTLAKE *BOTHER* YOU?

IS *THAT* IT?

"HECK, MOM, HE'S MY GEOMETRY TEACHER!"

"THE LAST THING I NEED IS FOR THE TWO OF YOU TO GANG UP ME.

"BESIDES, HE'S *FAT* AND *BALD.*"

OH, BABY, YOU'RE *SO* YOUNG.

AS YOU GET OLDER, YOU'LL LEARN THAT THERE'S SO MUCH *MORE* TO LIFE THAN JUST PHYSICAL APPEARANCE.

MR. WESTLAKE IS AN INTELLIGENT, CARING MAN. A BIT ON THE *SHY* SIDE, PERHAPS, BUT...

WELL, THEY CAN'T *ALL* BE LIKE BARRY LOCATELLI.

PLEASE, MOM! DON'T EVEN *MENTION* THAT CREEP'S NAME!

OH, I'M SORRY, HONEY. WHAT HAPPENED?

I DON'T WANNA TALK ABOUT IT.

THAT PHONY LITTLE... WELL, SHE AIN'T FOOLIN' *ME* WITH THAT. "SWEET" ACT.

I COULDA BEEN A CHEERLEADER.

SO I FELL THAT ONE LITTLE TIME. BIG DEAL. THE COACH'S LEG WASN'T BROKEN *THAT* BAD.

LUCY SPEARS AIN'T SO HOT.

LUCY SPEARS?

MOM! I TOLD YA I DON'T WANNA TALK ABOUT IT!

THAT DUMB JOCK. ALL GOOGLY-EYED OVER THAT... THAT... *BIMBO.*

BETCHA SHE STUFFS TISSUES IN HER BRA, TOO.

AND THAT BLOND HAIR. DON'T TELL *ME* THAT'S REAL.

"NESSIE, I KNOW HOW UPSET YOU MUST BE..."

"MOM! I-DON'T-WANT-TO-TALK-ABOUT-IT.' OKAY!?

"JUST LEAVE ME ALONE!"

12

NOW YOU JUST *WHOA* THERE, YOUNG LADY! I DON'T HAVE TO TAKE *THAT* KIND OF TALK FROM YOU!

I'M SORRY YOU'RE SO UPSET, BUT THAT DOESN'T EXCUSE THAT KIND OF BEHAVIOR!

I'M YOUR *MOTHER*, VANESSA. I'M ON *YOUR* SIDE. AND ALWAYS WILL BE.

I - I'M SORRY, MOM. I DIDN'T *MEAN*...

I KNOW YOU DIDN'T, BABY. BELIEVE IT OR NOT, I WAS YOUR AGE ONCE, AND I HAD MY SHARE OF ROTTEN BOYFRIENDS, TOO.

EACH TIME, YOUR GRANDMA WOULD SAY THAT I'D GET OVER IT.

I DIDN'T BELIEVE *HER*, EITHER.

BUT A LITTLE OF HER BAKLAVA USUALLY...

HEY! WHERE'D EVERYBODY GO!?

EH?

OH MY GOD!

WE'RE UP IN THE AIR!

DIANA! MOM, IT'S *DIANA*!

DIANA? I SHOULD HAVE KNOWN.

BUT WHY?

THE AMAZON PRINCESS MERELY SMILES REASSURINGLY AS SHE CONTINUES TO CARRY THE STATION WAGON OVER THE SKIES OF BOSTON.

13

PLYMOUTH, MASSACHUSETTS; AT THE PLYMOUTH ROCK MEMORIAL.

BENEATH THE MARBLE CANOPY, OBLIVIOUS TO ITS HISTORICAL SIGNIFICANCE, A LONE FIGURE GAZES UPWARD THROUGH A PAIR OF FIELD GOGGLES...

...AT A SPECTACLE MILES BEYOND THE BINOCULARS' RANGE.

THE FAMILIAR STAR-STUDDED ARMOR STOKES MANY A FUMING MEMORY...

...MEMORIES WHICH BURN IN THE WATCH-ER'S SOUL.

EXCUSE ME?

FELLA!

HEY, PAL, THESE OTHER TOURISTS SAY YOU CHASED 'EM OUTTA THIS HERE SHRINE.

SORRY TO TELL YA, BUDDY, BUT THIS AIN'T NO PRIVATE LOOK-OUT POINT. THEY GOT THE RIGHT TO BE HERE TOO, Y'KNOW?

HEY, FELLA! I'M TALKIN' TO YOU!

GO AWAY!

SEE, OFFICER? I TOLD YOU!

TAKE IT EASY, MA'AM. I'LL HANDLE THIS.

OKAY, FELLA, LET'S GO. YOU AND ME'S GONNA HAVE A LITTLE TALK.

C'MON, PAL, DON'T MAKE ME HAVE TO...

UPSTART! I WARNED YOU!

GO AWAY!!

TERROR.

TERROR WHICH SEARS THE SKIN...

...WHICH CLUTCHES THE THROAT.

TERROR BEYOND REASON.

WHICH SENDS FRANTIC FEET SCRAMBLING TO HOPEFUL SAFETY.

TERROR INCARNATE.

WHICH STANDS SOLITARY ONCE MORE.

14

WAKEFIELD, MASSACHUSETTS:

MOM! WE'RE *HOME!*

YES, BABY, I CAN SEE THAT.

OH, *DARN!*

WHATSA MATTER?

ALL THIS TIME WE WERE UP IN THE AIR I'VE HAD THE ENGINE RUNNING.

WE'RE OUT OF *GAS.*

WOW, DIANA, THAT WAS SO RADICAL! I'M SO GLAD TO SEE YOU!

YES, SWEETIE, THAT WAS A MOST *SINGULAR* EXPERIENCE.

I SUPPOSE THAT NOW I'LL HAVE TO GO BACK TO *MR. LINO* TO HAVE HIM TOUCH UP THESE *NEW* GRAY HAIRS OF MINE.

I'M SORRY IF I FRIGHTENED YOU, JULIA, BUT I WAS JUST SO *EXCITED* THAT I *HAD* TO TALK TO YOU AS SOON AS POSSIBLE.

BESIDES, THE LOOKS ON YOUR FACES WERE PRICELESS!

HMMM. FOR AN AMAZON YOU'RE DEVELOPING A PARTICULARLY NASTY SENSE OF HUMOR.

A LITTLE TOO MUCH DAVID LETTERMAN, I THINK.

SO THEN, WHAT'S THIS EXCITING NEWS YOU WANTED TO TELL US?

JULIA, NESSIE. I WANT YOU TO *COME* WITH ME... TO *THEMYSCIRA.*

15

GOOD LORD. THEN YOUR SISTERS VOTED *FOR* CULTURAL EXCHANGE?

YES, AND IT'S UP TO ME TO DECIDE WHO SHALL BE THE *FIRST* FROM PATRIARCH'S WORLD TO SET FOOT ON PARADISE ISLAND.

I COULD THINK OF NO *WORTHIER* CHOICES.

Y'MEAN WE'LL *ACTUALLY* GET TO MEET YOUR *MOM* AND ALL THE OTHER AMAZONS?

WHEN? WHEN DO WE GO?

THIS WEEKEND. WILL THAT BE ALL RIGHT?

ALL *RIGHT!?* IT'S *PERFECT!*

OH. MOM. GEE, I GUESS YOU'LL HAVE TO CANCEL WITH MR. WESTLAKE, HUH?

OH DEAR, THAT'S *RIGHT.*

WELL, I'M SURE HE'LL UNDERSTAND.

GREAT! YOU CALL HIM AFTER I CALL ALL O' MY FRIENDS.

THEY'RE ALL GONNA *DIE* WHEN I TELL 'EM!

LET'S SEE LUCY SPEARS TOP *THAT!*

GOD! WHAT A *FABULOUS* DAY!

MY WORD. WHAT AN INCREDIBLE TRANS-FORMATION!

DIANA, YOU CERTAINLY HAVE THE KNACK FOR LIFTING A GIRL'S SPIRITS.

NESSIE MENTIONED A MR. WESTLAKE. DID I SUGGEST AN INCONVENIENT TIME?

EH? OH, NO, NO. HORACE IS A *TEACHER* AS WELL.

HE'LL BE POSITIVELY *DELIGHTED* WHEN I TELL HIM ABOUT THIS UNIQUE EDUCATIONAL OPPORTUNITY.

I HOPE.

WONDERFUL. I'LL BE BACK AS SOON AS I CAN.

GOING BACK TO *THEMYSCIRA* ALREADY?

NO. TO *HANSCOM AIR FORCE BASE.*

THERE'S SOMEONE *SPECIAL* I HAVE TO SEE.

16

HANSCOM A.F.B.

HANSCOM AFB ADMINISTRATION

"GENERAL HILLARY?"

"YES, LIEUTENANT, WHAT IS IT?"

SIR, PRINCESS DIANA OF THEMYSCIRA IS HERE TO SEE YOU.

WONDER WOMAN? TO SEE ME? THAT'S ODD.

SEND HER IN.

YES, SIR.

HELLO, GENERAL HILLARY.

YOUR HIGHNESS. THIS IS AN UNEXPECTED HONOR. I HAVEN'T SEEN YOU IN MONTHS.

ALTHOUGH LT. CANDY DID INFORM ME OF HOW YOU ASSISTED HER AND STEVE TREVOR AT PALMER AIRCRAFT IN TEXAS. PLEASE, HAVE A SEAT.

NOW THEN, WHAT CAN I DO FOR YOU?

WELL, SIR. I WAS ACTUALLY LOOKING FOR ETTA CANDY, BUT YOUR AIDE SAID THAT I SHOULD TALK TO YOU FIRST.

CAN YOU TELL ME WHERE I MAY FIND HER?

I'M AFRAID NOT, YOUR HIGHNESS. LT. CANDY'S ON SPECIAL ASSIGNMENT. A CONFIDENTIAL ASSIGNMENT. I HOPE YOU UNDERSTAND.

YES, I SEE. THAT'S UNFORTUNATE.

NO. IT'S MORE OF A PERSONAL MATTER.

THOMAS HILL

WILL SHE BE BACK BY THIS WEEKEND?

IT ISN'T AN EMERGENCY, IS IT?

OFFICIALLY, I CAN'T ANSWER THAT, BUT PERSONALLY, I WOULDN'T BET THE THE FARM ON IT.

I'M AFRAID IT IS, YOUR HIGHNESS.

IS THAT A NO?

OH.

BY THE WAY, HOW'S TREVOR DOING? IS HE ENJOYING HIS NEW JOB AS A SAFETY AND SECURITY INVESTIGATOR?

I BELIEVE SO. I'VE TRIED TO CONTACT HIM, TOO, BUT I ONLY GOT HIS ANSWERING MACHINE.

I GUESS IT'S JUST NOT YOUR DAY, EH?

17

WELL, IF AND WHEN YOU DO TALK TO THAT OLD AIR JOCKEY, TELL HIM HIS POKER-PLAYING PALS *MISS* HIM.

WE ALWAYS MADE QUITE A BUNDLE OFF *HIM*.

YES, I'LL TELL HIM.

THANK YOU FOR YOUR TIME, GENERAL.

MY PLEASURE, YOUR HIGHNESS. I ONLY WISH I COULD HAVE BEEN OF MORE ASSISTANCE.

GOOD AFTERNOON, PRINCESS.

"GOOD AFTERNOON, GEN. HILLARY."

SIR?

YES, LIEUTENANT?

SIR, I HOPE YOU DIDN'T *OBJECT* TO MY DIRECTING WONDER WOMAN HERE, BUT SHE SEEMED QUITE DETERMINED.

AT EASE, LIEUTENANT. YOU DID THE CORRECT THING.

WONDER WOMAN'S FROM A *WARRIOR* RACE. SHE UNDERSTANDS THE CALLS OF *DUTY*.

BESIDES, LT. CANDY *VOLUNTEERED* FOR THE ASSIGNMENT.

SIR, YOU DON'T REALLY GIVE ANY *CREDENCE* TO LT. CANDY'S ASSERTIONS, DO YOU, SIR?

LIEUTENANT, AFTER THE *ARES AFFAIR*, I'VE LEARNED NEVER TO CLOSE MY MIND TO *ANYTHING*, NO MATTER *HOW* LUDICROUS IT SEEMS.

18

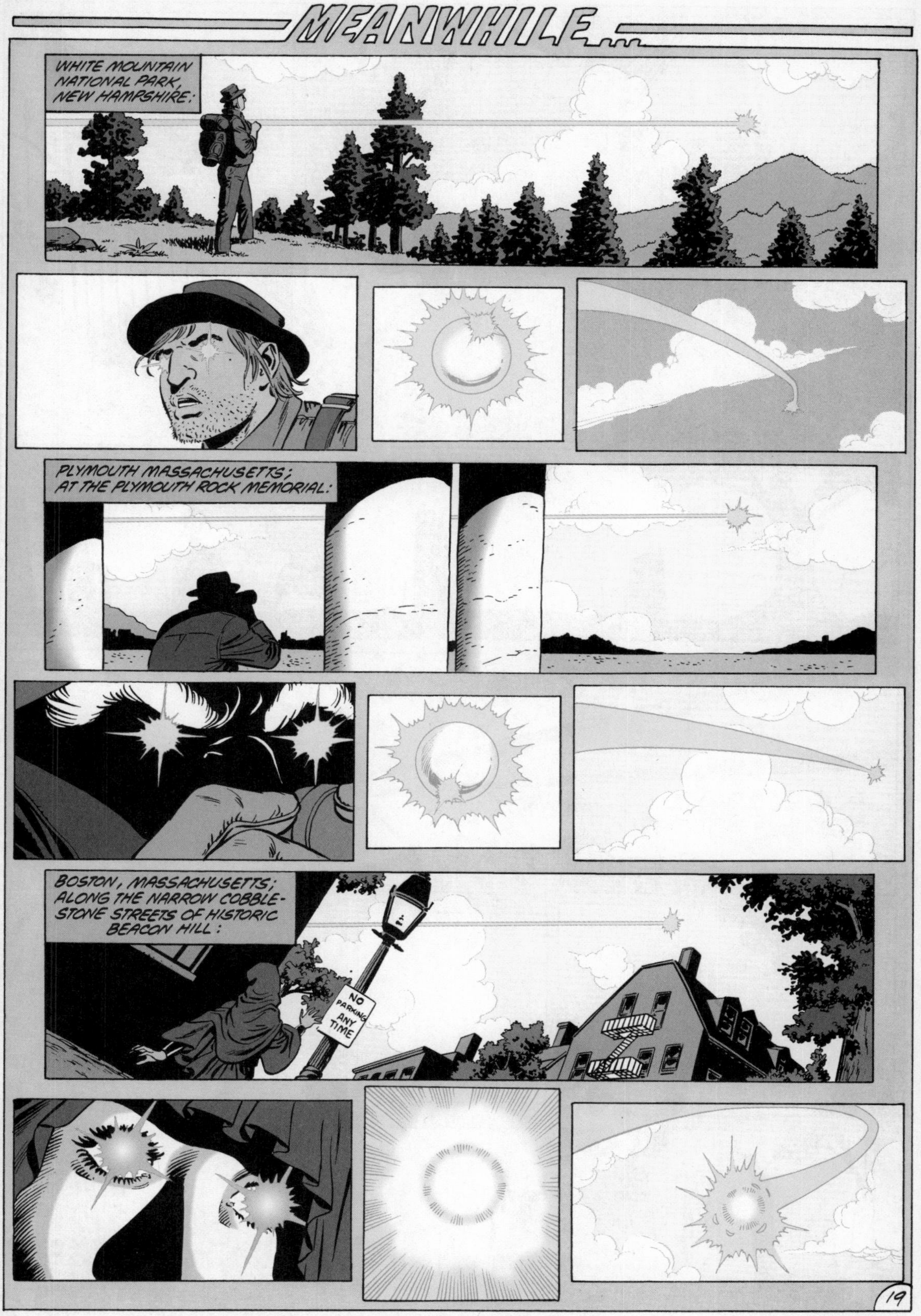
MEANWHILE....
WHITE MOUNTAIN NATIONAL PARK, NEW HAMPSHIRE:
PLYMOUTH MASSACHUSETTS; AT THE PLYMOUTH ROCK MEMORIAL:
BOSTON, MASSACHUSETTS; ALONG THE NARROW COBBLE-STONE STREETS OF HISTORIC BEACON HILL:
NO PARKING ANY TIME
19

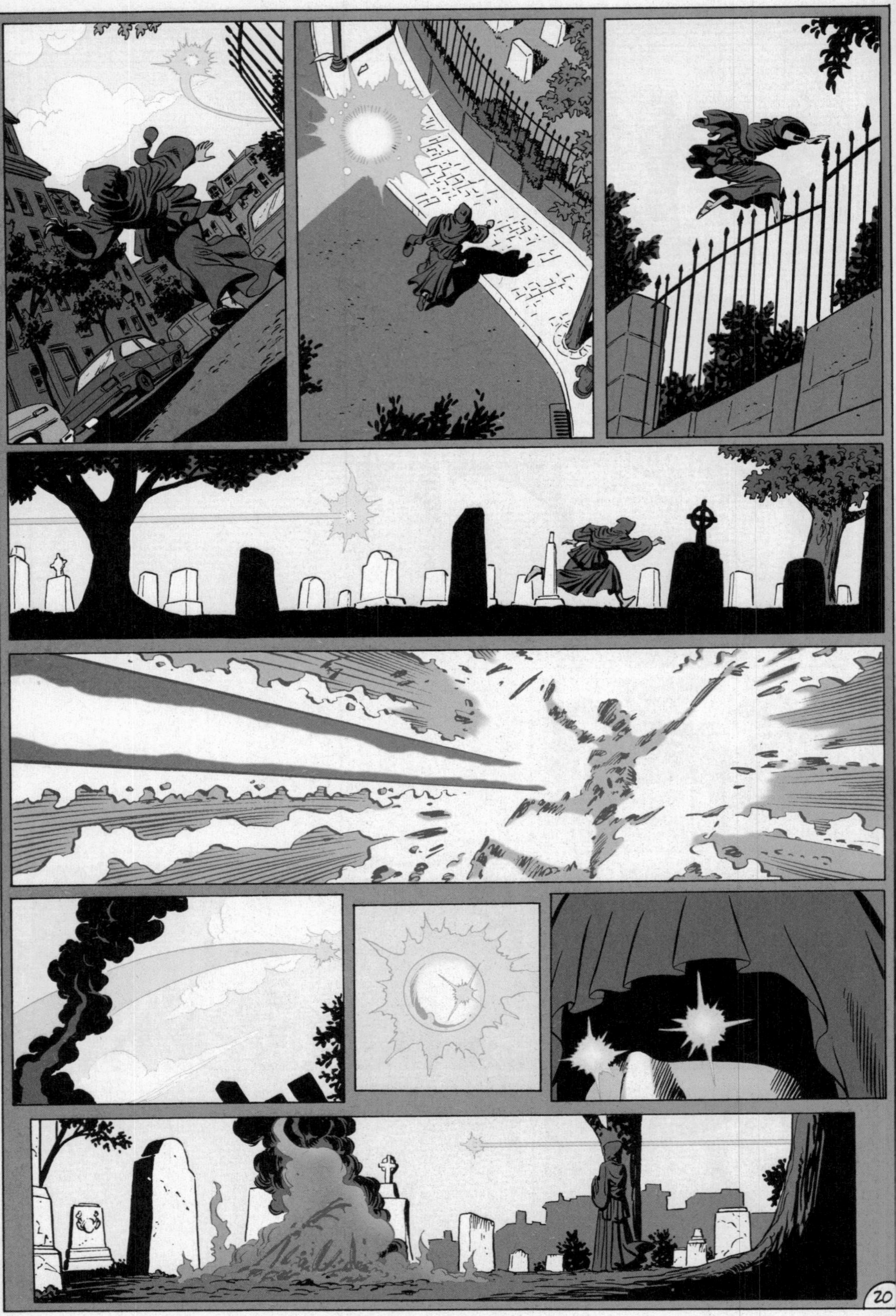
20

FRIDAY NIGHT IN FRAMINGHAM, MASS.

BZZZZZZZT

BZZZZZZZT

BZZZZZZZT

CLICK

HELLO. YOU HAVE REACHED THE RESIDENCE OF STEPHEN R. TREVOR. I AM UNABLE TO COME TO THE PHONE AT PRESENT, BUT IF YOU LEAVE YOUR NAME, NUMBER, TIME, AND PURPOSE OF YOUR CALL, I'LL TRY TO GET BACK TO YOU AS SOON AS POSSIBLE. THANK YOU.

BEEP!

HELLO, STEVE. IT'S DIANA AGAIN. I GUESS YOUR LATEST ASSIGNMENT HAS BEEN KEEPING YOU QUITE BUSY. I'M SORRY THAT I'VE LEFT SO MANY MESSAGES ON YOUR MACHINE, BUT I HAD HOPED THAT WE'D BE ABLE TO TALK BEFORE THIS WEEKEND.

IT WASN'T AN EMERGENCY, SO PLEASE DON'T WORRY. IT WAS JUST...WELL...

SIDE A

COMING MESSAGE

I'LL BE AWAY THIS WEEKEND WITH JULIA AND NESSIE, SO I WILL TRY TO CALL YOU AGAIN NEXT WEEK.

THE GLORY OF GAEA BE WITH YOU.

'BYE.

CLICK

STILL NO LUCK?

NO.

I'M SORRY YOU COULDN'T REACH HIM, BUT IT IS RATHER SHORT NOTICE.

I KNOW. IT'S JUST THAT IT WOULD HAVE MEANT SO *MUCH* FOR HIM TO MEET MY MOTHER AND SISTERS.

PERHAPS WE SHOULD POSTPONE IT?

NO. THAT WOULD BE UNFAIR TO YOU AND NESSIE. STEVE AND ETTA CAN ACCOMPANY ME NEXT TIME.

AFTER ALL, NESSIE BOUGHT ALL THAT *FILM* FOR HER CAMERA.

AND EVEN *I* WOULD NOT WANT TO BE THE ONE WHO DISAPPOINTS HER.

NOW, I MUST GO BACK TO THEMYSCIRA AND HELP WITH THE PREPARATIONS.

DIANA?

YES, JULIA?

I SIMPLY WANTED TO REITERATE JUST HOW GRATEFUL I AM TO YOU FOR THIS.

JULIA, YOU'VE BEEN MY GUIDE, MENTOR AND CONFIDANTE IN THIS STRANGE, WONDROUS WORLD. IT IS *I* WHO AM GRATEFUL THAT YOU WOULD NOW ALLOW ME TO SHARE *MY* WORLD WITH *YOU*.

I LOVE YOU.

21

JULIA STARES UPWARD AT THE NIGHT SKY ABOVE HER WAKEFIELD HOME. SOARING THROUGH THE EXPANSE OF COTTON AND INDIGO IS HER DEAREST FRIEND DIANA, A MAJESTIC BEAUTY WITH WINGED FEET.

AS THE BILLOWY CLOUDS PART TO GRANT THE PRINCESS' LIGHTED ENTRY, JULIA'S HEART RACES WITH ANTICIPATION OF THE NEXT NEW DAY.

THE DAY SHE, TOO, WILL BE ALLOWED TO JOURNEY THROUGH DESTINY'S DOOR.

22

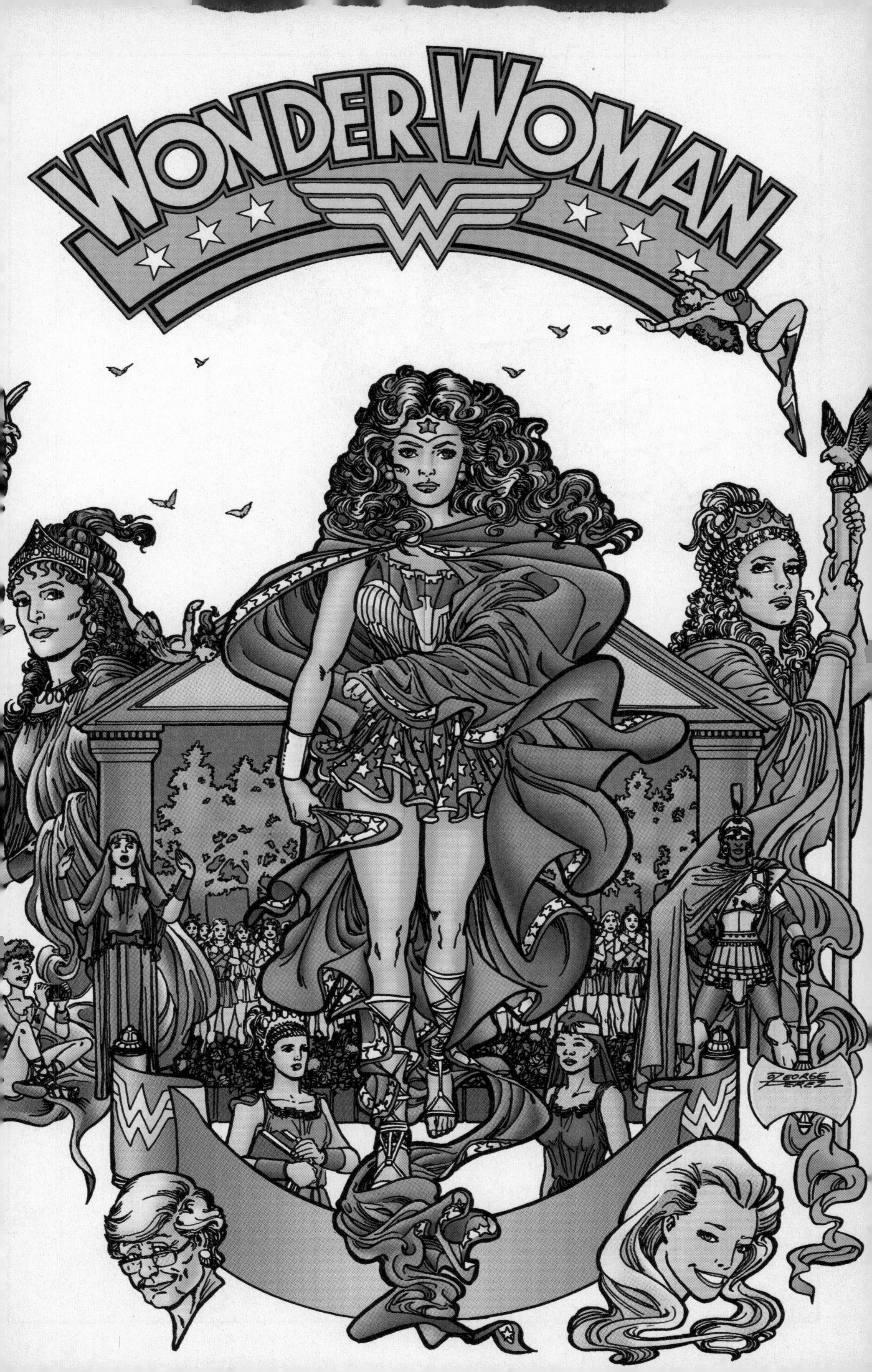
WONDER WOMAN

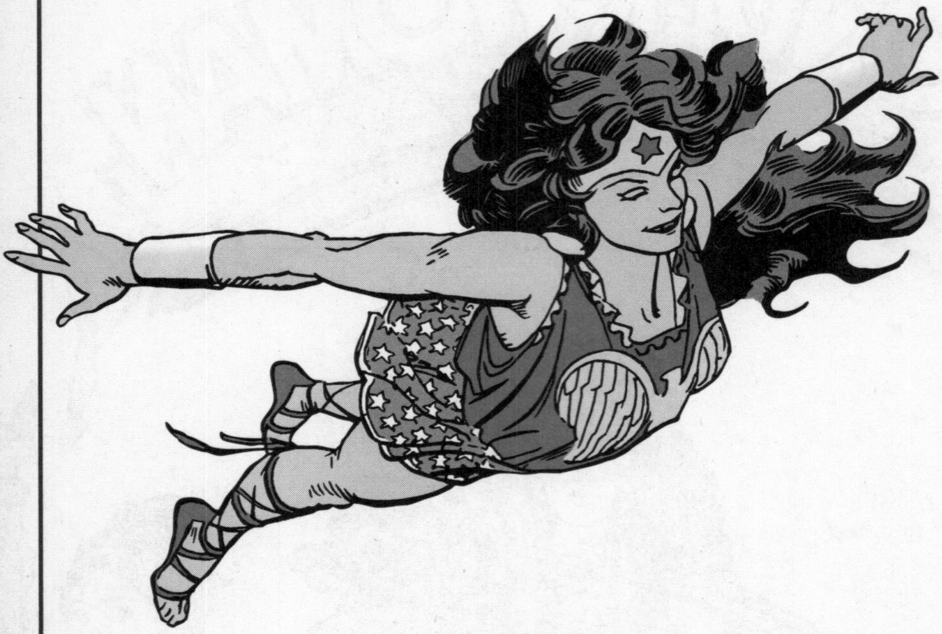

WONDER WOMAN

CHAPTER FOUR

OVER THE NEW ENGLAND SKY SHE SOARS, A JOYOUS SMILE ACCENTUATING A FACE AS BEAUTIFUL AS APHRODITE AND AZURE EYES SPARKLING WITH THE WISDOM OF ATHENA AND THE KEENNESS OF ARTEMIS.

ON HER HIP HANGS HESTIA'S MAGIC LASSO OF TRUTH, FORGED FROM GAEA'S GIRDLE. UPON HER FEET ARE THE WINGED SANDALS OF HERMES, WHICH ALLOW HER TRANSIT BETWEEN BOTH HER WORLDS: ONE WORLD SYMBOLIZED BY HER STAR-SPANGLED ARMOR, THE STANDARD OF *WONDER WOMAN*, HERO OF PATRIARCH'S WORLD.

THE OTHER BY HER GOLDEN TIARA AND SILVER BRACELETS, WHICH PROCLAIM TO ONE AND ALL THAT SHE IS *PRINCESS DIANA OF THEMYSCIRA*, ONE OF THE HOLY SISTERHOOD KNOWN THROUGHOUT HISTORY AND LEGEND AS...

AMAZONS

TITLE PAGE ILLUSTRATED BY *BRIAN BOLLAND & MARK FARMER*

PROLOGUE
ILLUSTRATED BY CHRIS MARRINAN & WILLIE BLYBERG

JULIA! EVERY-THING IS READY! THE GREAT MOMENT HAS FINALLY ARRIVED!

OH, DEAR LORD. THEN IT'S ALL *REALLY* GOING TO HAPPEN?

WAKEFIELD, MASSACHUSETTS. TWO EAGER FACES EXCHANGE JOYOUS, KNOWING SMILES.

WHERE ELSE? ON THE PHONE AGAIN.

VANESSA! DIANA'S HERE!

WE'RE READY TO GO!

OH WOW.

NESSIE? ARE YOU STILL THERE? NESSIE?

YES, MY DARLING FRIEND. WHERE'S *NESSIE*?

HERE I AM! HERE I AM!

I PACKED THREE CAMERAS AND FIFTEEN ROLLS O' FILM. LET'S *GO*.

I'M SORRY YOU COULDN'T BRING THE CAMCORDER, NESSIE, BUT THAT KIND OF ELECTRONIC DEVICE JUST DOESN'T FUNCTION ON THEMYSCIRA.

ARE YOU BOTH READY?

HEADS BOUNCE IN AFFIRMATIVE NODS. THE ASSENT IS GIVEN.

AND THE ASCENT BEGINS.

÷GULP÷ I NEVER CAN GET USED TO TAKE-OFFS.

SHIMMERING CLOUDS ROLL ASIDE LIKE SCATTERING SHEEP...

...TO BID THE TRAVELERS *WELCOME*.

②

THE SERENE NEW ENGLAND SKY IS GONE, SUPPLANTED BY THE RAW, BRUTAL, BOISTEROUS AIR OF *CHAOS.*

DIANA! ARE YOU *SURE* THIS IS SAFE?!

MAYBE WE MADE A WRONG TURN OR...

TAKE IT EASY, BABY. REMEMBER WHAT DIANA TOLD US? THIS IS THE MYSTIC ANTECHAMBER WHICH CONNECTS THEMYSCIRA TO PATRIARCH'S WORLD.

IT MAY LOOK PORTENTIOUS, BUT WE'RE PERFECTLY SAFE, AS LONG AS WE'RE WITH DIANA.

SHE'S A SORT OF *PASSPORT* FROM THE GODS. RIGHT, DIANA?

YES, NESSIE. IT ALSO ALLOWS US TO *HEAR* EACH OTHER OVER THIS ROARING THUNDER.

FEEL SAFER NOW?

MAYBE.

WHEN DO WE GET OUT?

NOW.

JULIA, NESSIE. WELCOME TO MY WORLD!

OH... DIANA...

I-IT'S MORE BEAUTIFUL THAN... I EVER COULD HAVE IMAGINED.

IT'S LIKE... WE'VE CROSSED OVER... INTO *HISTORY.*

OH... WOW...

③

THE ROYAL PALACE.

‹GAEA'S GLORY BE WITH YOU, SISTERS!›*

‹ON BEHALF OF THE ENTIRE AMAZON NATION, I, QUEEN HIPPOLYTE, WELCOME YOU TO THE ISLAND PARADISE OF THEMYSCIRA!›

‹YOUR ROYAL HIGHNESS, WE HUMBLY THANK YOU FOR YOUR FAVOR. MAY MY DAUGHTER AND I BE WORTHY OF YOUR KINDNESS AND TRUST.›

*TRANSLATED FROM THEMYSCIRAN.

‹YOU SPEAK OUR TONGUE! AND SO WELL!›

‹MOTHER, YOU WILL FIND THAT JULIA IS A MOST REMARKABLE WOMAN INDEED.›

‹YOUR DAUGHTER FLATTERS ME, YOUR HIGHNESS.›

‹I REALLY AM QUITE ORDINARY.›

‹HMM. WE SHALL SEE.›

‹AND THIS, MOTHER, IS NESSIE. I'M AFRAID SHE DOESN'T SPEAK OUR LANGUAGE.›

‹THEN PERHAPS WE SHALL TEACH EACH OTHER. WELCOME, NESSIE. BY THE GODS, YOU ARE SO YOUNG.›

UM...HI... YOUR MAJESTY.

THAT PLATINUM-HAIRED AMAZON...

SHE LOOKS... FAMILIAR SOMEHOW.

AND THE WAY SHE'S LOOKING AT ME, AS IF SHE TOO...

OH, JULIA, SNAP OUT OF IT. IT'S JUST THE EXCITEMENT. IT HAS TO BE.

A WAVE OF THE ROYAL SCEPTRE FILLS THE MORNING WITH FLOWERS AND SONG.

AND, FOR TODAY AT LEAST, TWO WORLDS SING OUT AS ONE.

82

PART 1: THE DIVING BIRD

ILLUSTRATED BY ARTHUR ADAMS

A WARM, NEW MORNING BY THE CLIFFS OF POSEIDON.

AS HER SISTERS WATCH INTENTLY, THE AMAZON *VENILIA* CHANTS A SACRED PRAYER TO THE *SEA DEITIES*, THE CEREMONIAL PRELUDE TO THE *DIVE OF THE NEREIDS*.

STEEL-MUSCLED LEGS PUSH OUT AND SHE GRACEFULLY PLUNGES TOWARD THE GLISTENING AQUAMARINE BELOW.

IT IS A DIVE VENILIA, LIKE *ALL* THE AMAZONS, HAS PERFORMED *COUNTLESS* TIMES. BUT, *THIS* DAY IS *DIFFERENT*...

...AS *NEW* EYES WITNESS THE RITUAL FOR THE *FIRST* TIME.

OH WOW

CLICK! CLICK!

THE DIVE IS *PERFECT* AND THE SACRAMENT *COMPLETED*.

SPLISH

<BEAUTIFUL! THE SEA GODS MUST BE INCREDIBLY FLATTERED BY *THAT* TRIBUTE!>

<THAT WAS ABSOLUTELY *BREATHTAKING*!>

<I DO BELIEVE THAT YOU AND VANESSA *INSPIRED* HER, JULIA.>

<THAT WAS VENILIA'S BEST DIVE *EVER*!>

THAT WAS *AWESOME*! MOM, WHY DON'T *YOU* TRY IT?

IT'LL MAKE A REALLY COOL *PICTURE*!

<JULIA?>

<NO WAY! MY OLYMPIC DIVING DAYS ARE LONG PAST!>

HOW ABOUT *YOU*, NESSIE? *EUBOEA* WILL SHOW YOU.

YOU'LL BE PERFECTLY *SAFE*.

WHO, *ME*?! YOU MEAN... I...

...WELL... OKAY.

HOW BAD COULD IT *BE*, RIGHT?

5

YIPE.

NESSIE, JUST DO AS EUBOEA *SHOWS* YOU!

THREE OF MY *SISTERS* WILL BE IN THE *WATER*! YOU HAVE NOTHING TO *FEAR*!

YEAH, SURE.

I STAND LIKE *THIS*, RIGHT?

N-NOW I'M SUPPOSED TO *PRAY*, RIGHT??

YEAH, IT'S DEFINITELY A GOOD TIME FOR *THAT*.

DEAR GODS: PLEASE MAKE THE ROCKS *SOFT*.

GERONIMO!

SPLASH

YAY-AAAAHH!

WOW! DID YA *SEE* ME? I WAS FREAKIN' *GREAT*!

TRY 'N' TOP *THAT*, DIANA!

OKAY, NESSIE, I'LL *TRY*.

‹EUBOEA, I'LL DIVE NOW.›

‹OH? YOU *WILL* TRY TO HIT THE *WATER* THIS TIME, WON'T YOU, PRINCESS?›

‹WHAT'S SO *FUNNY*?›

WITH DIANA AND JULIA TRANSLATING FOR VANESSA, EUBOEA EXPLAINS.

‹WELL, IT WAS A SHORT WHILE AGO, WHEN PRINCESS DIANA WAS A SMALL *CHILD*.›

‹DIANA WAS SUCH AN *OBEDIENT* AND *DUTIFUL* STUDENT, POSSESSING A GREAT *LOVE* FOR *LEARNING*. WE ALL TOOK TURNS TEACHING HER.›

‹WE NEVER HAD AN *INFANT* GROWING UP ON THE ISLAND BEFORE, SO *EDUCATING* HER IN THE WAYS OF THE AMAZONS WAS BOTH *EXCITING* AND *CHALLENGING*.›

‹WHEN IT WAS TIME FOR HER TO LEARN THE *RITES OF THE NEREIDS*, I, BEING CHAMPION DIVER AT THE TIME, WAS TO BE HER INSTRUCTOR.›

‹I SOON LEARNED THAT OUR LITTLE PRINCESS POSSESSED A HEALTHY AMOUNT OF *STUBBORN-NESS* AS WELL.›

‹BUT, EUBOEA, I DON'T *WANT* TO DIVE.›

‹HUSH, PRINCESS. YOU MUST LEARN TO PAY TRIBUTE TO THE SEA GODS WHO PROTECT OUR ISLAND.›

‹IT IS PART OF BEING AN *AMAZON*.›

‹DIVING INTO THE *WATER*?›

‹I DON'T UNDERSTAND THAT AT *ALL*.›

‹PLEASE, DIANA. JUST DO AS I DO.›

‹YES, EUBOEA.›

‹NOW, SAY YOUR PRAYER AND DIVE.›

‹YES, EUBOEA.›

"‹DIANA'S TINY FEET PUSHED OFF FROM THE CLIFF.›

"‹IT WOULD HAVE BEEN A *PERFECT* DIVE...›

"‹...WERE IT NOT FOR *ONE SMALL PROBLEM*...›

"‹SHE NEVER HIT THE *WATER*.›

"‹YOU SEE, *FLYING* WAS AN ABILITY THAT WAS DIANA'S *ALONE* AMONG THE AMAZONS.›"

‹SHE SO *CHERISHED* THE SENSATION OF BEING ONE WITH THE BIRDS THAT SHE FELT DIVING WAS A *WASTE* OF HER *ABILITIES*.›

‹REMEMBER WHAT YOU SAID, DIANA? "WATER IS FOR *BATHING* AND *SWIMMING*. WHY DO I HAVE TO *DIVE* INTO IT?"›

‹I REMEMBER. I ALSO SAID, "WHEN MY FEET LEAVE THE GROUND IT'S TO *FLY*, NOT *SINK*."›

7

"< YES, PRINCESS, YOU WERE QUITE THE *PRECOCIOUS* ONE.>

"< AS LITTLE DIANA SOARED HAPPILY THROUGH THE AIR, SHE COULDN'T--OR *WOULDN'T*--HEAR ME *ADMONISHING* HER.>

"< I WAS FACED WITH A GREAT DILEMMA. SHE *HAD* TO BE MADE AWARE OF THE RELIGIOUS *IMPORTANCE* OF PERFORMING THE DIVING RITUAL.>

"< OTHERWISE, I FEARED LORD POSEIDON WOULD BE GREATLY *OFFENDED* BY THE PRINCESS' *OBSTINANCE*.>

YET, HOW DOES ONE REASON WITH A *CHILD*?>

"< THAT NIGHT, IN THE TEMPLE OF *ATHENA*, I PRAYED FOR *GUIDANCE*.>

"< THE GODDESS OF WISDOM *ANSWERED* MY PRAYERS.>

"< REMEMBER WHAT HAPPENED THE NEXT MORNING, DIANA?>"

"< OH, YES, EUBOEA. *THAT* I CAN *NEVER* FORGET.>

"< AS I WATCHED, EUBOEA MADE THE *CLUMSIEST* DIVE I HAD EVER SEEN.>

"< IN FACT, IT WAS *RIDICULOUS*.>

"< I COULDN'T HELP BUT LAUGH. *THIS* WAS OUR *CHAMPION DIVER*?>

"< I WAITED FOR HER TO RESURFACE.>"

EUBOEA?

EUBOEA!

"< SHE DIDN'T COME UP. I WAS *TERRIFIED*.>

"< WITHOUT HESITATION, I *DIVED* OFF THE SMALL CLIFF...>

"< ...AND INTO THE *WATER*.>"

"⟨I COULDN'T FIND HER. THE SEA WAS AS CLEAR AS GLASS, YET EUBOEA WAS NOWHERE TO BE SEEN.⟩"

"⟨EVEN THOUGH I WAS *UNDERWATER*, I COULD STILL FEEL THE *TEARS* WELLING UP IN MY EYES. I STARTED TO *PANIC*.⟩"

"⟨BUT SUDDENLY, A STRANGE *EUPHORIA* TOOK HOLD OF ME. STIRRING THROUGH THE SEA ITSELF WAS AN ALLURING, MAGICAL *MELODY*. A WONDROUS SONG WHICH FILLED MY VERY *SOUL* WITH *STRENGTH* AND *JOY*.⟩"

"⟨MY EYES WIDENED AS I BEHELD THE MOST *BEAUTIFUL* THING I HAD EVER SEEN.⟩"

WEEP NOT, DEAR CHILD OF PARADISE. EUBOEA IS *SAFE*.

WE ARE *THE NEREIDS*, GODDESSES OF THE SEA, ATTENDANTS OF *LORD POSEIDON*.

I AM *PANOPEA*.

YOUR *SELFLESS COURAGE* IN DIVING AFTER YOUR SISTER HAS *HONORED* ALL OF US.

THE *REWARDS* OF THE SEA ARE YOURS.

AS THEY SHALL *ALWAYS* BE GIVEN TO THOSE WHO *HONOR* HER THROUGH THE RITES OF THE NEREIDS.

THE SEA IS THE *WELL OF LIFE*. THOSE WHO DRINK FROM HER SHALL SHARE IN HER BENEFITS.

SHE WILL *STRENGTHEN* YOU. *PROTECT* YOU. *LOVE* YOU.

SHE WILL BECOME *HOME* TO YOU. ONE *WITH* YOU.

"⟨PANOPEA'S WORDS WERE *TRUE*. I FELT THE SEA *WITHIN* ME. IT WAS *GLORIOUS*!⟩"

9

87

"<I SWAM BACK UP TO THE SURFACE AND FOUND EUBOEA WAITING BY THE SHORE. I KNEW THAT SHE HAD *TRICKED* ME, BUT I DIDN'T CARE. >"

<I FINALLY *UNDERSTOOD* WHY MY SISTERS SO HONORED THE SEA. >

<I NEVER TOOK HER FOR GRANTED AGAIN. >

<WHEN I WAS INJURED AFTER MY CONFRONTATION WITH *ARES*, IT WAS THE *SEA* WHO *HEALED* ME. >

<I OWE HER MY *LIFE*. >

CLICK!
CLICK!

ATOP THE HIGHEST CLIFF, DIANA CHANTS HER SACRED PRAYER.

THEN...THE SILENCE OF FLIGHT...

...THE SOFT BREAKING OF WATER...

...AND THE SEA WELCOMES THE *DIVING BIRD* HOME.

10

PART 2:
DUST

ILLUSTRATED BY
JOHN BOLTON

THEMYSCIRA, LATER IN THE DAY...

THE ROYAL PALACE:

<MOTHER? WHY DO YOU STARE OUT SO? YOU SEEM SO MELANCHOLY.>

<DO I? YES, I SUPPOSE I DO.>

<THERE'S NO NEED FOR CONCERN, DEAR DAUGHTER. NOTHING IS WRONG.>

<IT'S JUST THAT THE SIGHT OF OUR GUESTS JULIA AND VANESSA RIDING TOGETHER ON HORSEBACK BROUGHT BACK SUCH SOMBER MEMORIES.>

<MEMORIES OF ANTIOPE...>

<...AND OF A LESSON WE LEARNED TOO LATE.>

<MOTHER, I DON'T UNDERSTAND.>

<I KNOW, DIANA. WE AMAZONS HAVE HAD A VERY LONG HISTORY. THERE IS STILL MUCH YOU HAVE NOT LEARNED.>

<PLEASE. SIT NEXT TO ME. I WILL TELL YOU ABOUT A DAY LONG PAST. BEFORE WE CAME TO THIS ISLAND. THE DAY WHEN MY SISTER AND I CAME ACROSS ANOTHER MOTHER AND DAUGHTER ON HORSEBACK.>

"<WE WERE LEADING A SQUADRON OF SOLDIERS BACK TO THE CAPITAL CITY WHEN WE MET THEM.>

"<THEY WERE RIDING WITH AN OLD MAN WHOSE LINED FACE WAS A MAP OF EXPERIENCE AND WHOSE DEEP EYES WERE WELLS OF WISDOM.>

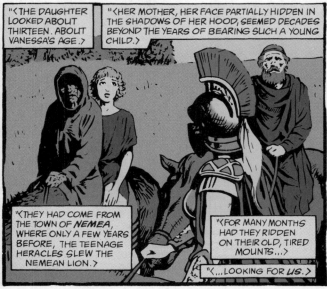

"<THE DAUGHTER LOOKED ABOUT THIRTEEN. ABOUT VANESSA'S AGE.>

"<HER MOTHER, HER FACE PARTIALLY HIDDEN IN THE SHADOWS OF HER HOOD, SEEMED DECADES BEYOND THE YEARS OF BEARING SUCH A YOUNG CHILD.>

"<THEY HAD COME FROM THE TOWN OF NEMEA, WHERE ONLY A FEW YEARS BEFORE, THE TEENAGE HERACLES SLEW THE NEMEAN LION.>

"<FOR MANY MONTHS HAD THEY RIDDEN ON THEIR OLD, TIRED MOUNTS...>

"<...LOOKING FOR US.>

"<THE OLD WOMAN FINALLY RAISED HER FACE TO THE PITILESS SUN.>

"I CAN STILL FEEL MY NECK TIGHTEN AT THE SIGHT. SHE WAS SCARRED AND RAVAGED BY SOME HIDEOUS LEPROSY. AND HER VOICE WAS DRY AS DUST.>"

<PLEASE, MERCIFUL QUEENS, DO NOT TURN US AWAY. YEARS AGO, I, TOO, WAS BEAUTIFUL.>

<I AM HYPSIPYLE, FORMER QUEEN OF LEMNOS. THIS IS MY DAUGHTER, PHTHIA.>

<WE SEEK YOUR HELP.>

11

⟨AYE, MOST ROYAL HIGHNESSES, SHE SPEAKS THE TRUTH. SHE *IS* HYPSIPYLE.⟩

⟨JUST AS *I AM CALCHAS*, A HUMBLE SOOTHSAYER WHO ONCE TRAVELED WITH THE MIGHTY JASON AS ONE OF HIS ARGONAUTS.⟩

"⟨IT WAS ON ONE OF THESE TRAVELS THAT WE CAME UPON THE ISLE OF LEMNOS.⟩

"⟨LEMNOS WAS A MATRIARCHY, MUCH LIKE YOUR OWN THEMYSCIRA, EXCEPT THAT IT ESTABLISHED ITS GYNECOCRATIC SOCIETY THROUGH BLOODY REVOLUTION. ALL THE LEMNOS MEN WERE KILLED, SAVE ONE. THE NEW QUEEN--HYPSIPYLE--COULD NOT KILL HER OWN FATHER. SO KING THOAS WAS BANISHED TO A PRISON TOWER WHERE HE EVENTUALLY WENT MAD. THE WOMEN OF LEMNOS RESOLVED TO WAR NO MORE AND TO FORBID MEN FROM EVER DEFILING THEIR SHORES AGAIN. AND SO THEY DID, FOR MANY YEARS.⟩

"⟨UNFORTUNATELY, THEY DIDN'T RECKON WITH THE CHARMS OF THE CAPTAIN OF THE ARGO.⟩

"⟨I KNEW HOW CHARIS-MATIC AND PERSUASIVE OUR CAPTAIN JASON COULD BE. THE SAME FIRE WHICH KINDLED THE SPIRIT OF ADVEN-TURE AMONG THOSE WHO SAILED WITH HIM SOON MELTED THE ICY SHIELD OF THE LEMNOSIAN WOMEN.⟩

"⟨UNTIL IT ROARED AS A BLAZING PASSION.⟩

"⟨FROM THOSE FLAMES WERE FORGED MANY OFFSPRING, INCLUDING TWINS FOR THE CAPTAIN AND THE QUEEN. A SON AND A DAUGHTER. THAT DAUGHTER WAS PHTHIA.⟩

"⟨HOWEVER, JASON WAS A DRIVEN MAN AND HE WOULD NOT ABANDON HIS QUEST. WITHOUT EXPLANATION, HE DISREGARDED HIS VOW OF FIDELITY TO HYPSIPYLE AND ORDERED US AWAY FROM LEMNOS.⟩"

"⟨YES, CALCHAS. ABANDONING THOSE WHO HAD *LOVED* YOU. THOSE WHOM YOU *BETRAYED*.⟩

12

"〈I WAS BLAMED FOR THE SINS OF JASON. IN ONE NIGHT OF TERROR, THE WOMEN OF LEMNOS SLAUGHTERED ALL THE MALES ON THE ISLAND. 〉

"〈INCLUDING MY POOR MAD FATHER ...〉

"〈AFTER BRANDING ME WITH A CURSE WHICH AGED AND ROTTED MY FLESH, MY FORMER SUBJECTS BANISHED ME AND MY DAUGHTER. WE EVENTUALLY SETTLED IN NEMEA WHERE WE SURVIVED... AS BEGGARS.〉

"〈... AND MY SON.〉

"〈IT WAS THERE THAT THE NOW-REPENTANT CALCHAS FOUND US. HE TOLD US THAT WE MUST NOW RETURN TO LEMNOS. THAT THE GODS HAD DECREED THAT A GREAT TRUTH AWAITS US THERE.〉"

〈BUT, ACCORDING TO THE PROPHECY, I MUST BE ESCORTED BY A WARRIOR QUEEN. ONLY THUS CAN THE LESSON BE LEARNED.〉

〈SURELY, MY RETURN TO LEMNOS SIGNIFIES AN END TO MY CURSE. THE END OF THIS HORRIBLE, PAINFUL LEPROSY.〉

〈THAT IS WHY WE'VE JOURNEYED SO LONG AND FAR. TO BEG YOU...〉

〈YOU NEED NOT BEG US, QUEEN HYPSIPYLE.〉

〈I AM ANTIOPE, QUEEN OF THE AMAZONS, AND I WILL PROUDLY CONDUCT YOU BACK TO YOUR RIGHTFUL THRONE.〉

〈OH, THE GODS BE PRAISED. THANK YOU! THANK YOU, OH MOST NOBLE QUEEN!〉

〈ANTIOPE, I HAVE A STRANGE SENSE OF FOREBODING ABOUT THIS.〉

〈A SISTER NEEDS OUR HELP, HIPPOLYTE. WE CANNOT REFUSE.〉

〈MEN'S SICKNESSES HAVE ALL BUT DESTROYED THE LAND OF LEMNOS. AS USUAL, IT IS FOR US AMAZONS TO REMEDY THOSE AFFLICTIONS.〉

"〈I STAYED BEHIND TO GOVERN THEMYSCIRA AS YOUR AUNT LED A CREW OF AMAZON SAILORS ON A LONG JOURNEY BACK TO THE HOME OF THE DYING HYPSIPYLE.〉

"〈IT WOULD BE MONTHS BEFORE I LEARNED OF THE EVENTS OF THAT VOYAGE...〉

13

"‹OF THAT ANXIOUS MORNING WHEN HYPSIPYLE LED THEM UP TO THE CITY OF HER YOUTH...›

"‹...ONLY TO BE BLOCKED BY AN AWESOME WINGED SENTINEL...›

"‹...A FOUL-SMELLING, SHRIEKING *HARPY!*›

"‹ A RUSH OF FETID BREATH ESCAPED FROM THE GAPING JAWS OF THE PINIONED BEAST. ITS TEETH WERE JAGGED STALACTITES JUTTING FROM THE EDGES OF A DEEP BLACK CAVE. ITS TONGUE LASHED OUT SPASTICALLY IN RAVENOUS ANTICIPATION OF A FEAST OF HUMAN MEAT.›

"‹HOWEVER, YOUR SISTERS SHOWED THAT THIS MEAT WAS TOO TOUGH EVEN FOR THE SHARP TEETH OF THE HARPY.›

"‹ANTIOPE ORDERED THE ARCHERS TO LET FLY...›

"‹...AND ENDED THE MONSTER'S HUNGER PANGS ONCE AND FOR ALL.›

"‹AS THE CLIFFS SHOOK WITH THE CREATURE'S DEATH SCREAMS, ANTIOPE PONDERED THE *REASON* FOR THE HARPY'S PRESENCE IN LEMNOS.›

"‹AFTER ALL, HARPIES WERE *SCAVENGERS.* THEIR TERRITORY WAS USUALLY LIMITED TO PLACES WHERE THE *DEAD* HAD BEEN LEFT *UNATTENDED.*›

⑭

"<AS THAT QUESTION RACED THROUGH ANTIOPE'S MIND, PHTHIA HELPED HER DECREPIT MOTHER THROUGH THE CITY GATES...>

"<...AND FOUND THE ANSWER.>

"<ALL DURING THAT LONG VOYAGE, HYPSIPYLE SPOKE OF THE BEAUTY OF LEMNOS. OF THE TALL, FULL CYPRESS TREES AND THE LUSH, FLOWERY GARDENS; OF WORKS OF ART BEYOND THE SENSES; OF PRECIOUS MELODIES THAT DANCED SWEETLY OFF COOL MARBLE WALLS. SHE SPOKE OF THE LEMNOS OF HER YOUTH, REFRESHING AS A SUMMER'S RAIN.>

"<A LEMNOS LONG DEAD.>

"<THERE WERE NO COOL MARBLE WALLS NOW. NO MUSIC OR FLOWERS. NO LIFE. JUST CRUMBLING RUINS HALF BURIED IN A BASIN OF DUST. POWDERY SKELETONS LAY IN MYRIAD INTERTWINING POSITIONS AS IF THEY HAD BEEN IN THE THROES OF BATTLE. THE WOMEN OF LEMNOS HAD KILLED EACH OTHER.>

"<HYPSIPYLE'S VOICE CRACKED WITH ANGUISH. 'WHY?' SHE SCREAMED. 'WHY HAVE THE GODS BROUGHT ME BACK TO WITNESS THIS?' HER FRAIL BODY TREMBLED AS THE IRON VISE OF GRIEF CLUTCHED HER HEART, SQUEEZING TIGHTLY, RELENTLESSLY...>

"<...UNTIL THE FRAIL PUMP FINALLY EXPLODED.>

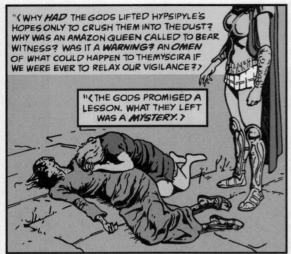

"‹ WHY *HAD* THE GODS LIFTED HYPSIPYLE'S HOPES ONLY TO CRUSH THEM INTO THE DUST? WHY WAS AN AMAZON QUEEN CALLED TO BEAR WITNESS? WAS IT A *WARNING?* AN *OMEN* OF WHAT COULD HAPPEN TO THEMYSCIRA IF WE WERE EVER TO RELAX OUR VIGILANCE? ›

"‹ THE GODS PROMISED A LESSON. WHAT THEY LEFT WAS A *MYSTERY.* ›

"‹THAT NIGHT, THE QUEEN OF LEMNOS WAS SENT ON HER JOURNEY TO THE AFTERLIFE. PHTHIA PRAYED FOR CHARON TO FERRY HYPSIPYLE TO THE ELYSIAN FIELDS, WHERE HER SUBJECTS WOULD GREET HER AS THEIR BEAUTIFUL QUEEN ONCE MORE. ›

"‹ SHE PRAYED THAT HER MOTHER WOULD, FINALLY, BE FREE OF *PAIN.* ›

"‹ YOUR AUNT TOOK PHTHIA AS HER OWN AND TAUGHT HER THE WAYS OF THE AMAZONS. WHEN ANTIOPE REFUSED TO COME WITH ME TO BUILD PARADISE ISLAND AND WENT OUT TO SEEK REVENGE ON THE MEN WHO ENSLAVED US, PHTHIA WENT WITH HER ›

"‹ I GUESS I'LL NEVER KNOW WHAT BECAME OF THAT CHILD. ›"

‹POOR ANTIOPE. HER CHAUVINISM TOWARD MEN BLINDED HER TO THE *MEANING* OF THAT GRIM NIGHT IN LEMNOS. ›

‹UNLIKE THEMYSCIRA, THE MATRIARCHY OF LEMNOS WAS BORN OF HATE AND FEAR. AFTER THE ARGONAUTS LEFT, AND ALL THOSE INNOCENT MALE CHILDREN WERE BUTCHERED, THERE WAS NOBODY LEFT ON THE ISLAND TO FIGHT. ›

‹EXCEPT EACH OTHER. ›

‹WITH VIOLENCE AND PREJUDICE AS CORNERSTONES, ANY SOCIETY, MALE *OR* FEMALE, MUST EVENTUALLY COLLAPSE ONTO ITSELF. ›

‹AND CRUMBLE INTO *DUST.* ›

‹IN THE END, DESPITE ALL HER AMBIVALENCE TOWARD MEN, DEATH CAME TO HER IN THE SHAPE OF A MADDENED *WOMAN.* ›

‹THE LESSON WAS LEARNED *TOO LATE.* ›

‹OH MY POOR, DEAR SISTER. ›

‹BUT THE PAST IS IRRETRIEVABLE. COME. LET US NOW SEE TO YOUR FRIENDS. ›

‹IF MAN AND AMAZON *ARE* TO FINALLY SHARE THIS WORLD IN PEACE AND EQUALITY...›

‹...THERE ARE STILL MANY *MORE* LESSONS TO BE LEARNED. ›

16

PART 3
THE FIRST STATUE

ILLUSTRATED BY
JOSÉ LUIS GARCIA-LÓPEZ

THE AFTERNOON BREEZE WHISTLES GENTLY AGAINST THE SKIN OF THE PRINCESS OF PARADISE AS SHE SOARS OVER HER BELOVED THEMYSCIRA.

NEAR THE CENTER OF THE CAPITAL CITY RESTS THE SACRED AND SOMBER *TEMPLE OF HADES*, THE SHRINE HONORING THE *AMAZON DEAD*.

INTO ITS HALLOWED HALLS DIANA DESCENDS.

‹PRINCESS, I AM SO HAPPY YOU CAME.›

‹VANESSA HAS BEEN QUITE CURIOUS ABOUT THE FIRST STATUE, BUT HER MOTHER WAS CALLED AWAY TO THE LIBRARY BY *MNEMOSYNE*.›

‹PLEASE, WOULD YOU...?›

‹HER NAME WAS *EGERIA*.›

‹PHILIPPUS, I WAS TOLD YOU WANTED TO SEE ME?›

HI, DIANA! BOY, AM I GLAD TO SEE *YOU*!

‹OF COURSE, DEAR SISTER. I WILL GLADLY *TRANSLATE*.›

‹THEMYSCIRA'S FIRST *CAPTAIN OF THE GUARDS*.›

"‹OUR FIRST YEARS ON THE ISLAND WERE DEDICATED TO BUILDING THE CAPITAL CITY AND OUR HOMES.›"

"‹WHILE THE QUEEN AND *CONSIVIA*, THE CHIEF ARCHITECT, OVERSAW THE ACTUAL CONSTRUCTION...›"

⑰

"‹...EGERIA, WITH ME AS HER *LIEUTENANT*, WAS CHARGED WITH THE FELLING OF THE TREES FOR LUMBER.›"

"‹SO IT WAS WHEN *IT* HAPPENED ONE FATEFUL AFTERNOON IN THE FOREST OF DRYOPE.›"

"‹AS MY SISTERS AND I PREPARED TO HAUL A NEW LOAD OF FALLEN TIMBER TO THE CITY...›"

"‹...I HEARD IT.›"

"‹AN EERIE, HAUNTING MELODY IN THE WIND. IT *MESMERIZED* ME.›"

"‹*BECKONED* ME.›"

‹PHILIPPUS? WHERE ARE YOU *GOING*?›

‹*PHILIPPUS!*›

‹CAPTAIN, SHE'S HEADING TOWARD *DOOM'S DOORWAY!*›

‹GREAT GAEA! THERE'S A BLACK SMOKE ESCAPING FROM IT.›

‹THE SEAL HAS BEEN BROKEN!›

"‹THE GODDESSES HAD TOLD US THAT THE ISLAND RESTED OVER A DUNGEON OF PROFANE DEMONS, THAT WE WERE TO GUARD ITS GATE. BUT, THE HUGE BOULDER COVERING THE CAVE WAS NOT *ENOUGH*.›"

"‹AS MY STEED WHIFFED THE ACRID FUMES, SHE *BOLTED*.›"

"‹MY TRANCE WAS FINALLY BROKEN BY THE IMPACT OF MY HITTING THE HARD, STONY GROUND.›"

"‹I CAN STILL HEAR THE SCREAMS OF MY POOR HORSE AELLA AS SHE WAS ENGULFED BY THE BLISTERING MIST.›"

"‹I CAN STILL SMELL HER FLESH *BURNING*.›"

18

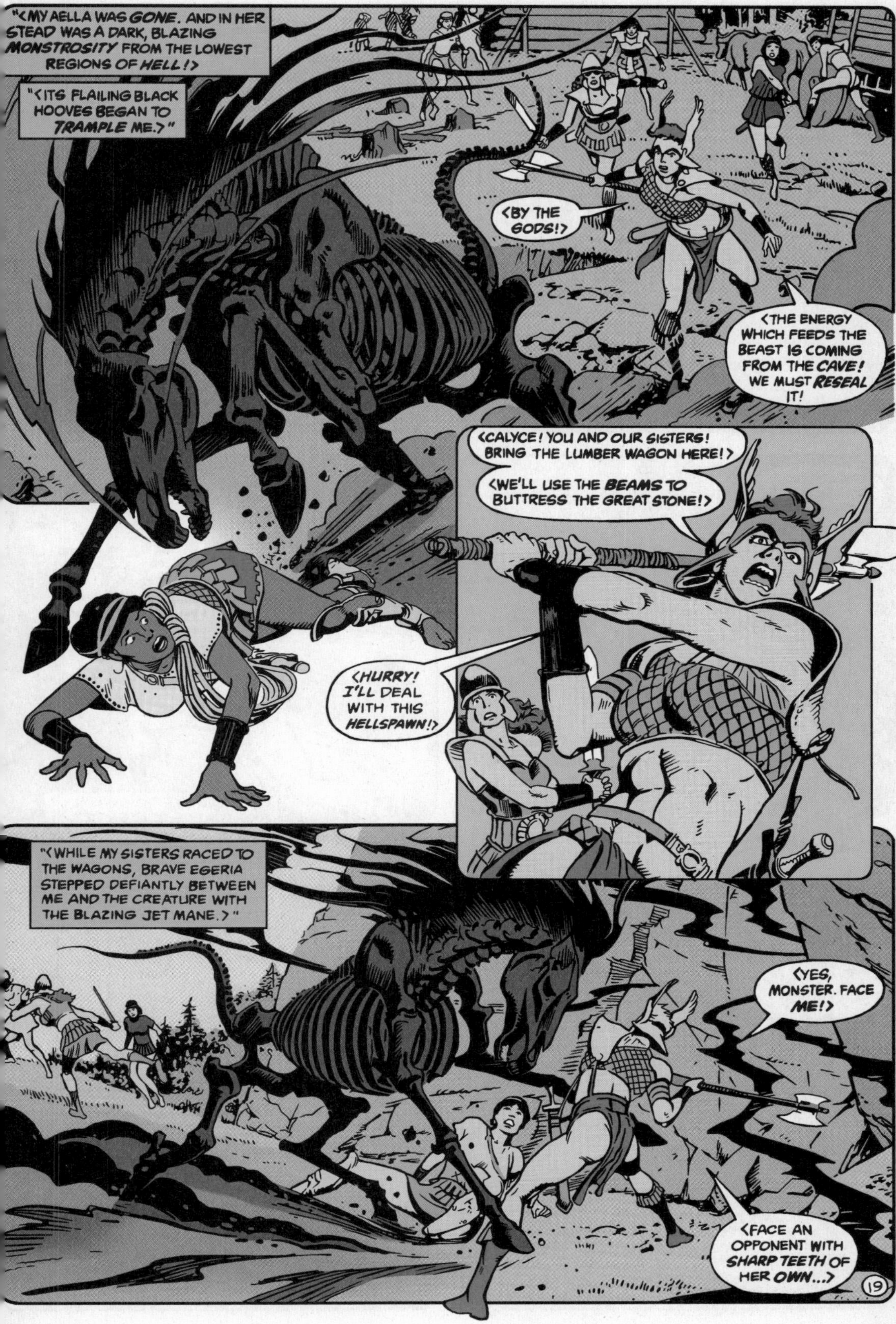
"<MY AELLA WAS GONE. AND IN HER STEAD WAS A DARK, BLAZING MONSTROSITY FROM THE LOWEST REGIONS OF HELL!>
"<ITS FLAILING BLACK HOOVES BEGAN TO TRAMPLE ME.>"
<BY THE GODS!>
<THE ENERGY WHICH FEEDS THE BEAST IS COMING FROM THE CAVE! WE MUST RESEAL IT!
<CALYCE! YOU AND OUR SISTERS! BRING THE LUMBER WAGON HERE!>
<WE'LL USE THE BEAMS TO BUTTRESS THE GREAT STONE!>
<HURRY! I'LL DEAL WITH THIS HELLSPAWN!>
"<WHILE MY SISTERS RACED TO THE WAGONS, BRAVE EGERIA STEPPED DEFIANTLY BETWEEN ME AND THE CREATURE WITH THE BLAZING JET MANE.>"
<YES, MONSTER. FACE ME!>
<FACE AN OPPONENT WITH SHARP TEETH OF HER OWN...>
19

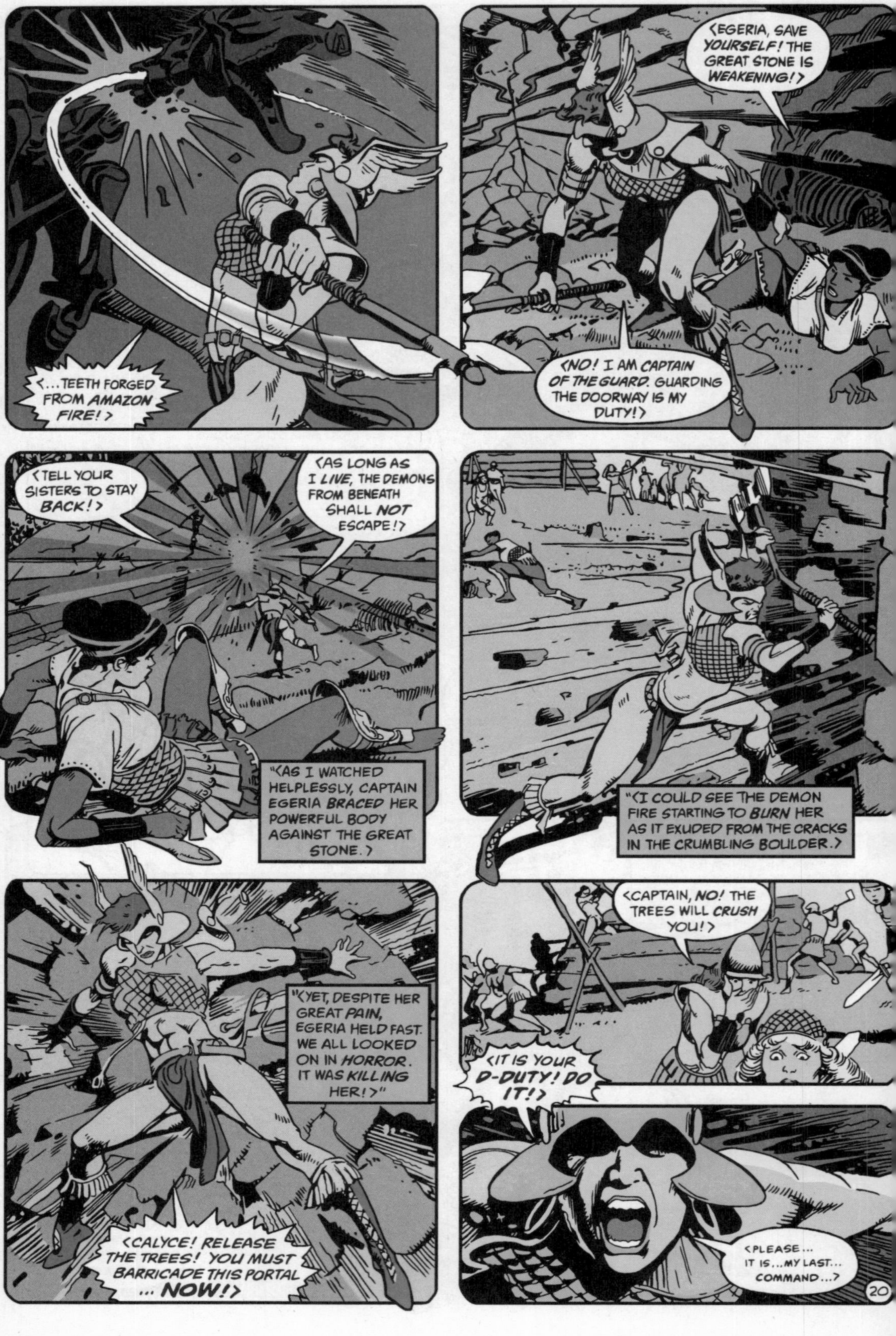

<...TEETH FORGED FROM AMAZON FIRE!>
<EGERIA, SAVE YOURSELF! THE GREAT STONE IS WEAKENING!>
<NO! I AM CAPTAIN OF THE GUARD. GUARDING THE DOORWAY IS MY DUTY!>
<TELL YOUR SISTERS TO STAY BACK!>
<AS LONG AS I LIVE, THE DEMONS FROM BENEATH SHALL NOT ESCAPE!>
"<AS I WATCHED HELPLESSLY, CAPTAIN EGERIA BRACED HER POWERFUL BODY AGAINST THE GREAT STONE.>
"<I COULD SEE THE DEMON FIRE STARTING TO BURN HER AS IT EXUDED FROM THE CRACKS IN THE CRUMBLING BOULDER.>
"<YET, DESPITE HER GREAT PAIN, EGERIA HELD FAST. WE ALL LOOKED ON IN HORROR. IT WAS KILLING HER!>"
<CALYCE! RELEASE THE TREES! YOU MUST BARRICADE THIS PORTAL ... NOW!>
<CAPTAIN, NO! THE TREES WILL CRUSH YOU!>
<IT IS YOUR D-DUTY! DO IT!>
<PLEASE... IT IS...MY LAST... COMMAND...>
20

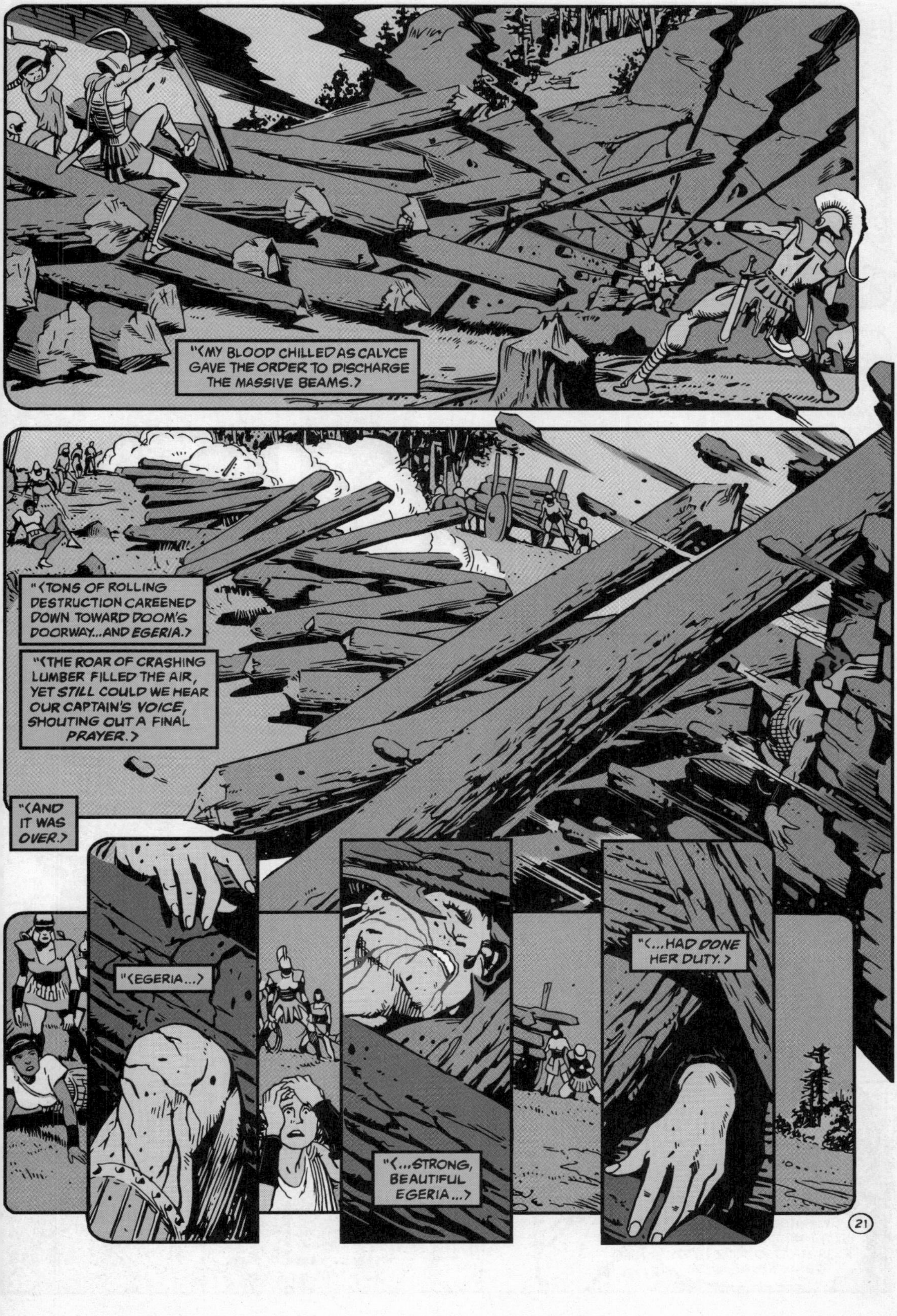
"<MY BLOOD CHILLED AS CALYCE GAVE THE ORDER TO DISCHARGE THE MASSIVE BEAMS.>
"<TONS OF ROLLING DESTRUCTION CAREENED DOWN TOWARD DOOM'S DOORWAY...AND EGERIA.>
"<THE ROAR OF CRASHING LUMBER FILLED THE AIR, YET STILL COULD WE HEAR OUR CAPTAIN'S VOICE, SHOUTING OUT A FINAL PRAYER.>
"<AND IT WAS OVER.>
"<EGERIA...>
"<...STRONG, BEAUTIFUL EGERIA...>
"<...HAD DONE HER DUTY.>
21

"(FROM THAT DAY FORWARD, PARADISE WAS NEVER THE *SAME*. EGERIA'S VALIANT DEATH HAD *REMINDED* US ALL OF THE TERRIBLE *RESPONSIBILITY* THE GODDESSES HAD ENTRUSTED US WITH.)

"(NEVER AGAIN WOULD WE RELAX OUR VIGILANCE.)

"(EGERIA MUST NOT HAVE DIED IN VAIN.)

"(AFTER AN ELIMINATION TOURNAMENT, I BECAME THE *NEW* CAPTAIN OF THE GUARD.)

"(AND MY *FIRST* DUTY WAS TO BUILD A *PERMANENT* SEAL FOR DOOM'S DOORWAY...)

"(...TO *PROTECT* OURSELVES AND ALL THE *WORLD* FROM THE DENIZENS OF THIS ODIOUS *PANDORA'S BOX*.)"

(WE HONORED EGERIA WITH A WARRIOR'S FUNERAL SO THAT SHE COULD PROPERLY BE WELCOMED INTO THE ELYSIAN FIELDS...)

(...AND WITH A MEMORIAL STATUE IN THIS SACRED TEMPLE.)

(ALAS, THROUGH THE AGES, WE'VE HAD TO ERECT *OTHER* SUCH STATUES. THE GUARDING OF THE GATE COST US MANY PRECIOUS SOULS.)

(THIS *LAST* MEMORIAL HONORS *DIANA TREVOR*, THE ONLY *OUTWORLDER* TO BE SO GLORIFIED.)

OH WOW THAT'S *STEVE'S* MOM, ISN'T IT?

YES. AND MY *NAMESAKE*

YEAH, THANKS TO *YOU*.

MAN, THIS IS SO AWESOME.

BUT TO PHILIPPUS, THEY ARE SO MUC*H* *MORE*. THEY ARE *MEMORIES*. REMEMBRANCES OF BELOVED SISTERS WHO STILL *LIVE*, ETERNALLY, IN HER HEART.

DOOM'S DOORWAY IS GONE NOW NO SISTER WILL EVER HAVE TO DIE IN ITS DEFENSE AGAIN.

DIANA AND VANESSA GAZE WONDROUSLY AT THE MARBLE FACES OF AMAZON *HISTORY*.

GARCIA LOPEZ 88

22

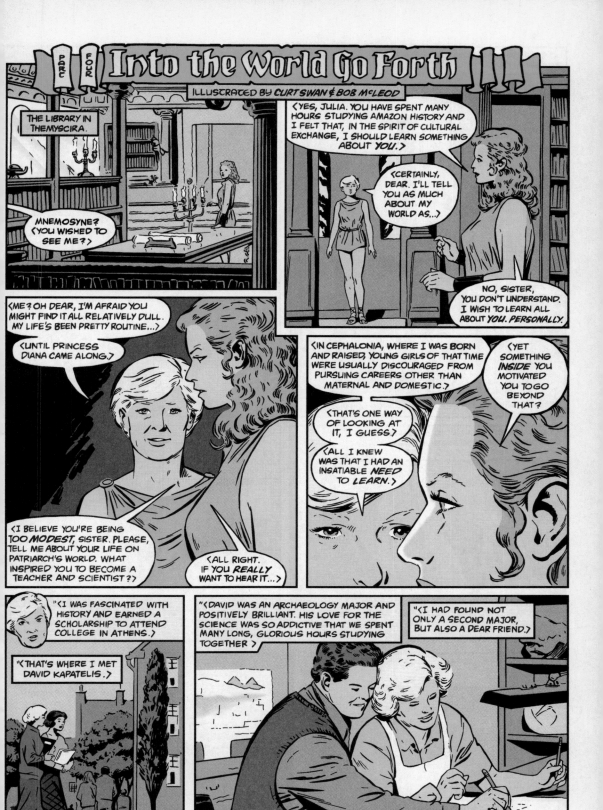

Into the World Go Forth

PART FOUR

ILLUSTRATED BY *CURT SWAN* & *BOB McLEOD*

THE LIBRARY IN THEMYSCIRA.

MNEMOSYNE? ⟨YOU WISHED TO SEE ME?⟩

⟨YES, JULIA. YOU HAVE SPENT MANY HOURS STUDYING AMAZON HISTORY AND I FELT THAT, IN THE SPIRIT OF CULTURAL EXCHANGE, I SHOULD LEARN SOMETHING ABOUT *YOU.*⟩

⟨CERTAINLY, DEAR. I'LL TELL YOU AS MUCH ABOUT MY WORLD AS...⟩

NO, SISTER, YOU DON'T UNDERSTAND. I WISH TO LEARN ALL ABOUT *YOU. PERSONALLY.*

⟨ME? OH DEAR, I'M AFRAID YOU MIGHT FIND IT ALL RELATIVELY DULL. MY LIFE'S BEEN PRETTY ROUTINE...⟩

⟨UNTIL PRINCESS DIANA CAME ALONG.⟩

⟨I BELIEVE YOU'RE BEING *TOO MODEST,* SISTER. PLEASE, TELL ME ABOUT YOUR LIFE ON PATRIARCH'S WORLD. WHAT INSPIRED YOU TO BECOME A TEACHER AND SCIENTIST?⟩

⟨ALL RIGHT. IF YOU *REALLY* WANT TO HEAR IT...⟩

⟨IN CEPHALONIA, WHERE I WAS BORN AND RAISED, YOUNG GIRLS OF THAT TIME WERE USUALLY DISCOURAGED FROM PURSUING CAREERS OTHER THAN MATERNAL AND DOMESTIC.⟩

⟨YET SOMETHING *INSIDE* YOU MOTIVATED YOU TO GO BEYOND THAT?⟩

⟨THAT'S ONE WAY OF LOOKING AT IT, I GUESS.⟩

⟨ALL I KNEW WAS THAT I HAD AN INSATIABLE *NEED* TO *LEARN.*⟩

"⟨I WAS FASCINATED WITH HISTORY AND EARNED A SCHOLARSHIP TO ATTEND COLLEGE IN ATHENS.⟩"

"⟨THAT'S WHERE I MET DAVID KAPATELIS.⟩"

"⟨DAVID WAS AN ARCHAEOLOGY MAJOR AND POSITIVELY BRILLIANT. HIS LOVE FOR THE SCIENCE WAS SO ADDICTIVE THAT WE SPENT MANY LONG, GLORIOUS HOURS STUDYING TOGETHER⟩"

"⟨I HAD FOUND NOT ONLY A SECOND MAJOR, BUT ALSO A DEAR FRIEND.⟩"

"⟨MY PARENTS WERE OVERJOYED WHEN WE FELL IN LOVE.⟩" 23

"⟨I SUPPOSE THEY HAD HOPED THE MARRIAGE WOULD END MY WANDERLUST AND SETTLE ME DOWN TO HOME AND HEARTH.⟩

"⟨BUT DAVID KNEW BETTER.⟩

"⟨THE WORLD BEYOND THE GREEK ISLES WAS FULL OF WONDROUS HISTORY AND ADVENTURE...⟩

"⟨AND WE EXPLORED IT TOGETHER.⟩

"⟨PAST CIVILIZATIONS CAME ALIVE THROUGH THE EPIGRAPHS ON ANCIENT WALLS...⟩

"⟨ETCHED BY SCRIBES LONG GONE.⟩

"⟨AT THOSE MOMENTS, I FELT LIKE TIME WAS ENTRUSTING ITSELF TO US. THAT THE PAST WOULD LIVE ON, THROUGH DAVID AND ME.⟩

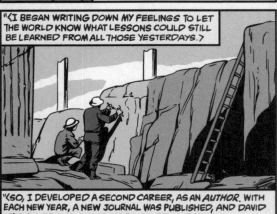

"⟨I BEGAN WRITING DOWN MY FEELINGS TO LET THE WORLD KNOW WHAT LESSONS COULD STILL BE LEARNED FROM ALL THOSE YESTERDAYS.⟩

"⟨SO, I DEVELOPED A SECOND CAREER, AS AN *AUTHOR*. WITH EACH NEW YEAR, A NEW JOURNAL WAS PUBLISHED, AND DAVID WAS SO *PROUD*. THOSE WERE GLORIOUS TIMES.⟩

"⟨YET, NO TIME WAS MORE THRILLING FOR DAVID AND ME THAN THAT DAY IN SCOTLAND, FOURTEEN YEARS AGO.⟩

"⟨THE DAY OUR DAUGHTER WAS CONCEIVED.⟩

"⟨DAVID WAS AN INCORRIGIBLE PUNSTER AND WANTED TO NAME HER *NESSIE* AFTER A SCOTTISH LEGEND WE WERE INVESTIGATING.⟩

"⟨WE COMPROMISED ON *VANESSA*.⟩

"⟨SIX YEARS LATER, WHILE EXCAVATING IN EGYPT, DAVID DIED.⟩

"⟨AND SUDDENLY EVEN THE *PYRAMIDS* SEEMED INSIGNIFICANT.⟩

"⟨I THOUGHT I COULDN'T GO ON WITHOUT HIM. BUT I *DID*. IT WOULD HAVE BEEN AN INSULT TO HIS MEMORY IF I HADN'T. AN INSULT TO EVERYTHING THAT I EVER STRUGGLED FOR. THE WORLD HAD TO BE SHOWN THAT PROFESSOR JULIA KAPATELIS COULD MAKE IT ON HER OWN. FOR DAVID. FOR VANESSA. FOR MY PARENTS. BUT MOST OF ALL, FOR *ME*.⟩"

(24)

‹I FINALLY SETTLED IN BOSTON WITH VANESSA WHEN I BECAME THE DEAN OF HISTORY AND GEOLOGY AT HARVARD UNIVERSITY.›

‹BEING A WOMAN IN A MAN'S WORLD MADE THE PROCESS A LITTLE MORE DIFFICULT, BUT I FEEL THAT I'VE MANAGED TO SUCCEED FOR THE MOST PART.›

‹TRULY. AUTHOR, SCIENTIST, EXPLORER, TEACHER. MOTHER.›

‹THE GODS COULD NOT HAVE CHOSEN DIANA'S MENTOR MORE WISELY.›

‹YES, JULIA, AND I COULD NOT BE ANY PROUDER.›

‹EH? YOU'RE PYTHIA, THE AMAZON I WAS STARING AT WHEN WE ARRIVED YESTERDAY.›

‹AS IF...WE'D MET BEFORE SOMEHOW.›

‹SEE, MNEMOSYNE, I WAS RIGHT. IT MUST BE SHE!›

‹WHAT DO YOU MEAN? WHAT'S GOING ON HERE?›

‹THEN, YOU FELT IT, TOO?›

‹TAKE PYTHIA'S HANDS IN YOURS, DEAR JULIA, AND ALL SHALL BE MADE CLEAR TO YOU.›

‹WITHIN THE DEEPEST RECESSES OF YOUR MIND LIE SEQUESTERED MEMORIES. MEMORIES WHICH SHALL NOW BE FREED FROM THEIR SUBCONSCIOUS HAVEN.›

‹YES! YES, I SEE IT. I FEEL IT!›

"‹I'M WITH MY PARENTS AND MY BROTHER ON PAPA'S BOAT!›"

‹OPEN YOUR MIND, JULIA.›

‹LET THE PAST BECOME ONE WITH THE PRESENT...›

‹...AND REMEMBER.›

25

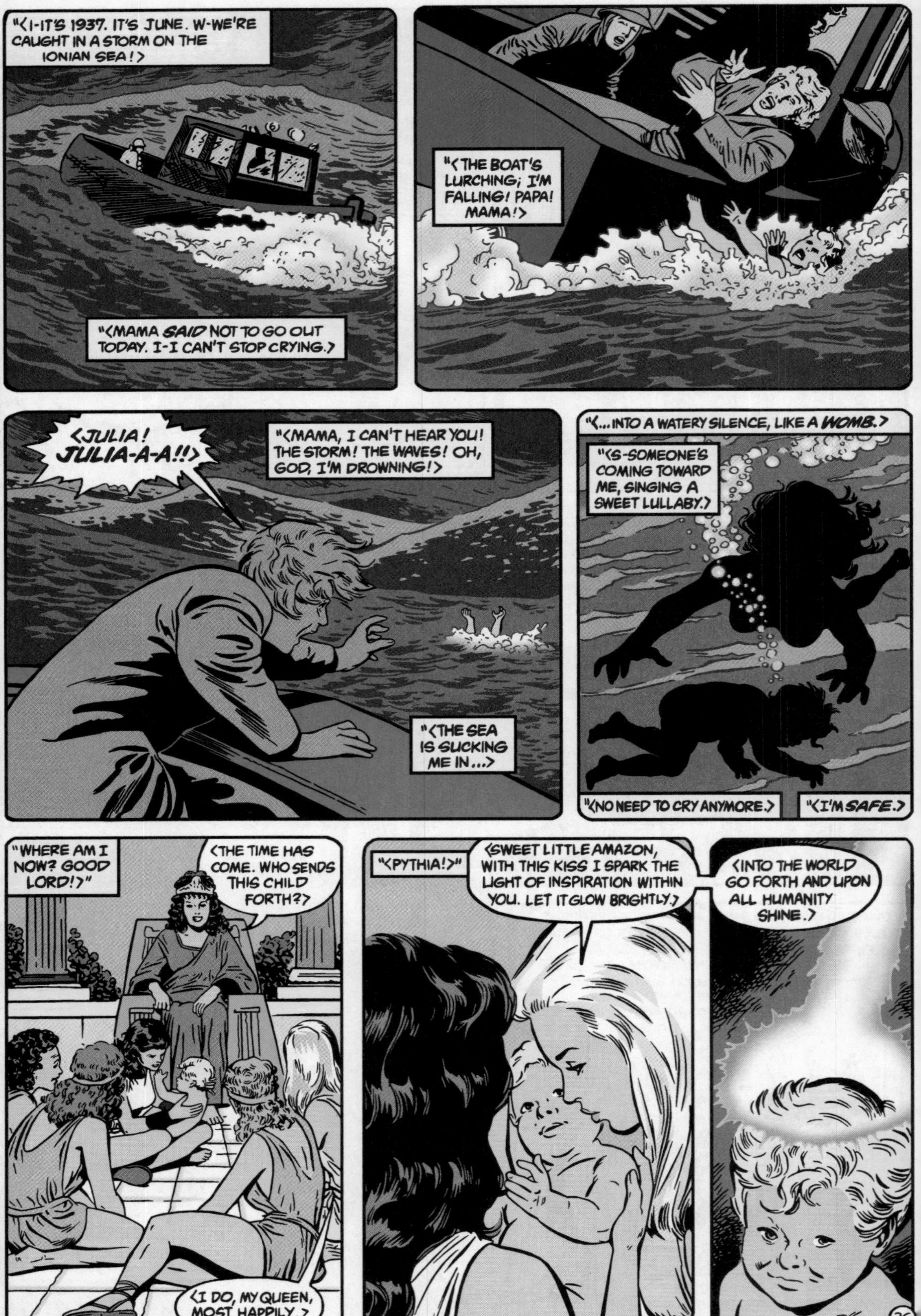
"<I-IT'S 1937. IT'S JUNE. W-WE'RE CAUGHT IN A STORM ON THE IONIAN SEA!>
"<MAMA SAID NOT TO GO OUT TODAY. I-I CAN'T STOP CRYING.>
"<THE BOAT'S LURCHING; I'M FALLING! PAPA! MAMA!>
<JULIA! JULIA-A-A!!>
"<MAMA, I CAN'T HEAR YOU! THE STORM! THE WAVES! OH, GOD, I'M DROWNING!>
"<THE SEA IS SUCKING ME IN...>
"<...INTO A WATERY SILENCE, LIKE A WOMB.>
"<S-SOMEONE'S COMING TOWARD ME, SINGING A SWEET LULLABY.>
"<NO NEED TO CRY ANYMORE.>
"<I'M SAFE.>
"WHERE AM I NOW? GOOD LORD!>"
<THE TIME HAS COME. WHO SENDS THIS CHILD FORTH?>
<I DO, MY QUEEN, MOST HAPPILY.>
"<PYTHIA!>"
<SWEET LITTLE AMAZON, WITH THIS KISS I SPARK THE LIGHT OF INSPIRATION WITHIN YOU. LET IT GLOW BRIGHTLY.>
<INTO THE WORLD GO FORTH AND UPON ALL HUMANITY SHINE.>
26

"〈AS THE GODS DID BRING YOU TO US, SO MUST WE NOW RETURN YOU. YOU WILL NOT REMEMBER ME, LITTLE AMAZON, BUT I, AND THE GLORY OF GAEA SHALL BE WITH YOU ALWAYS.〉"

"〈WHY ARE YOU PUTTING ME ON THE BEACH? I DON'T WANT TO GO. I WANT TO STAY.〉"

"〈PLEASE, LET ME STAY.〉"

"〈THE SURF, SO WARM AND STRONG. PULLING ME IN.〉"

"〈WRAPPING ME IN ITS ARMS.〉"

"〈REASSURING ME. YES. THIS IS FOR THE BEST.〉"

"〈I HAVE TO GO BACK.〉"

"〈HOME ...〉"

"〈I RESURFACED IN THE SPOT WHERE I HAD DISAPPEARED BENEATH THE WAVES. ACCORDING TO MAMA AND PAPA, I HAD ONLY BEEN GONE FOR SECONDS.〉"

〈OH MY GOD! PYTHIA! WHEN THOSE IMAGES WHIRLED THROUGH MY HEAD AS I TOUCHED HARMONIA'S AMULET, IT WAS *YOUR* FACE I SAW!〉

〈THEN, *THAT'S* WHY THE GODS CHOSE ME TO HELP DIANA.〉

〈YES, BECAUSE YOU WERE *ALREADY* ONE OF THE AMAZON SISTERHOOD.〉

27

‹THROUGHOUT THE AGES SINCE OUR SETTLING THIS ISLAND, THE GODS HAVE CHARGED US WITH AN HONORED DUTY.›

‹A DUTY SIGNALED BY THE ROAR OF ZEUS' TEMPER.›

"‹IN THE EVENT OF SOME SEA DISASTER MANIFESTED BY THE OLYMPIAN LORD'S RAGE, THE SEA DEITY THETIS WOULD RESCUE AN INFANT DOOMED TO DROWN OTHERWISE.›

"‹WHILE MALE CHILDREN WERE TAKEN TO SAFETY ELSEWHERE ...›

"‹...THE FEMALES WERE BROUGHT HERE.›

"‹AT THE ISLAND OF HEALING, OUR CHIEF PHYSICIAN EPIONE WOULD TAKE THE BABY IN AND MINISTER TO HER.›

"‹THEN SHE WOULD BE TAKEN TO THE ROYAL CHAMBER WHERE ONE AMAZON IS SELECTED AS HER GUARDIAN OF INSPIRATION.›

‹ONCE SENT BACK, THE SUBLIMINAL AMAZON TEACHINGS OF PEACE AND EQUALITY WOULD HOPEFULLY BE SPREAD BY THEM, OR THEIR DESCENDANTS, THROUGHOUT PATRIARCH'S WORLD.›

‹IN ESSENCE, THE WORLD OUTSIDE HAS SEEN THE INSPIRED LIGHT OF MANY AMAZONS, FEMALE AND MALE.›

‹YOU, JULIA, WERE THE LAST OF THE HUNDREDS OF BABIES TO BE RESCUED.›

‹AND THE ONLY ONE EVER TO RETURN.›

"‹SINCE THEN, TWO OTHER OUTWORLDERS HAD BEEN BROUGHT TO THEMYSCIRA THROUGH THE MERCY OF THETIS, NEITHER OF THEM INFANTS.›

"‹THE FIRST WAS THE HEROIC DIANA TREVOR WHO DIED WHILE SAVING A SISTER AMAZON FROM DOOM'S DOORWAY.›

"‹AND THE SECOND WAS HER SON, STEPHEN, PLUCKED FROM THE SEA BY PRINCESS DIANA ...›

‹IF YOU ARE AN EXAMPLE OF HOW BRILLIANTLY OUR LIGHT HAS SHONE, THEN PERHAPS THE WORLD OUTSIDE IS READY FOR US.›

‹WELCOME HOME, LITTLE AMAZON.›

‹THANK YOU, PYTHIA.›

‹IT'S GOOD TO BE BACK.›

28

PART 5:

Flight of the Icarus

ILLUSTRATED BY
ROSS ANDRU &
GEORGE PÉREZ

ON THIS COOL FINAL EVENING OF THE KAPETELISES' VISIT, THE SMILING FACES OF AMAZON SISTERS BATHE IN THE WARMTH OF AN OPEN FIRE.

THEMYSCIRA AT NIGHT, LUSTROUSLY GLEAMING WITH THE GLOW OF ARTEMIS' SILVER MOON.

THESE HAVE BEEN DAYS OF GREAT SHARING. TWO WORLDS, IN MANY WAYS SO DIFFERENT...

...YET WITH A COMMON *BOND*...

...A *BOND* WHICH PORTENDS GREAT PROMISE WITH EACH COMING DAWN.

‹DIANA, THESE DAYS HAVE BEEN SO WONDERFUL AND ENLIGHTENING THAT I NEVER ASKED *WHY* THE MAN STEPHEN TREVOR DID NOT COME AS WELL.›

‹I SO LOOKED FORWARD TO MEETING THE SON OF THE DIANA WHOSE NAME YOU BEAR.›

‹MOTHER, HE *WOULD* HAVE COME IF HE COULD, BUT HIS NEW DUTIES COMMAND SO MUCH OF HIS TIME.›

‹SINCE LEAVING THE MILITARY, STEVE IS NOW A SAFETY INSPECTOR AND ENGINEERING ADVISOR SPECIALIZING IN MILITARY AIRCRAFT.›

"‹DAUGHTER, AREN'T THESE THE *SAME* KIND OF CRAFT THAT STEPHEN TREVOR HIMSELF FLEW WHEN MAD ARES NEARLY HAD HIM DESTROY OUR ISLAND??›"

‹YES, MOTHER. STEVE STILL DEEPLY REGRETS THAT, EVEN THOUGH I'VE TOLD HIM THAT HE WAS NOT TO BLAME.›

29

<HE WAS JUST SO GRATEFUL FOR THE MYSTIC PROTECTIVE SHIELD WHICH MADE HIS PLANE'S CONTROLS GO BERSERK AND THUS SAVED OUR HOME.>

<IN FACT, IT WAS THE MEMORIES OF THAT DAY THAT GAVE ME A SENSE OF WHAT THE OUTWORLDERS CALL *DÉJÀ VU* WHEN STEVE WAS CALLED IN TO INVESTIGATE RECENT CRASHES OF MILITARY AIR-CRAFT IN THE AMERICAN STATE OF TEXAS.>

"<STEVE HAD COME TO CONSOLE ME ABOUT THE DEATH OF MYNDI MAYER, WHEN HIS LOVER ETTA TOLD HIM ABOUT THE CRASHES. YOU SEE, ETTA'S WITH THE AERIAL BRANCH OF THEIR MILITARY AND WANTED TO GIVE STEVE AN ASSIGNMENT WHICH WOULD HELP ESTABLISH HIS REPUTATION.>

"<I SUPPOSE THEY THOUGHT THAT I NEEDED A 'CHANGE OF SCENERY', SO THEY ASKED ME TO ACCOMPANY THEM.>"

UH, HERE, LIEUTENANT. BUT I TELL YA THERE'S NO WAY THESE PLANES COULD HAVE HAD ANY STRUCTURAL DEFECTS. I WENT OVER THESE BABIES *MYSELF*.

WELL, SIR, THAT'S WHY MR. TREVOR IS HERE. IF YOUR FIRM HOPES TO CONTINUE DEALING WITH THE AIR FORCE, I SUGGEST YOU COOPERATE.

MA'AM, I LOST TWO GOOD *PILOTS*. I INTEND TO HELP ANY WAY I CAN.

HELLO THERE, FOLKS! WELCOME TO *PALMER AIRCRAFT*. MR. TREVOR, I PRESUME?

I'M P.J. PALMER, MANAGER OF THIS HERE PLANT AND...

...WONDER WOMAN?

PUT YOUR EYES BACK IN YOUR HEAD, MR. PALMER. THE PRINCESS IS WITH *US*.

I'M LT. CANDY, U.S. AIR FORCE. WHERE'S THE WRECKAGE?

<AND SO, STEVE WENT TO WORK.>

"<ALTHOUGH I DIDN'T UNDERSTAND WHAT STEVE WAS ACTUALLY DOING, I COULD NOT HELP BUT MARVEL AT THE CONFIDENCE HE SHOWED. HE WAS LIKE A SKILLED CRAFTSMAN, IMPECCABLE IN HIS ATTENTION TO DETAIL.>

"<HE LABORED FOR DAYS, UNTIL...>"

WELL?

WELL, I'LL TELL YA, MR. PALMER. THE MILITARY DIDN'T WASTE THEIR MONEY BY HIRING *YOU*. THIS BIRD WAS *PERFECT*.

AIN'T NO WAY IN *HELL* THAT THIS PLANE SHOULD'VE CRASHED. LOOKS LIKE *SABOTAGE*.

I JUST WISH I COULD FIGURE OUT *HOW*.

"<I CONFESS TO HAVING *MIXED* FEELINGS ABOUT STEVE'S FINDINGS.>

30

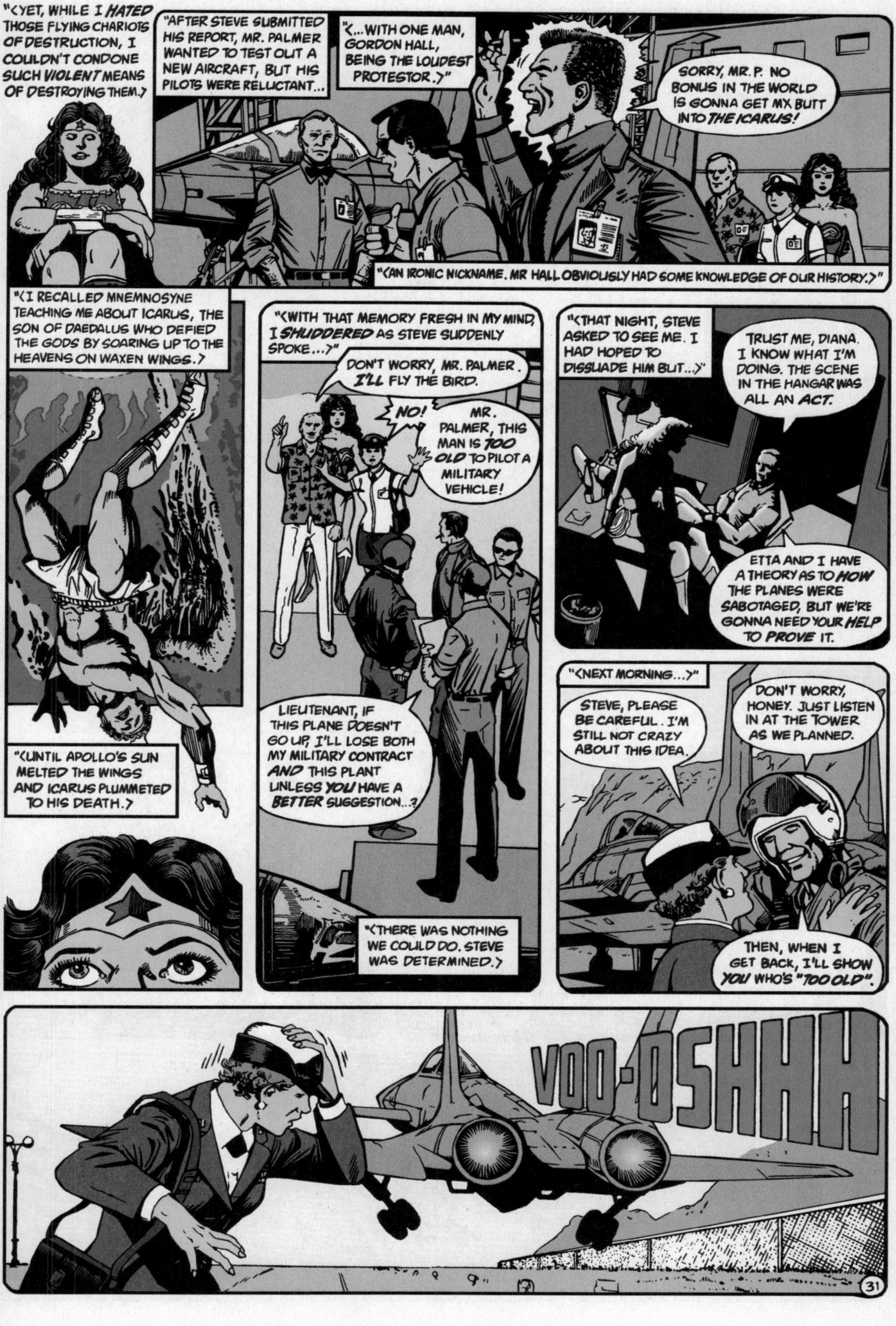
"<YET, WHILE I HATED THOSE FLYING CHARIOTS OF DESTRUCTION, I COULDN'T CONDONE SUCH VIOLENT MEANS OF DESTROYING THEM.>
"AFTER STEVE SUBMITTED HIS REPORT, MR. PALMER WANTED TO TEST OUT A NEW AIRCRAFT, BUT HIS PILOTS WERE RELUCTANT...
"<...WITH ONE MAN, GORDON HALL, BEING THE LOUDEST PROTESTOR.>"
SORRY, MR. P. NO BONUS IN THE WORLD IS GONNA GET MY BUTT INTO THE ICARUS!
"<AN IRONIC NICKNAME. MR HALL OBVIOUSLY HAD SOME KNOWLEDGE OF OUR HISTORY.>"
"<I RECALLED MNEMNOSYNE TEACHING ME ABOUT ICARUS, THE SON OF DAEDALUS WHO DEFIED THE GODS BY SOARING UP TO THE HEAVENS ON WAXEN WINGS.>
"<UNTIL APOLLO'S SUN MELTED THE WINGS AND ICARUS PLUMMETED TO HIS DEATH.>
"<WITH THAT MEMORY FRESH IN MY MIND, I SHUDDERED AS STEVE SUDDENLY SPOKE...>"
DON'T WORRY, MR. PALMER. I'LL FLY THE BIRD.
NO!
MR. PALMER, THIS MAN IS TOO OLD TO PILOT A MILITARY VEHICLE!
LIEUTENANT, IF THIS PLANE DOESN'T GO UP, I'LL LOSE BOTH MY MILITARY CONTRACT AND THIS PLANT UNLESS YOU HAVE A BETTER SUGGESTION...?
"<THERE WAS NOTHING WE COULD DO. STEVE WAS DETERMINED.>
"<THAT NIGHT, STEVE ASKED TO SEE ME. I HAD HOPED TO DISSUADE HIM BUT...>"
TRUST ME, DIANA. I KNOW WHAT I'M DOING. THE SCENE IN THE HANGAR WAS ALL AN ACT.
ETTA AND I HAVE A THEORY AS TO HOW THE PLANES WERE SABOTAGED, BUT WE'RE GONNA NEED YOUR HELP TO PROVE IT.
"<NEXT MORNING...>"
STEVE, PLEASE BE CAREFUL. I'M STILL NOT CRAZY ABOUT THIS IDEA.
DON'T WORRY, HONEY. JUST LISTEN IN AT THE TOWER AS WE PLANNED.
THEN, WHEN I GET BACK, I'LL SHOW YOU WHO'S "TOO OLD".
VOO-OSHHH
31

"<AS ETTA ARRIVED AT THE CONTROL TOWER, SHE LISTENED AS MR. PALMER KEPT CONTACT WITH STEVE AND THE PLANE.>"

TOWER TO TREVOR. YOU'RE LOOKIN' GOOD OUT THERE. ANY TROUBLE WITH THE BIRD YET? OVER.

ROGER, TREVOR. WE'VE GOT YOU ON OUR SCOPES, CLIMBING TO 22,000.

STILL LOOKIN' GOOD. OVER.

YEAH, BUT NOT FOR LONG, OLD MAN.

AWRIGHT, CORBIN. LET'S MELT THE ICARUS' WINGS.

WITH PLEASURE, MR. HALL.

OUR FOREIGN BUDDIES ARE GONNA PAY US PLENTY FOR THIS CRASH.

THAT'S A NEGATIVE, TOWER. THE BIRD'S HANDLING SMOOTH AS SILK. I'M TAKING HER UP ANOTHER TWO THOUSAND. OVER.

UH-OH.

TREVOR TO TOWER. THE BIRD'S STARTING TO KICK. THE CONTROLS AREN'T RESPONDING. OVER.

TREVOR TO TOWER. COME IN. OVER.

TREVOR TO TOWER! COME IN!! OVER!!

IKARUS!! YOIARTHRA!

HUH? WHAT'S HE SAYING...?

WONDER WOMAN!

DAMN! I'M GETTIN' OUTTA HERE!

"<IT TOOK GORDON HALL SOME TIME TO TRAVERSE THE LENGTH OF THE HANGAR.>

"<LONG ENOUGH FOR ETTA TO BE READY FOR HIM.>"

UNNGHH!

"<MEANWHILE, THE MYSTIC FIRE OF HESTIA'S LASSO WAS BURNING DOWN THE WALLS OF DECEIT FROM HALL'S ACCOMPLICE.>"

YOU MUST TELL ME! WHAT HAVE YOU DONE TO STEVE'S PLANE?

W-WE'RE TRANSMITTING A DISRUPT SEQUENCE TO OVERRIDE THE ICARUS' COMPUTER CONTROL SYSTEMS. TH-THEY WON'T RESPOND TO PILOT COMMAND.

WHAT ABOUT MANUAL CONTROLS?

USELESS. THEY ONLY WORK WHEN THE COMPUTER'S DEACTIVATED. AND THAT CAN NOW ONLY BE DONE FROM THIS TERMINAL.

W-WE DON'T HAVE THAT ACCESS CODE.

ETTA? DIANA? ARE YOU THERE?

32

THE CANOPY RELEASE IS INOPERATIVE. I CAN'T *EJECT.*

ETTA, HONEY, I THINK I'M IN *BIG* TROUBLE. OVER.

DIANA, YOU HAVE TO GET TO THAT PLANE. I'LL FIND THE BACK DOOR TO THIS SYSTEM.

ETTA? DIANA? ARE YOU READING ME? OVER.

LADIES, I COULD DEFINITELY USE SOME HELP UP HERE. OVER.

AH! FINALLY! MY OWN PERSONAL *GUARDIAN ANGEL.*

OKAY, DIANA. I DON'T KNOW IF YOU CAN STILL HEAR ME, BUT I SURE HOPE YOU REMEMBER WHAT I TAUGHT YOU.

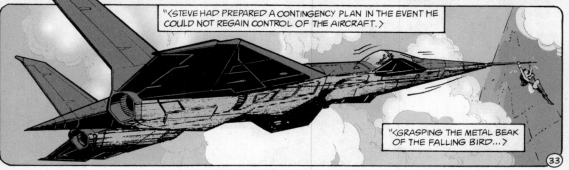

"‹STEVE HAD PREPARED A CONTINGENCY PLAN IN THE EVENT HE COULD NOT REGAIN CONTROL OF THE AIRCRAFT.›

"‹GRASPING THE METAL BEAK OF THE FALLING BIRD...›

33

"<MAKING MYSELF A HUMAN *PROPELLER*.>

"<...I BEGAN *SPINNING*. FASTER. AND *FASTER*.>"

"<...UNTIL I FINALLY MANAGED TO HALT THE PLANE'S FALL AND LEVEL IT.>"

"<THEN, I HEARD ETTA'S VOICE.>"

ETTA TO STEVE! ETTA TO STEVE!

I *DID* IT! I'VE BROKEN INTO THE SYSTEM! THE COMPUTER'S *DOWN*!

SHE'S ALL *YOURS*, BABY. OVER.

SWEETHEART, I COULD *KISS* YOU.

OKAY, PRINCESS, LET 'ER GO. I'VE GOT HER ON MANUAL NOW.

I'LL SHOW THEM WHAT AN "OLD MAN" CAN DO.

<YOU SEE, I WAS ABLE TO KEEP THE JET FROM *CRASHING* UNTIL STEVE COULD REGAIN CONTROL.>

<HE WANTED TO PROVE THAT THE AIR-CRAFT'S BASIC *DESIGN* WAS SOUND, THAT PALMER AIRCRAFT WAS NOT AT FAULT.>

"<SO, STEVE BROUGHT THE PLANE THEY'D PREMATURELY CALLED *THE ICARUS* TO A PERFECT, SAFE LANDING.>"

34

‹STEVE SUSPECTED SABOTAGE FROM *WITHIN* THE COMPLEX, AND THAT THE SABOTEURS WOULD HAVE TO MONITOR THE RADIO COMMUNICATION EVEN AFTER THE CONTROLS WERE DISRUPTED TO CONFIRM THEIR SUCCESS.›

‹I MERELY KEPT MY EARS ALERT FOR STEVE'S *SIGNAL.*›

"‹THE STAFF OF PALMER AIRCRAFT HAILED STEVE AS A HERO, AND ETTA COLLECTED ON THE KISS HE PROMISED.›

"‹THEY ARE BOTH SUCH BRAVE, NOBLE PEOPLE, MOTHER, WITH A GREAT SENSE OF HONOR AND DUTY.›

‹THE *THEMYSCIRAN* WORDS: THIS IS *ICARUS! HELP* ME!›

‹IT'S JUST A TRAGEDY THAT SUCH POTENTIAL CANNOT BE CHANNELED IN A WORLD WITHOUT NEED OF FLYING DEATH MACHINES.›

‹BUT THEN, ISN'T THAT THE *PURPOSE* OF THIS CULTURAL EXCHANGE?›

DIANA?

YES, NESSIE?

CAN YOU 'N' YOUR MOM GO OVER TO THAT TEMPLE SO I CAN GET ONE LAST GROUP SHOT?

AS YOUNG VANESSA GAZES THROUGH THE LENS OF HER SMALL CAMERA, HER SKIN TINGLES AS SHE STUDIES THE BEAUTIFUL, MOON-LIT FACES OF *HISTORY* AND *HOPE.*

EVEN HER MOTHER JULIA. A FACE THAT HAS BEEN SO *FAMILIAR* NOW SEEMS SO WONDROUSLY *NEW.* SO MUCH LIKE A *PART* OF THIS GLORIOUS PARADISE ISLAND.

VANESSA COCKS HER HEAD FORWARD AND UTTERS THE THEMYSCIRAN WORD SHE HAS LEARNED TO USE OFTEN ON THIS MOST UNIQUE WEEKEND.

‹SMILE!›

㉟

EPILOGUE

ILLUSTRATED BY
*BRIAN BOLLAND &
MARK FARMER*

DAWN: APOLLO'S OVERTURE TO THE SYMPHONY OF A NEW DAY. AND, SADLY, THE TUNE WHICH MARKS THE END OF THE KAPATELISES' VISIT.

TWO WORLDS, LONG SEPARATED AND NOW REUNITED, MUST PART COMPANY ONCE MORE...

...THIS TIME NOT WITH *"GOODBYE"*...

...BUT WITH *"TILL NEXT WE MEET."*

AS PRINCESS DIANA CARRIES MOTHER AND CHILD BACK TO THE WORLD OF MAN...

AMAZON EYES, SQUINTING THROU[GH] PANES OF TEARS, GLIMMER WITH HO[PE] AND INSPIRATION.

AND THEY HEAR APOLLO'S MUSIC IN THE AIR.

THE DAWN...

...OF A NEW AGE.

36

114

TESTAMENT

"PRINCESS DIANA, ARE YOU OKAY?"

WHAT? OH. YES, MR. FELDMAN. I WAS JUST LOST IN THOUGHT.

I CAN IMAGINE. THIS MUST ALL BE PRETTY *NEW* TO YOU.

YOU SEEMED RATHER *CONFUSED* WHEN I CALLED ON YOU LAST TUESDAY...

...TO INFORM YOU THAT YOU HAVE BEEN NAMED AS A *BENEFICIARY* IN THE WILL OF THE LATE *MYNDI MAYER*.

"BENEFICIARY"?

YES. THE READING WILL BE THIS FRIDAY. YOUR ATTENDANCE WILL BE APPRECIATED.

WELL, UNTIL FRIDAY THEN.

GOOD DAY, PRINCESS.

GOOD DAY, MR. FELDMAN.

HI, DIANA.

HI, CHRISSIE.

STRANGE RITUAL, ISN'T IT?

WELL, DON'T LET IT THROW YOU. *VIDEO WILLS* ARE PRETTY COMMONPLACE THESE DAYS.

THANK YOU FOR COMING, PRINCESS. NOW IF WE MAY *BEGIN*.

KLLK

Hello, darlings. Well, it looks like I didn't make it to fifty after all. Knowing me, I probably died during one hell of a party with some gorgeous hunk of man-flesh.

There are certainly **worse** ways to go.

Stanley Feldman is taking care of my business dealings separately. This tape is strictly between me and **you**...

My precious family, and closest, dearest friends.

115

As all you sweethearts know, I'm a sucker for theatrics. I wouldn't be the Star of Publicists if I weren't, would I? Well, sit back and relax, darlings. The curtain's going up.

We're going to take a trip down **Memory Lane**, courtesy of the Mayer Film Archives. Ah! Here's our family portrait, the only one taken of all of us the year Momma died.

Poor Momma. She worked so hard to please Poppa, until it **killed** her. Believe it or not, folks, she was only **twenty-seven** in this photo. I swore that wasn't going to happen to me.

But **you**, Lili, my sweet, self-sacrificing little sister, you were Poppa's **perfect** little daughter. Cooking, cleaning, ironing. And you were always quick to remind Poppa of how lazy and self-centered I was. A sorry excuse for a Jewish daughter.

MOMMY, THIS IS *BORING.* CAN'T WE GO WATCH SOME *REAL* TV?

SHUT UP, LEO. I'M TRYING TO *HEAR* THIS.

MOMMY! MOMMY! I GOTTA *GO*!

I TOLD YOU BOTH TO SHUT UP!

THAT LITTLE *TRAMP!* SHE ISN'T GETTING AWAY WITH *THIS!*

I CAN'T BELIEVE THAT SHE IS MYNDI'S *SISTER.*

THEY *HATED* EACH OTHER SO MUCH.

I DON'T KNOW IF I'D REALLY CALL IT *HATE.*

JEALOUSY, ON THE OTHER HAND...

Yes, Lili, I admit I was **jealous** of Poppa's affection for you, but I couldn't pay the price you were paying. Besides, you didn't fool me. You wanted out as badly as I did. That's why you married Irwin so young. To **escape**. Ha! Some escape! Five obnoxious brats and a boorish husband.

My escape was in books, and movies... and yes, **boys**. Being an early bloomer had its advantages. Of course, baby sister always made sure Poppa got all the sordid details.

So, little sister, in a way **you're** responsible for starting me up that ladder of success. My independence, business, all those young leading men. All because of **you**.

To my darling sister Lili I bequeath the sum of $500,000...

On one condition:

That you and Irwin move back to Chicago. To be with **Poppa.**

NO! TH-THAT'S *EXTORTION!*

Lili, you did me a great **favor**. Getting kicked out was the **best** thing that ever happened to me.

And Myndi Mayer **knows** how to express her **gratitude**.

EXTORTION? WHY WOULD ANY CHILD NEED TO BE *BRIBED* TO BE NEAR HER PARENT?

WELL, I PERSONALLY NEVER *MET* MR. MAYER.

ALTHOUGH MYNDI DID *TALK* ABOUT HIM FROM TIME TO TIME. 38

THE FIRST TIME WAS THE DAY WE *MET* AS ROOM-MATES IN COLLEGE. MYNDI ALWAYS BELIEVED IN STRONG *FIRST* IMPRESSIONS.

HER FATHER COULDN'T JUST BE A *TAILOR*. OH NO. SHE HAD TO MAKE HIM...

AN *INTERNATIONAL FASHION CONSULTANT*. HE'S CLOTHED SOME OF THE GREATEST CROWNED HEADS IN EUROPE.

HE MADE ME *THIS* DRESS FOR MY EIGHTEENTH BIRTHDAY. WHAT DO YOU THINK?

I THINK IT'S GORGEOUS. I THOUGHT SO THE *FIRST* TIME I SAW IT.

IN THE WINDOW AT *SAKS FIFTH AVENUE*.

OH.

You always **could** see through me, Chrissie. I'll always be grateful for the day you divorced that turkey and came to work for me.

You were **more** to me than a secretary. You were my **conscience**.

You kept me honest. **Most of** the time, anyway. I can't think of a better person to inherit the controlling shares of Mayer Publicists.

Give yourself a raise, Ms. Fenton. You've **earned** it.

Congratulations, Chrissie.

eh?

OH. KEVIN. I THOUGHT YOU'D BE WITH LILI.

I SAID "CONGRATULATIONS," CHRISSIE.

NAH. LILI AND I DON'T TALK MUCH ANYMORE.

PRINCESS, WE MET IN PASSING AT MYN'S FUNERAL.

I'M *KEVIN MAYER*.

My adorable baby brother. You and I shared a lot of laughs. And a lot of tears. We also shared the need to be different. Thanks, Kev. Thanks for being there when nobody else wanted to be. Thanks for loving me for who **I** am.

I'm sorry we'll never get to blow out those eighty candles, Kev. I hope you forgive me. Even though I haven't shown it lately, I love you, baby...with all my heart.

No inheritance could ever express that enough.

BUT, DAMN IT, KEVIN, SHE SHOULD HAVE LEFT YOU *SOMETHING*.

NAH. SHE KNEW HOW I FELT ABOUT THAT.

MYN, I WANT YOU TO BE AROUND TO BLOW OUT THE CANDLES ON MY EIGHTIETH BIRTHDAY CAKE. IF NOT, I DON'T WANT *ANYTHING* ELSE FROM YOU. NOT EVEN IN YOUR WILL. OKAY?

OH, ALL RIGHT, KEV. BUT ONLY 'CAUSE YOU'LL *NEED* MY HELP TO BLOW THEM OUT THEN.

IF ONLY I COULDA *HELPED* HER. IF ONLY SHE'D LISTEN...

OH GOD. I'M GONNA MISS HER SO MUCH.

I KNOW, KEVIN. I KNOW.

KEVIN, I FEEL SO AWKWARD. MAYBE *YOU'D* LIKE TO HAVE THIS.

AFTER ALL, I BARELY KNEW HER.

AND IT'S SO *PERSONAL*.

39

Princess Diana, out of all my clients, I've never known one whose respect I value more than yours. I hope that my contribution to the **Wonder Woman Foundation** can help in earning that respect and that it will convince you to honor this last request:

To take this gaudy urn which, when **you** get it, should be filled with my ashes...

...and scatter them into the waters around Paradise Island.

BUT, *WHY?*

YOU MEAN WHY DID SHE *WANT* IT? OR WHY SHOULD YOU *DO* IT?

KEVIN...

NO! I'M TIRED OF ALL THE CRAP I'VE BEEN HEARIN' ABOUT MY SISTER!

YOU WANNA KNOW ABOUT MYNDI MAYER, PRINCESS? WHO SHE *REALLY* WAS? HUH? *DO YA?*

WELL, SHE *WASN'T* NO SAINT. BUT SHE WASN'T NO *DEVIL* EITHER.

I guess I was just a **rebel**. **Different.** And Poppa couldn't **handle** that. Just like he couldn't handle **you** being different, Kev.

I GUESS THAT'S WHY ME AND HER GOT ALONG SO WELL.

SHE WAS THE ONLY ONE IN THE FAMILY WHO DIDN'T HATE ME FOR BEING *GAY.*

I DIDN'T WANT POPPA TO FIND OUT, BUT LIL TOLD HIM.

AT FIRST, THEY WOULDN'T EVEN LET ME COME TO LIL'S WEDDING. BUT MYN THREATENED TO MAKE A BIG STINK IF THEY DIDN'T.

AND HOW WOULD IT ALL *LOOK* IN THE LOCAL PAPERS, DARLING LILI?

UH-HMM. WHY, LILI DEAR. HOW *KIND* OF YOU TO INVITE US!

KEVIN AND I WILL CHECK OUR CALENDAR AND LET YOU KNOW, OKAY?

OF COURSE, THAT STUNT DIDN'T HELP MEND ANY FENCES BETWEEN POPPA AND US.

BUT, IT DID FINALLY GIVE ME *COURAGE.* MYN TOLD ME THAT...

YOU CAN'T KEEP HIDING WHO YOU ARE. IF YOU DO, YOU'LL ALWAYS BE DUCKING INTO ALLEYWAYS. AFRAID OF BEING FOUND OUT.

HEY, BELIEVE ME, I KNOW WHAT THEY SAY ABOUT *ME* -- SOME OF IT EVEN *TRUE.*

BUT, I'M NOT *ASHAMED* OF WHO I AM...

...AND NEITHER SHOULD *I* BE.

WHEN I CAME OUTTA THE CLOSET, MY BOSSES TRIED TO *FIRE* ME. MYNDI SICKED HER *LAWYERS* ON 'EM.

THAT WAS MY MYN, A REGULAR LITTLE FIRECRACKER.

40

THEN WE LEARNED POPPA HAD *ALZHEIMER'S*. DAMN. WE THOUGHT HE WAS JUST GETTIN' OLD, THAT'S ALL. ANYWAY, MYN AND I WANTED TO GO BACK TO CHICAGO TO HELP...

...BUT POPPA ONLY WANTED HIS DARLING LILI.

SO, DESPITE IRWIN'S COMPLAINTS, LIL TOOK POPPA INTO HER HOME AND PLAYED THE MARTYR. I THINK SHE DID IT JUST TO *SPITE* MYN AND ME.

UNTIL POPPA GOT WORSE. THEN, WITHOUT EVEN CONSULTING US, THEY DUMPED POOR POPPA INTO SOME *SNAKE PIT*.

IT'S *NOT* A SNAKE PIT! IT'S THE BEST HOME WE COULD *AFFORD*!

LILI, THAT PLACE ISN'T *EQUIPPED* TO HANDLE ALZHEIMER PATIENTS.

THEN *YOU* PAY FOR SOME PLACE THAT *WILL!*

IRWIN'S BEING TRANSFERRED TO L.A. A BIG PROMOTION. HE CAN'T HAVE SOME SENILE OLD MAN HOLDING HIM BACK.

I'VE TAKEN CARE OF POPPA FOR OVER TWENTY YEARS. I'VE *DONE* MY TIME!

NOW IT WAS *MYN'S* TURN. SHE PUT POPPA IN THE BEST CLINIC MONEY COULD BUY. AND AT FIRST, SHE VISITED HIM EVERY WEEK.

I GUESS SHE FELT THAT WAS THE ONLY WAY SHE COULD GET POPPA'S LOVE...

BY *BUYING* IT.

BUT HE DIDN'T EVEN KNOW SHE WAS THERE.

LILI... IS THAT YOU?... MY DARLING LILI...

LATER, MYN STOPPED VISITING AND BURIED HERSELF DEEPER IN HER WORK. SHE STARTED DRINKING MORE HEAVILY. AND THEN CAME THE *COCAINE*.

SHE CHANGED SO MUCH. ALL HER SELF-CONFIDENCE WAS NOW COMING FROM THAT DAMN WHITE POWDER.

TO HER IT WAS A LOVE THAT MONEY *COULD* BUY.

UNTIL IT *KILLED* HER.

KEVIN, YOU MISUNDERSTOOD MY QUESTION.

BUT YOU ANSWERED IT NEVERTHELESS.

"I WAS WONDERING *WHY* MYNDI FELT SHE HAD TO *PAY* ME TO HONOR HER FINAL WISH."

Diana, in this make-believe, laminated business of mine, finding true innocence is rare, true honesty even rarer, and true love nearly impossible.

Yet, you've known it all your life. All the happiness I've ever clawed and fought for, you were simply born into. On that wonderful Paradise Island. What I wouldn't **give** to know that kind of feeling.

To be part of a world of innocence, honesty and unequivocal love.

To be truly **happy**.

God, what I wouldn't give for **that**.

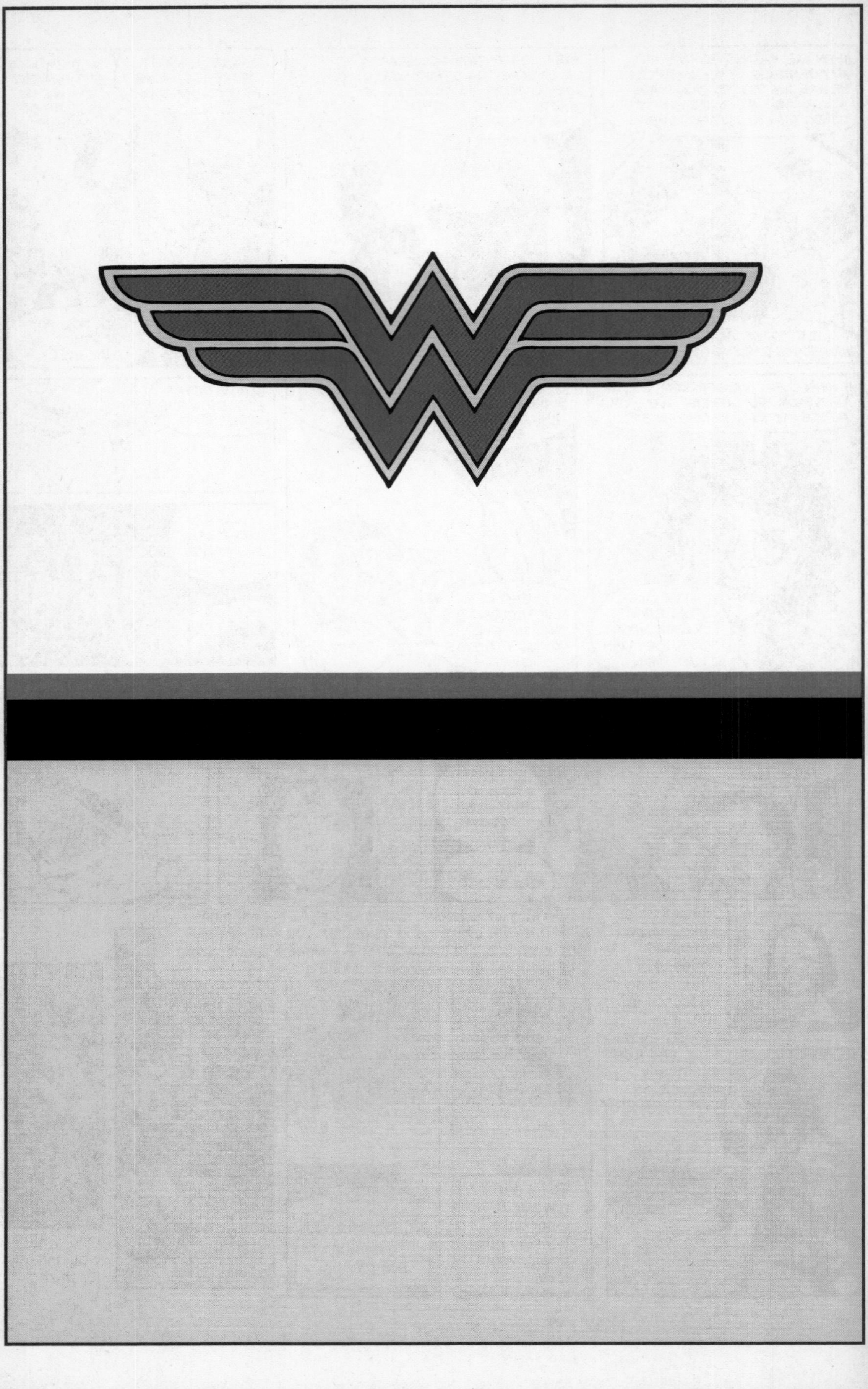

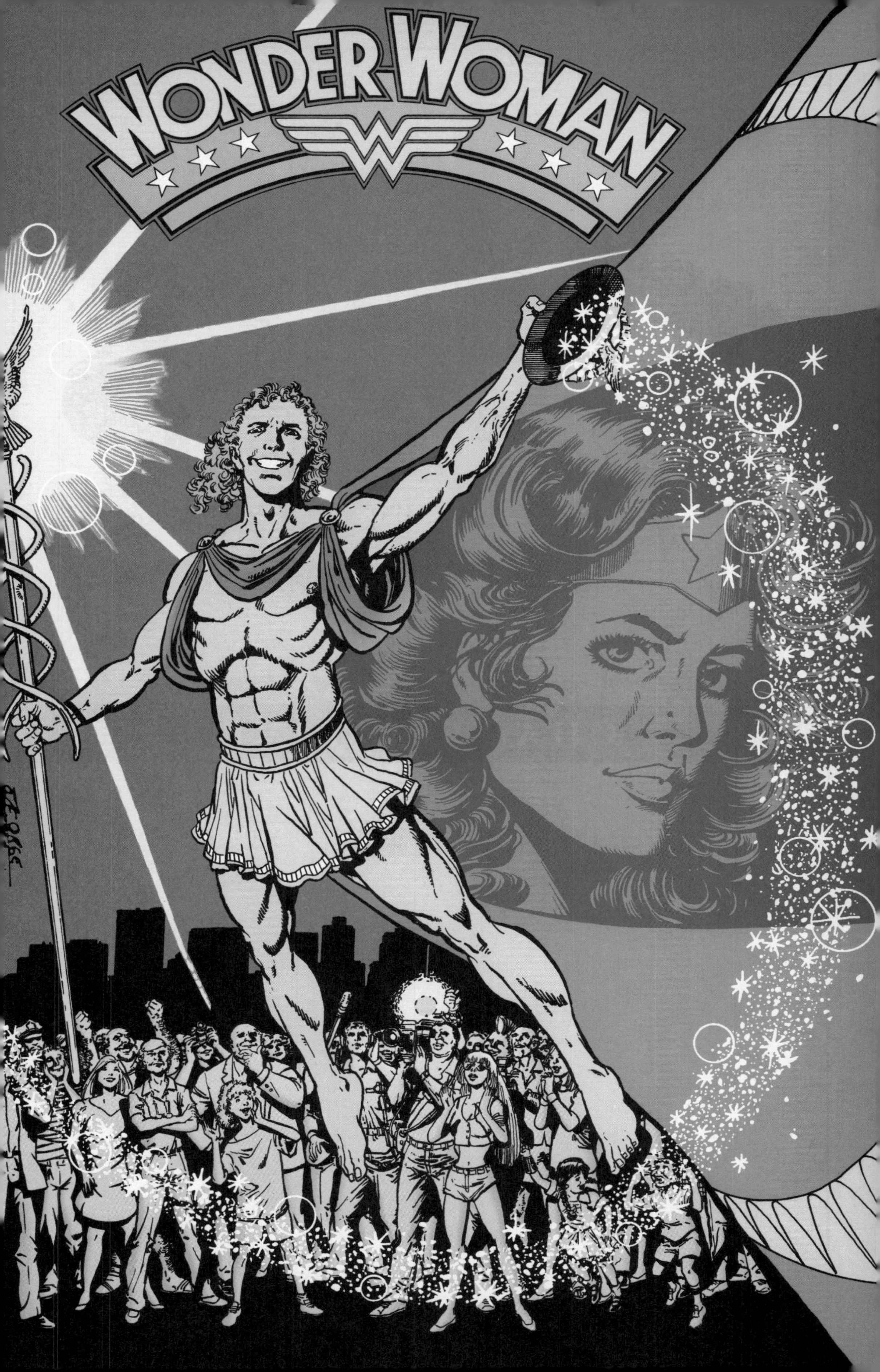
WONDER WOMAN

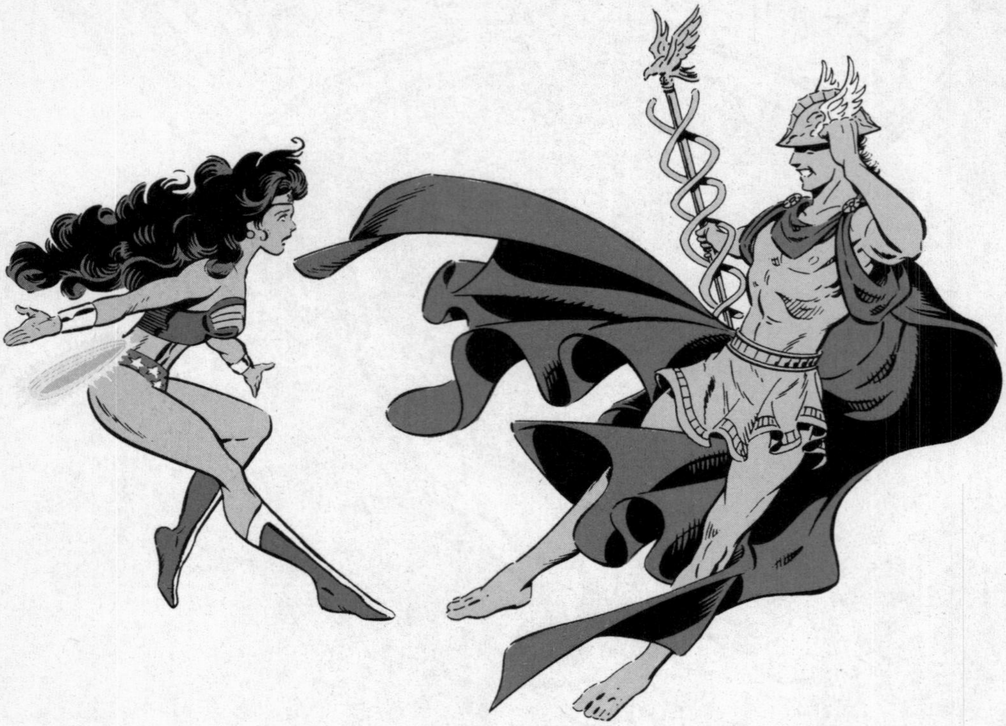

WONDER WOMAN

CHAPTER FIVE

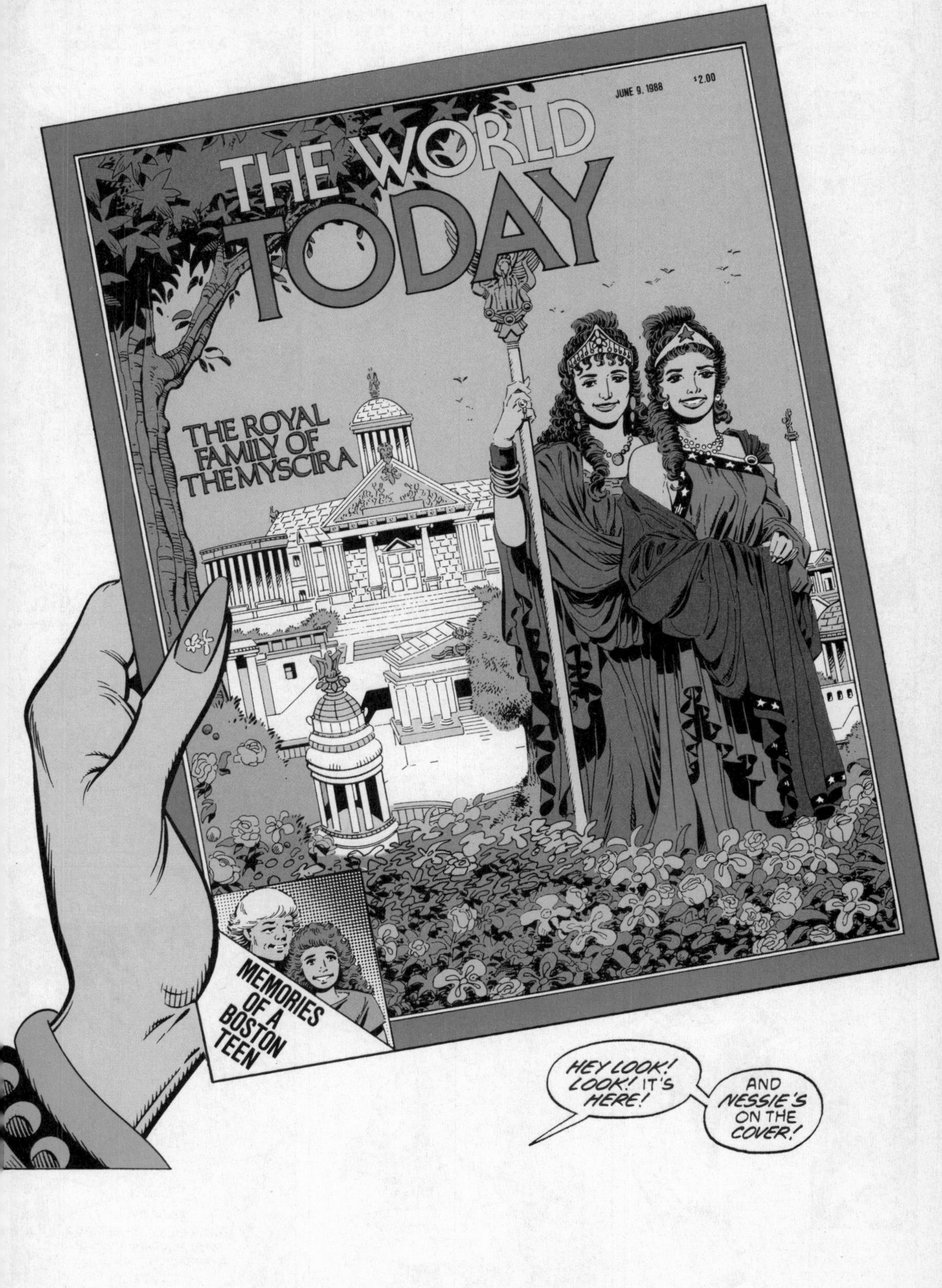
JUNE 9, 1988
$2.00
THE WORLD TODAY
THE ROYAL FAMILY OF THEMYSCIRA
MEMORIES OF A BOSTON TEEN
HEY LOOK! LOOK! IT'S HERE!
AND NESSIE'S ON THE COVER!

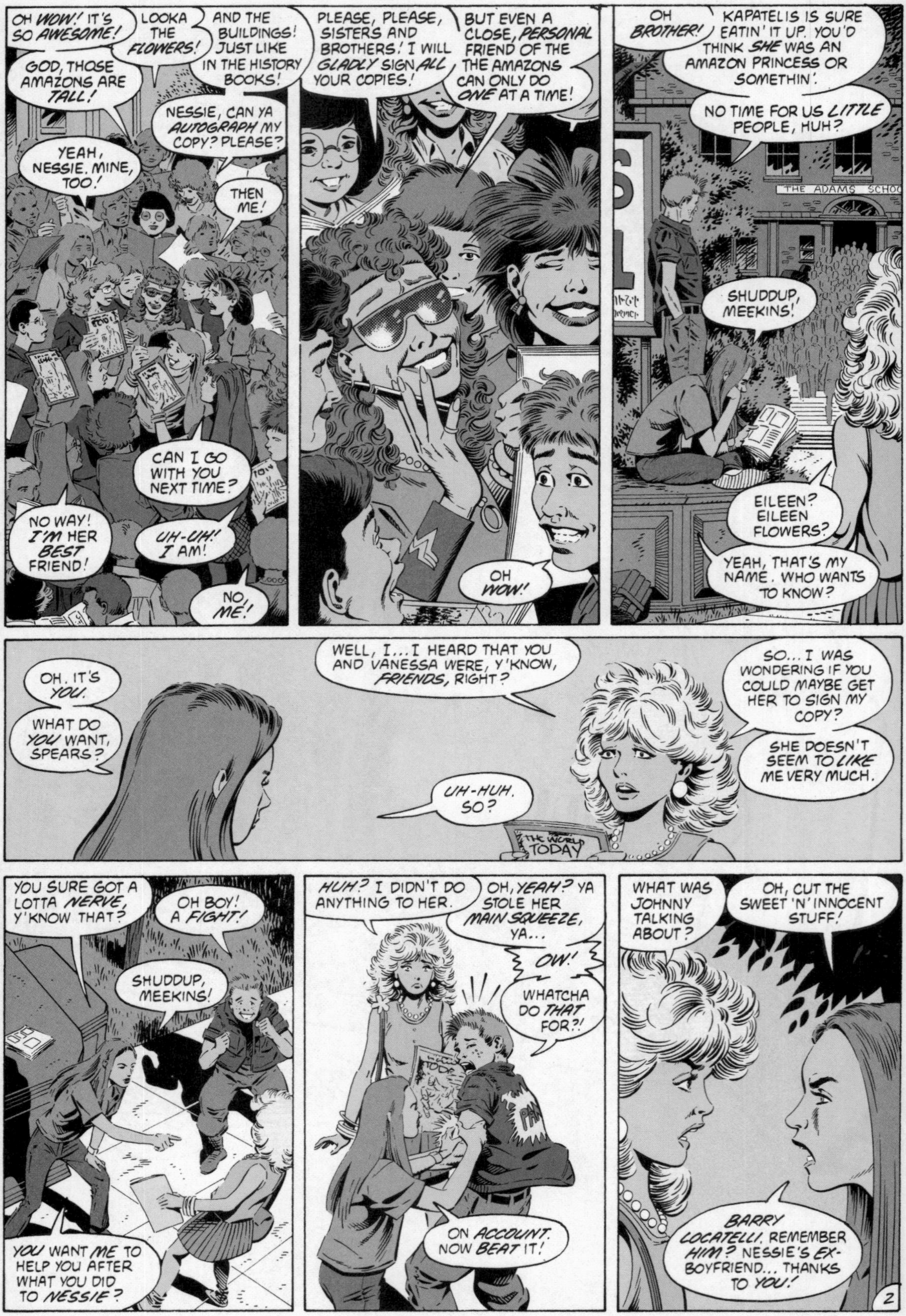
OH WOW! IT'S SO AWESOME!
LOOKA THE FLOWERS!
AND THE BUILDINGS! JUST LIKE IN THE HISTORY BOOKS!
GOD, THOSE AMAZONS ARE TALL!
NESSIE, CAN YA AUTOGRAPH MY COPY? PLEASE?
YEAH, NESSIE. MINE, TOO!
THEN ME!
CAN I GO WITH YOU NEXT TIME?
NO WAY! I'M HER BEST FRIEND!
UH-UH! I AM!
NO, ME!
PLEASE, PLEASE, SISTERS AND BROTHERS! I WILL GLADLY SIGN ALL YOUR COPIES!
BUT EVEN A CLOSE, PERSONAL FRIEND OF THE THE AMAZONS CAN ONLY DO ONE AT A TIME!
OH WOW!
OH BROTHER!
KAPATELIS IS SURE EATIN' IT UP. YOU'D THINK SHE WAS AN AMAZON PRINCESS OR SOMETHIN'.
NO TIME FOR US LITTLE PEOPLE, HUH?
THE ADAMS SCHO
SHUDDUP, MEEKINS!
EILEEN? EILEEN FLOWERS?
YEAH, THAT'S MY NAME. WHO WANTS TO KNOW?
OH. IT'S YOU.
WHAT DO YOU WANT, SPEARS?
WELL, I... I HEARD THAT YOU AND VANESSA WERE, Y'KNOW, FRIENDS, RIGHT?
UH-HUH. SO?
SO... I WAS WONDERING IF YOU COULD MAYBE GET HER TO SIGN MY COPY?
SHE DOESN'T SEEM TO LIKE ME VERY MUCH.
THE WORLD TODAY
YOU SURE GOT A LOTTA NERVE, Y'KNOW THAT?
OH BOY! A FIGHT!
SHUDDUP, MEEKINS!
YOU WANT ME TO HELP YOU AFTER WHAT YOU DID TO NESSIE?
HUH? I DIDN'T DO ANYTHING TO HER.
OH, YEAH? YA STOLE HER MAIN SQUEEZE, YA...
OW!
WHATCHA DO THAT FOR?!
ON ACCOUNT. NOW BEAT IT!
WHAT WAS JOHNNY TALKING ABOUT?
OH, CUT THE SWEET 'N' INNOCENT STUFF!
BARRY LOCATELLI. REMEMBER HIM? NESSIE'S EX-BOYFRIEND... THANKS TO YOU!
2

ME, I ALWAYS THOUGHT HE WAS A *JERK*. BUT, NESSIE...

WHOA! CHILL OUT! YOU MEAN THAT BARRY AND VANESSA...

I *DIDN'T*, EILEEN. I SWEAR.

BARRY TOLD ME THAT SHE...

THANKS, EILEEN. I'LL TALK TO YOU AND VANESSA LATER, OKAY?

AFTER I TALK TO BARRY LOCATELLI!

DAMN STRAIGHT. DON'T PRETEND YOU DIDN'T KNOW.

WHY THAT LITTLE *CREEP*...

EILEEN?

HI, NESSIE. READY TO GO?

WELL, *UM*, Y'SEE, EILEEN... MY FRIENDS HERE WANT ME TO GO TO A PARTY AT JOANNE ALBERT'S HOUSE. Y'KNOW, THE ONE WITH HORSES?

THEY WANT ME TO SHOW 'EM HOW AMAZONS RIDE 'N' EVERYTHING.

OH. CAN I COME?

WE ONLY HAVE ROOM IN *MOM'S* CAR FOR VANESSA. SORRY, FLOWERS.

MAYBE YOU AND ME CAN GO TO THE MOVIES NEXT WEEK, OKAY?

BESIDES, YOU GOTTA GET HOME IN TIME TO MAKE YOUR FOLKS DINNER, RIGHT?

LISSEN, EILEEN, I GOTTA GO. TALK TO YA TOMORROW, OKAY?

UH-HUH. SURE.

SEE YA.

YEAH, KAPATELIS IS REAL BROKEN UP ABOUT LOCATELLI, AIN'T SHE?

"OW! HEY! C'MON, FLOWERS! I WAS ONLY *PLAYIN'*!"

"*SHUDDUP,* MEEKINS!"

3

125

"HEY, PAL. YOU BUYING THAT MAG OR WHAT?

"THIS AIN'T NO LIBRARY YOU KNOW. THAT'LL BE TWO BUCKS!"

BUDDY, YA HEARD MY WIFE, DIDN'T YA? COUGH UP THE CASH OR PUT THE MAG BACK.

ROCCO, MAYBE HE'S DEAF OR SOMETHIN'?

NAAH. HE AIN'T DEEF! HE'S JUST A BUM. AIN'T YA, BUDDY?

AWRIGHT, BUDDY. HAND IT OV...

EH?

RR

IPP!

NOW LOOK WHAT YA DID! C'MON, COUGH UP THE TWO DOLLARS!

ARE YOU ALLUDING TO CURRENCY? I NEVER EVEN CONSIDERED THAT.

AND AS FOR THAT BOOKLET YOU SO CARELESSLY RENT...

OHHH. WISE GUY, HUH?

CALL A COP, ROCCO.

NAAH! I'LL TAKE CARE OF...

YOWW!

ROCCO!

I APOLOGIZE FOR THAT, BUT HE SHOULDN'T HAVE...

PLEASE, WOMAN, IF YOUR OBESE SPOUSE IS HURT, I WILL GLADLY...

POLICE!

KEEP AWAY, YOU THIEF!

THIEF!? YOU CALL THAT INSIGNIFICANCE THIEVERY? HOW INSULTING!

ENOUGH OF THIS FOOLISHNESS. YOU ASKED THAT I "COUGH UP" PAYMENT.

¿COUGH¿

WILL THIS SUFFICE?

ALL RIGHT. WHAT'S GOING ON HERE?

THAT UNIFORM. YOU ARE ONE OF THE LOCAL CENTURIONS?

I'M A POLICE OFFICER, MISTER. YOU FROM OUT OF TOWN?

I? OH YES.

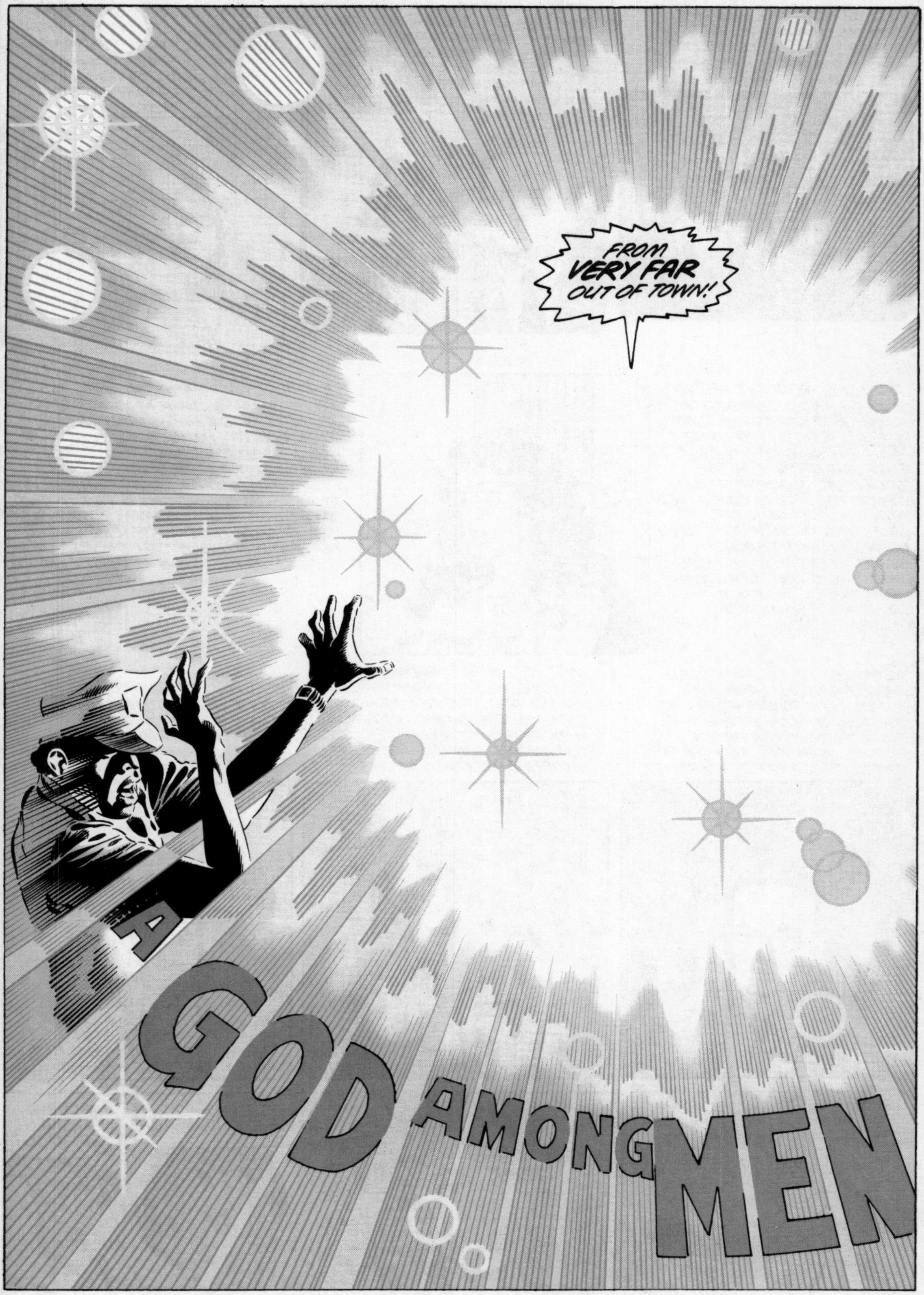
FROM VERY FAR OUT OF TOWN!
A GOD AMONG MEN

"WE INTERRUPT OUR REGULARLY SCHEDULED PROGRAM FOR THIS SPECIAL BULLETIN. FROM OUR NEWS ROOM IN NEW YORK, HERE'S BRIAN HATCHER."

"GOOD AFTERNOON. JUST MINUTES AGO, THE U.N. GENERAL ASSEMBLY HEARD A STIRRING SPEECH BY PRINCESS DIANA OF THEMYSCIRA, KNOWN THROUGHOUT THE WORLD AS 'WONDER WOMAN.'"

"SPEAKING ON BEHALF OF HER MOTHER, THE QUEEN OF THE AMAZONS, PRINCESS DIANA OFFICIALLY ANNOUNCED THE OPENING OF THEMYSCIRA'S GATES TO THE REST OF THE WORLD."

"TOO LONG HAVE THE WEEDS OF FEAR AND DISTRUST BEEN ALLOWED TO STRANGLE OUR WORLD'S GARDEN. NO LONGER MUST THE SINS OF THE PAST TAINT OUR HOPES FOR THE FUTURE. MY MOTHER, QUEEN HIPPOLYTE, HAS CHARGED ME WITH THE HOLY DUTY OF SELECTING THOSE WHO WILL REPRESENT PATRIARCH'S WORLD AS THE NEXT WAVE IN WHAT I HOPE WILL BE A CONTINUOUS TIDE OF CULTURAL EXCHANGE AND MUTUAL ENLIGHTENMENT.

"I PRAY I AM WORTHY OF THAT TRUST. AS THE AMBASSADOR TO YOUR WORLD, MY DUTY IS TO DEMONSTRATE THE SINCERITY OF MY NATION'S GOALS: TO TEACH, AND TO LEARN; TO LIVE TOGETHER PEACEFULLY, AND TO HONOR ALL EQUALLY; TO UNDERSTAND COMPASSIONATELY, AND TO LOVE UNEQUIVOCALLY. I'VE GROWN TO CHERISH THIS NEW WORLD, AND ALL OF YOU. DESPITE ALL OUR DIFFERENCES, I FERVENTLY BELIEVE THAT THE AGE OF GLOBAL COMMUNION IS JUST BEYOND THE HORIZON."

"RESPONSE TO THE PRINCESS'S SPEECH RANGED FROM THE ENTHUSIASTIC TO THE APATHETIC. STANDING BY LIVE AT THE U.N. IS CORRESPONDENT MARIAN BIFULCO. MARIAN, HAS WONDER WOMAN TALKED TO REPORTERS YET?"

"NOT YET, BRIAN, ALTHOUGH WE DO EXPECT HER MOMENTARILY. AS YOU SAID, THE REACTION TO DIANA'S SPEECH WAS MIXED, WITH THE MOST NEGATIVE COMMENTS COMING FROM THE MIDDLE EASTERN NATIONS.

"HOWEVER, FURTHER TALKS HAVE BEEN SCHEDULED TO DISCUSS HOW EACH NATION SHOULD...WAIT. BRIAN, I SEE WONDER WOMAN ENTERING THE HALL NOW." >

PRINCESS DIANA!

ARE YOU HAPPY WITH THE RECEPTION OF YOUR ANNOUNCEMENT?

WHAT WILL YOU SAY TO THE AMAZONS?

WHEN WILL QUEEN HIPPOLYTE BE COMING TO OUR WORLD?

WILL THE PRESIDENT GET TO GO?

PLEASE. ALLOW ME THE CHANCE TO ANSWER AT LEAST *ONE* QUESTION.

PRINCESS, ARE YOU CONCERNED ABOUT THE *CYNICISM* EXPRESSED BY SOME OF THE ASSEMBLY MEMBERS?

CONCERNED, YES, BUT NOT SURPRISED. I'VE LONG AGO LEARNED THAT, IN THIS WORLD, NEW IDEAS ARE NOT SO READILY EMBRACED.

EVEN IF THOSE IDEAS ARE *CENTURIES OLD.*

STILL, I AM OPTIMISTIC THAT THE NATIONS' LEADERS WILL SEE THAT...

IT WILL...

...SERVE...

AN *ICY CHILL* STIFFENS THE AMAZON PRINCESS AS SHE SENSES THE PRESENCE OF SOMETHING STRANGE, YET VAGUELY *FAMILIAR.*

SOMETHING BURIED IN THE SHADOWS OF A GRECIAN HOOD.

YOU... WHY DO I FEEL... I *KNOW* YOU?

BECAUSE YOU *MAY,* CHOSEN ONE...

BECAUSE...

NO.

"BY CRONUS... NO!"

YOU ARE *NOT* THE ONE!

WAIT! COME BACK!

DAMN IT ALL! I'VE WASTED SO MUCH TIME!

PLEASE! LET ME THROUGH!

WHO IS *SHE?*

WHO *WAS* THAT WOMAN?

• WAS SHE ANOTHER *AMAZON?*

DIANA, WOULD YOU...?

PLEASE!

LET ME THROUGH!!!

STOP! PLEASE! I WON'T HURT YOU!

ALL I WANT IS TO...

...TALK...?

SHE'S GONE! BUT HOW...?

THE MYSTERY WOMAN DISAPPEARS IN SEARCH OF DIANA'S "SISTER," DONNA TROY. BUT THAT'S A TALE FOR ANOTHER DAY...

WONDER WOMAN! WONDER WOMAN!

EH? MS. BIFULCO, I'M SORRY. I DIDN'T MEAN TO KNOCK ALL OF YOU OVER AS I DID.

OH, THAT. ALL PART OF THE NEWS GAME, PRINCESS.

BUT, YOU COULD MAKE UP FOR IT BY TELLING US ABOUT YOUR FRIEND IN BOSTON -- THE ONE WITH THE WINGED HELMET?

"WINGED HELMET?"
"YES, LIKE THE FTD MAN. HE CLAIMS TO KNOW YOU QUITE INTIMATELY AND THAT..."

"GREAT GAEA!"

"HUH?"

"PRINCESS DIANA? NOW WHERE DID SHE GO? DAMN! OH... UMMM... THIS IS MARIAN BIFULCO IN THE U.N. BACK TO YOU, BRIAN."

"WELL, ahem, THANK YOU, MARIAN. CURIOUSER AND CURIOUSER. SO. IT SEEMS A NEW WRINKLE HAS BEEN ADDED TO THE WONDER WOMAN ENIGMA.

DIANA'S SECRET WONDER MAN?

"WITH MORE NEWS ABOUT THE MYSTERIOUS MAN IN THE WINGED HELMET, WE GO NOW TO CORRESPONDENT JOHN SARDY...

"... AT OUR SISTER STATION WHGP IN BOSTON, MASSACHU-SETTS."

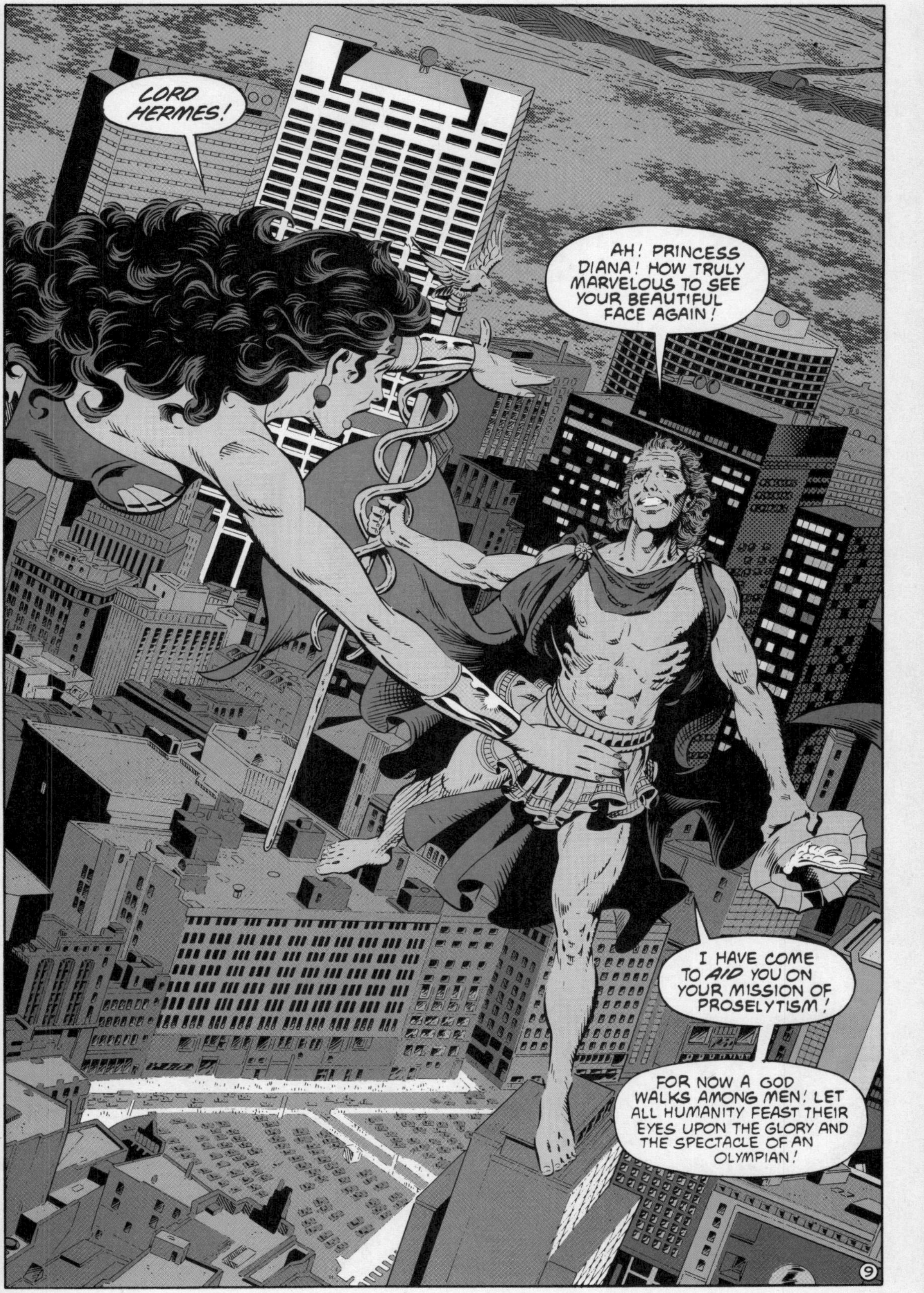
LORD HERMES!
AH! PRINCESS DIANA! HOW TRULY MARVELOUS TO SEE YOUR BEAUTIFUL FACE AGAIN!
I HAVE COME TO AID YOU ON YOUR MISSION OF PROSELYTISM!
FOR NOW A GOD WALKS AMONG MEN! LET ALL HUMANITY FEAST THEIR EYES UPON THE GLORY AND THE SPECTACLE OF AN OLYMPIAN!
9

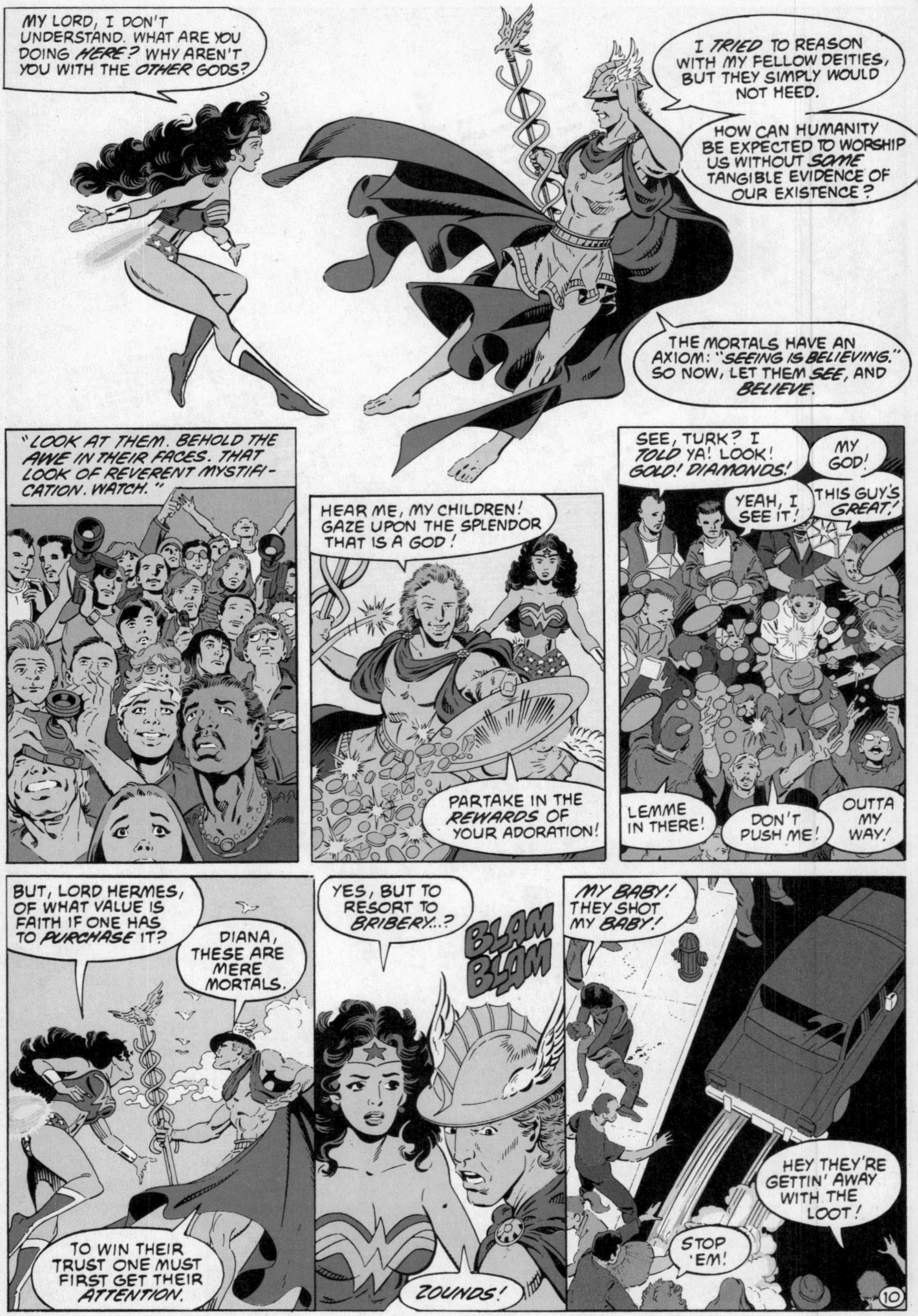

MY LORD, I DON'T UNDERSTAND. WHAT ARE YOU DOING HERE? WHY AREN'T YOU WITH THE OTHER GODS?
I TRIED TO REASON WITH MY FELLOW DEITIES, BUT THEY SIMPLY WOULD NOT HEED.
HOW CAN HUMANITY BE EXPECTED TO WORSHIP US WITHOUT SOME TANGIBLE EVIDENCE OF OUR EXISTENCE?
THE MORTALS HAVE AN AXIOM: "SEEING IS BELIEVING." SO NOW, LET THEM SEE, AND BELIEVE.
"LOOK AT THEM. BEHOLD THE AWE IN THEIR FACES. THAT LOOK OF REVERENT MYSTIFICATION. WATCH."
HEAR ME, MY CHILDREN! GAZE UPON THE SPLENDOR THAT IS A GOD!
PARTAKE IN THE REWARDS OF YOUR ADORATION!
SEE, TURK? I TOLD YA! LOOK! GOLD! DIAMONDS!
MY GOD!
YEAH, I SEE IT!
THIS GUY'S GREAT!
LEMME IN THERE!
DON'T PUSH ME!
OUTTA MY WAY!
BUT, LORD HERMES, OF WHAT VALUE IS FAITH IF ONE HAS TO PURCHASE IT?
DIANA, THESE ARE MERE MORTALS.
TO WIN THEIR TRUST ONE MUST FIRST GET THEIR ATTENTION.
YES, BUT TO RESORT TO BRIBERY...?
BLAM BLAM
ZOUNDS!
MY BABY! THEY SHOT MY BABY!
HEY THEY'RE GETTIN' AWAY WITH THE LOOT!
STOP 'EM!
10

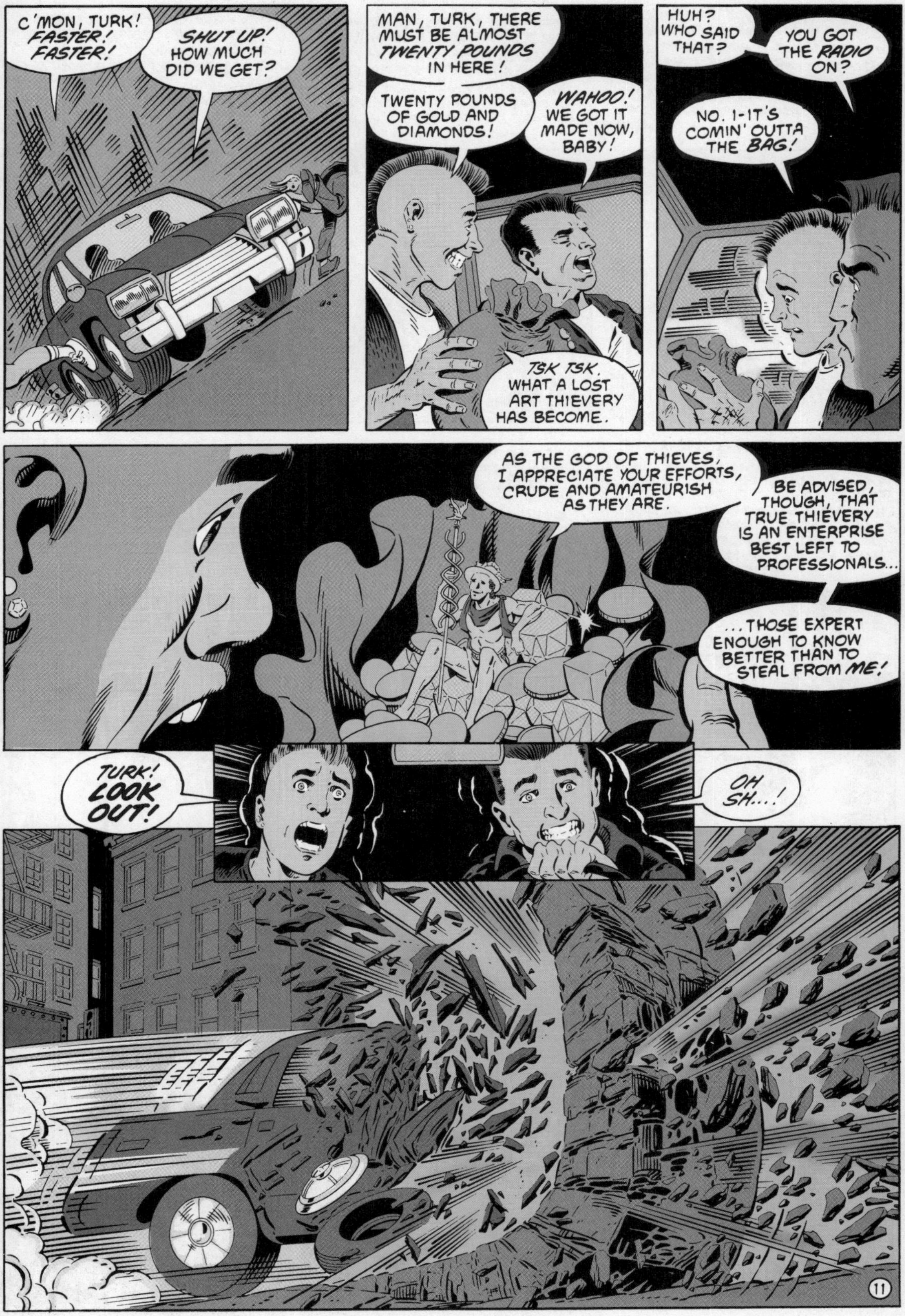
C'MON, TURK! FASTER! FASTER!
SHUT UP! HOW MUCH DID WE GET?
MAN, TURK, THERE MUST BE ALMOST TWENTY POUNDS IN HERE!
TWENTY POUNDS OF GOLD AND DIAMONDS!
WAHOO! WE GOT IT MADE NOW, BABY!
TSK TSK. WHAT A LOST ART THIEVERY HAS BECOME.
HUH? WHO SAID THAT?
YOU GOT THE RADIO ON?
NO. I-IT'S COMIN' OUTTA THE BAG!
AS THE GOD OF THIEVES, I APPRECIATE YOUR EFFORTS, CRUDE AND AMATEURISH AS THEY ARE.
BE ADVISED, THOUGH, THAT TRUE THIEVERY IS AN ENTERPRISE BEST LEFT TO PROFESSIONALS...
...THOSE EXPERT ENOUGH TO KNOW BETTER THAN TO STEAL FROM ME!
TURK! LOOK OUT!
OH SH...!
11

"HERMES, WHAT ARE YOU GOING TO DO?"
"WHAT A GOD DOES BEST, BEAUTIFUL ONE. I SHALL GIVE LIFE. NOW, STAND BACK, ALL OF YOU, EXCEPT THOSE WITH THE CAMERAS. NOW SHALL I PLACE THE EVIDENCE BEFORE YOUR EYES. WATCH NOW, AND BELIEVE!"

"IT WAS THE MOST INCREDIBLE THING I'VE EVER WITNESSED. HE JUST PLACED HIS HANDS ON THE OPEN WOUNDS, BLOOD STILL SPOUTING FROM THEM, AND A GLOW CAME OVER THE BOY. THE BLEEDING STOPPED. THEN, MR. HERMES DUG HIS FINGERS IN...

"...AND PULLED OUT THE TWO BULLETS. I-I'VE NEVER SEEN ANYTHING LIKE IT. THE CROWD WENT WILD! WHEN LITTLE TONY WAS EXAMINED LATER AT BOSTON GENERAL, DOCTORS COULDN'T EVEN FIND ANY SCARS ON HIM. IT WAS A MIRACLE."

WHILE MR. HERMES WAS EAGER TO TALK TO REPORTERS, HE WAS PULLED ASIDE BY WONDER WOMAN, WHO TALKED HIM INTO GOING WITH HER...

DESPITE BEING IN CRITICAL CONDITION, BOTH ROBBERS WERE COMPLETELY HEALED AND WALKED TO POLICE HEADQUARTERS. AN AMAZING DAY.

THANK YOU, JOHN. LATER ON, MR. HERMES ANNOUNCED PLANS TO APPEAR TOMORROW ON ALL THE MORNING SHOWS--SIMULTANEOUSLY. AS JOHN SAID, AN AMAZ...

...SO THAT HE COULD ALSO HEAL THE WOULD-BE ROBBERS.

WHICH MR. HERMES DID.

OH WOW.

JOHN SARDY, WHGP NEWS, ON THE STREETS OF BOSTON.

EH?

TURN IT OFF, VANESSA.

NOW, PLEASE.

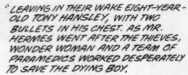

WHY DID YOU TURN IT OFF? THEY WERE STILL SPEAKING OF ME.

JULIA, WHAT'S WRONG? YOU LOOK SO *SOMBER.*

DO I? I'M SORRY.

OH WOW. FIRST AN AMAZON PRINCESS, 'N' NOW A *GOD!* LIVING WITH *US!*

THEY'LL MAKE ME *CLASS PRESIDENT* NOW!

MR. HERMES, CAN I ASK YOU SOMETHING?

MOST ASSUREDLY, MY CHILD.

AND IT'S *LORD* HERMES.

"OH. YEAH, THAT'S COOL. *LORD HERMES,* IS IT TRUE YOU CAN CONJURE UP ANYTHING?"

"YES."

"*AWESOME!* DO Y'KNOW WHAT A *VIDEO ENTERTAINMENT CENTER* IS?"

VANESSA! THAT'S *ENOUGH!*

WHAT!? I JUST FIGURED...

I *KNOW* WHAT YOU JUST FIGURED!

DON'T YOU HAVE HOMEWORK TO DO? IN YOUR *ROOM?*

ALREADY DONE IT.

THEN MAYBE YOU SHOULD GIVE *EILEEN* A CALL. SHE'S BEEN CALLING YOU ALL NIGHT.

B-R-R-OTHER! WHAT GOOD IS HAVING A GOD AROUND IF YOU CAN'T GET ANY *FUN* OUT OF IT?

WOMAN, WHAT TROUBLES YOU? I WOULD GLADLY HAVE GIVEN THE CHILD ANYTHING SHE DESIRED.

WITH ALL DUE RESPECT, LORD HERMES, I WOULD APPRECIATE YOUR NOT TRYING TO *BUY* MY DAUGHTER'S LOYALTY.

BEING A MOTHER IS DIFFICULT ENOUGH WITHOUT HAVING TO COMPETE WITH AN OLYMPIAN *SANTA CLAUS.*

ARE YOU *MOCKING* ME, WOMAN?

JULIA, PLEASE...

I'M SORRY, DIANA, BUT I'M NOT FLATTERED BY LORD HERMES' ASSERTIONS THAT FAITH IS *CHATTEL* WHICH WE HUMANS WOULD READILY SELL TO THE HIGHEST BIDDER.

AND, IT'S *PROFESSOR,* LORD HERMES, NOT *"WOMAN."*

13

135

YOU HAVE FIRE IN YOUR HEART, PROFESSOR. I ADMIRE THAT.

BUT *YOU* SAW THE CROWD. HISTORY HAS SHOWN THAT REWARD IS THE CORNERSTONE OF FAITH, WHETHER IT BE THE PROMISE OF AN AFTERLIFE...

...OR SOMETHING MORE *IMMEDIATE.*

YOUTH AND BEAUTY PERHAPS?

SORRY, NO DEAL.

WHAT YOU'RE TALKING ABOUT ISN'T REWARD, IT'S *RANSOM.*

IS THIS WHAT OLYMPUS HAS COME TO?

"THAT THE GODS MUST NOW BARTER FOR THE FAITH THEY CANNOT *EARN?*"

YOU *DARE!?*

LORD HERMES, NO! SHE DIDN'T MEAN...

THERE WAS NO CONFUSION IN HER VOICE.

EVERY WORD WAS *DELIBERATE.*

PLEASE MY LORD. JULIA IS MY FRIEND AND MENTOR HERE. ALL I HAVE LEARNED ABOUT HUMANITY, I'VE LEARNED FROM HER.

DIANA, PLEASE DON'T BEG...

AH! OF COURSE! IT'S ALL *CLEAR* NOW!

PROFESSOR IS *JEALOUS.* SHE SEES THAT THE TIME OF HER MENTORSHIP IS *ENDED.*

THIS IS YOUR HOME AND HEARTH, PROFESSOR. I WILL NOT STAY WHERE I AM NOT WELCOME.

BUT DIANA, YOU MUST COME *WITH* ME.

NO!!

MOM, DON'T! YA CAN'T JUST LET THEM LEAVE!

VANESSA! PLEASE, STAY OUT OF THIS!

JULIA, I DON'T WANT TO LEAVE.

BUT YOU MUST UNDERSTAND. LORD HERMES IS ONE OF MY GODS. I OWE MY EXISTENCE TO HIM.

CAN'T WE COMPROMISE?

PROFESSOR, DON'T FORCE ME TO TAKE YOUR FRIEND DIANA FROM YOU. ALL I ASK IS THAT YOU DO NOT CHALLENGE MY AUTHORITY.

WELL?

MOMMY?

I'M SORRY.

BUT I CAN'T DO THAT.

(14)

SO BE IT, THEN.

BUT FIRST, YOU MUST BE ATTIRED IN ROBES BEFITTING AN EMISSARY OF OLYMPUS.

THERE! NOW, LET US DEPART!

JULIA, NESSIE. I LOVE YOU.

BUT I HAVE MY DUTY.

"WHAT I DO NOW I AM *COMPELLED* TO DO:"

"FAREWELL."

A BLINDING LIGHT DAZZLES THE EYE AS A SOFT *ECHO* DANCES THROUGH THE EAR.

"FAREWELL..."

"FAREWELL..."

"FAREWELL..."

DAMN.

⑮

A WEEK LATER:

HORACE, WILL YOU *PLEASE* PUT THAT PAPER AWAY!

☐ BOSTON ◯ GLOBE

☆☆ SPECIAL EDITION ☆☆

HERMES & DIANA ON 'MIRACLE TOUR'

CURES ONLY TEMPORARY

"FAITH SHALL BE REWARDED"

RELIGIOUS LEADERS CALL IT TRICKERY

I'M SORRY, JULIA. IT'S JUST SO AMAZING.

HERMES CLAIMS HE CAN DO ANYTHING, EXCEPT MAYBE RAISE THE DEAD.

YES. *TEMPORARILY.* UNLESS YOU SELL YOUR SOUL TO HIM.

AND IT'S *LORD* HERMES.

WHAT?

NOTHING. I'M SORRY, HORACE, IT'S JUST THAT I'M WORRIED ABOUT DIANA. THAT... GOD... HAS SUCH A SPELL ON HER.

PEOPLE WERE STARTING TO *LISTEN* TO HER... BUT *NOW.*

HOW CAN YOU PREACH EQUALITY WHEN ONLY THE SO-CALLED FAITHFUL STAND TO REAP THE REWARDS?

JUST HAVE FAITH AND YOU NEED NEVER THINK FOR YOURSELF AGAIN. I THINK HE'S ALREADY CONVERTED VANESSA.

YES. I HAVE NOTICED A GREATER LACK OF MOTIVATION FROM HER LATELY.

UH, JULIA... PERHAPS WHAT YOU AND VANESSA NEED IS SOME TIME AWAY FROM THIS LORD HERMES IMBROGLIO. TO CHANNEL YOUR ENERGY INTO SOMETHING A LITTLE LESS...ENERVATING?

ER... DO YOU LIKE TO FISH?

FISHING. GOD, IT SEEMS LIKE AN ETERNITY.

DIANA *IS* A GROWN WOMAN, AFTER ALL. MAYBE I'M JUST AFRAID THAT SHE JUST DOESN'T NEED ME ANY MORE.

SUDDENLY...

EH?

THE EYES OF BOSTON DART UPWARD, JOLTED BY ELECTRIC WAVES OF ASTONISHMENT.

FACES GLEAM WITH THE WARM GLOW FROM ABOVE.

AS IF HEAVEN HAD OPENED ITS GATE TO A NEW SUN!'

16

CAN YOU FEEL IT, DIANA? CAN YOU FEEL THE MORTALS EMBRACING US FROM AFAR?

D'YA THINK THEY'LL TOSS US SOME GOLD FROM UP THERE?

I DON'T TRUST THEM. THEY'RE TRYING TO TAKE OVER.

I HEARD THAT HE'S A BIG FAKE, JUST LIKE THE WONDER WOMAN BROAD...

GOD, I WISH I HAD A ZOOM LENS.

HOW CAN YOU PREACH EQUALITY WHEN ONLY THE SO-CALLED FAITHFUL STAND TO REAP THE REWARDS?

DON'T WORRY, DIANA. MORTALS CAN SOMETIMES BE A STUBBORN LOT.

MY LORD, SOME FEAR OUR GOAL IS TO RULE OVER THEM!

HERMES-- PLEASE, NO MORE.

MY GORGEOUS ONE, WE ARE GODS.

WHAT ELSE WOULD WE DO?

"BUT LORD HERMES, I AM NOT A GOD."

I WAGER THEIR LIPS TREMBLE WITH SONGS OF WORSHIP AND ADULATION.

LISTEN.

THEY ARE MY SISTERS AND BROTHERS.

I AM ONE OF THEM.

NO, PRINCESS. YOU ARE MEANT FOR MUCH GREATER THINGS!

BUT IS NOT TEACHING PEACE, LOVE...AND EQUALITY...THE GREATEST OF ALL ENDEAVORS?

ISN'T THAT MY DESTINY?

FORGIVE ME, DIANA. I'VE PUSHED YOU TOO FAST.

YOU NEED TIME TO THINK... TO UNDERSTAND.

17

"HIE THEN TO OUR TEMPLE. I WILL JOIN YOU SHORTLY.

"BUT, FIRST I MUST ATTEND THIS MULTI-TUDE."

THANK YOU, MY LORD. I OBEY FOR THE GLORY OF GAEA.

HERMES' BLESSING BE ON YOU, MY BEAUTY.

DAMN MY FELLOW GODS! THEY'VE DONE NOTHING BUT CONFOUND HER. ALL THAT POTENTIAL .... BEING WASTED.

SO, MY CHILDREN. WHAT CAN LORD HERMES DO FOR YOU THIS DAY?

"ONE OF THEM" INDEED!

WELL, IF DIANA IS TO TEACH AMONG THIS RABBLE, THEN I SHALL SEE THAT THEY ARE WORTHY OF HER!

AS THE GOD OF MESSENGERS BASKS IN THE GLORIOUS ATTENTION DUE AN OLYMPIAN, A FIGURE WATCHES FROM THE SHADOWS.

EYES PEERING THROUGH MIRRORED GLASS.

< WHAT? YOU SPEAK CLASSICAL GREEK? >

< I HAVE SPOKEN IT ALL MY LIFE AS HAS MY FATHER BEFORE ME, AND HIS FATHER BEFORE HIM. PRAYING FOR THE DAY OF THE OLYMPIANS' RETURN. >

< AND NOW THAT DAY IS HERE! >

SMOOTH LEGS CROSSING SILENTLY THROUGH THE GLADE.

AND A VOICE, SWEET AS WARM HONEY.

< MY NAME IS EURY. >

< FOR CENTURIES HAVE WE KEPT THE FAITH, AND NOW MY HEART OVERFLOWS WITH GRATITUDE THAT I'VE REALIZED MY FAMILY'S DREAM. >

< MY JOY TEMPERED ONLY BY THE SORROW OF MY DEAR FAITH-FUL FATHER NOT BEING ABLE TO BEND HIS KNEE TO YOU. >

< O MOST NOBLE GOD OF OLYMPUS! >

< FOR...HE IS DYING. >

18

"< FATHER PLEADED WITH ME NOT TO BOTHER YOU, BUT I KNEW THAT YOU WOULD NOT TURN AWAY FROM ONE OF YOUR MOST LOYAL WORSHIPPERS. >

"< PLEASE, O MOST MAGNIFICENT OF BEINGS, WON'T YOU PLEASE FIND FAVOR WITH YOUR MOST DEVOUT WORSHIPPER, SO THAT HE MAY LIVE TO SHOUT YOUR PRAISES FOR MANY MORE YEARS TO COME?>

BY MIGHTY OLYMPUS! YES! YES!

THIS IS THE CHANCE I HAVE AWAITED! I WILL MORE THAN SAVE YOUR FATHER! I WILL MAKE HIM LIKE A GOD!

EVEN MIGHTY HERACLES WILL BLANCH WITH ENVY!

NEWSMEN! SEND A CAMERA CREW.

"JUST FOLLOW MY BEACON.

"I SHALL BE WAITING.

LATER...

OKAY, MR. HERMES. WE'RE ALL SET.

GOOD. LEAD ON, GIRL.

AND IT IS LORD HERMES.

THIS WAY, MY LORD.

SUCH SQUALOR! ONCE THE FAITH HAS BEEN WON, I SHALL PERSONALLY PUT AN END TO THIS PESTILENCE.

HEY, OMAR. ISN'T THERE SOMETHIN' STRANGE ABOUT THIS BUILDING?

I MEAN, DO YOU RECOGNIZE IT AT ALL?

NOPE. BUT THEN, I DON'T USUALLY GET TO THE COMBAT ZONE MUCH.

DO NOT WORRY, MY SONS. NOTHING SHALL HARM YOU WHILE YOU'RE UNDER MY CARE.

IT'S DOWN THESE STEPS, LORD HERMES.

PEE-YOO! WHAT A STENCH!

BY ALL THAT IS HOLY. HOW CAN ANY BEING LIVE LIKE THIS?

WE HAVE NO MONEY AND THE HOSPITALS WOULDN'T TAKE HIM.

< FATHER! HE'S HERE! LORD HERMES IS HERE! >

< LORD... HERMES...? OH... I AM NOT... WORTHY...? >

MY LORD PLEASE, HE'S SLIPPING AWAY.

YES, THE FAITHFUL SHALL BE REWARDED.

< HEAR ME, OLD ONE. BY THE POWER OF ASCLEPIUS, GOD OF HEALING, I BID YOU TO BEHOLD THE POWER OF THE CADUCEUS. >

< REACH OUT AND TAKE HOLD OF IT WHERE THE SERPENTS JOIN. >

< LET THE ENERGY OF THE FOUR ELEMENTS SURGE THROUGH YOUR VEINS... >

< FEEL THE POWER OF OLYMPUS! >

LAWD ALMIGHTY. I DON'T KNOW WHAT HE'S SAYING, BUT THIS IS HOT STUFF!

"AAAAAARRRGGG!!!"

"HEY, HE'S SCREAMIN'! IS THAT SUPPOSED TO HAPPEN?"

20

142

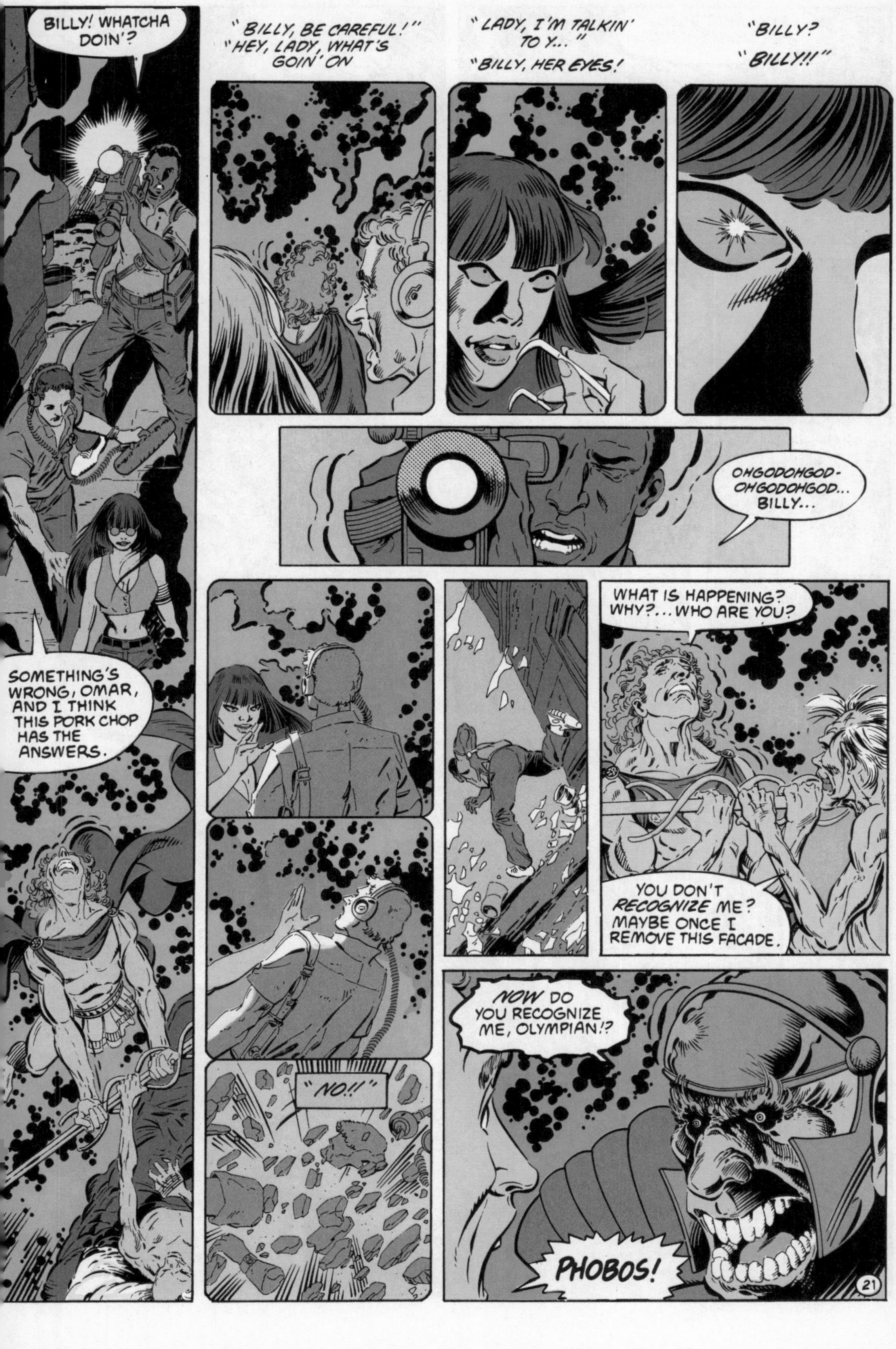
BILLY! WHATCHA DOIN'?
"BILLY, BE CAREFUL!"
"HEY, LADY, WHAT'S GOIN' ON
"LADY, I'M TALKIN' TO Y..."
"BILLY, HER EYES!
"BILLY?
"BILLY!!"
OHGODOHGOD-OHGODOHGOD... BILLY...
SOMETHING'S WRONG, OMAR, AND I THINK THIS PORK CHOP HAS THE ANSWERS.
WHAT IS HAPPENING? WHY?... WHO ARE YOU?
YOU DON'T RECOGNIZE ME? MAYBE ONCE I REMOVE THIS FACADE.
"NO!!"
NOW DO YOU RECOGNIZE ME, OLYMPIAN!?
PHOBOS!
21

AND WHAT ABOUT ME, 'LORD' HERMES?

EURY... BY ALL THE GODS... I SHOULD HAVE SEEN...

EURYALE!

YES, DOOMED IMBECILE. ONE OF THE IMMORTAL SISTERHOOD OF GORGONS!

THE FLOOR EXPLODES WITH A CRASH OF THUNDER AND THE ONCE MIGHTY GOD FALLS INTO THE DARKNESS.

UNTIL...

...HERRR... MEEESSS...

THAT VOICE! LIKE CRUMBLING EARTH.

IT CANNOT BE! NOT AFTER ALL THESE EONS!

HAHAHAHAHA!

IXION THE ASSASSIN!

22

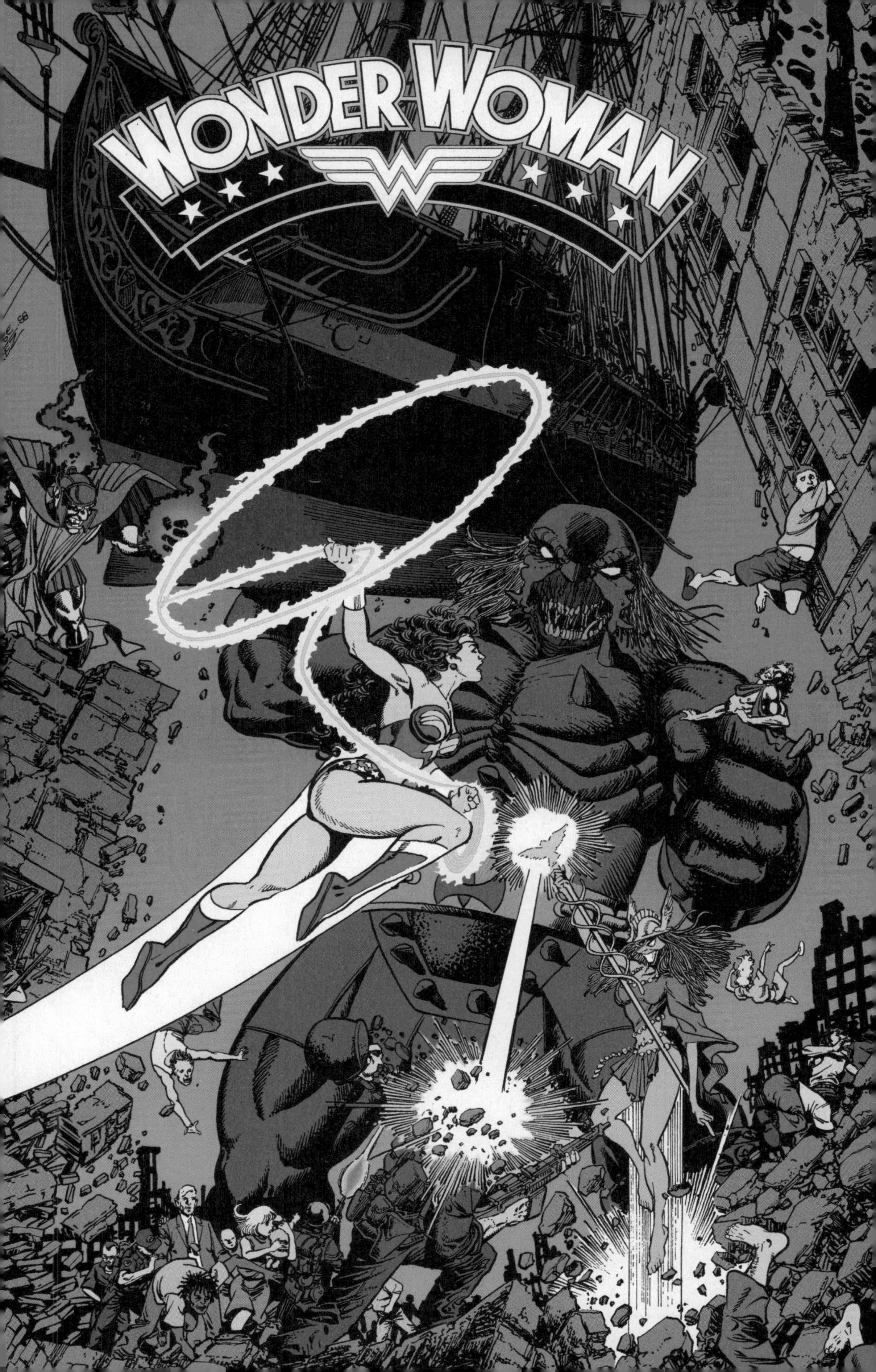
WONDER WOMAN

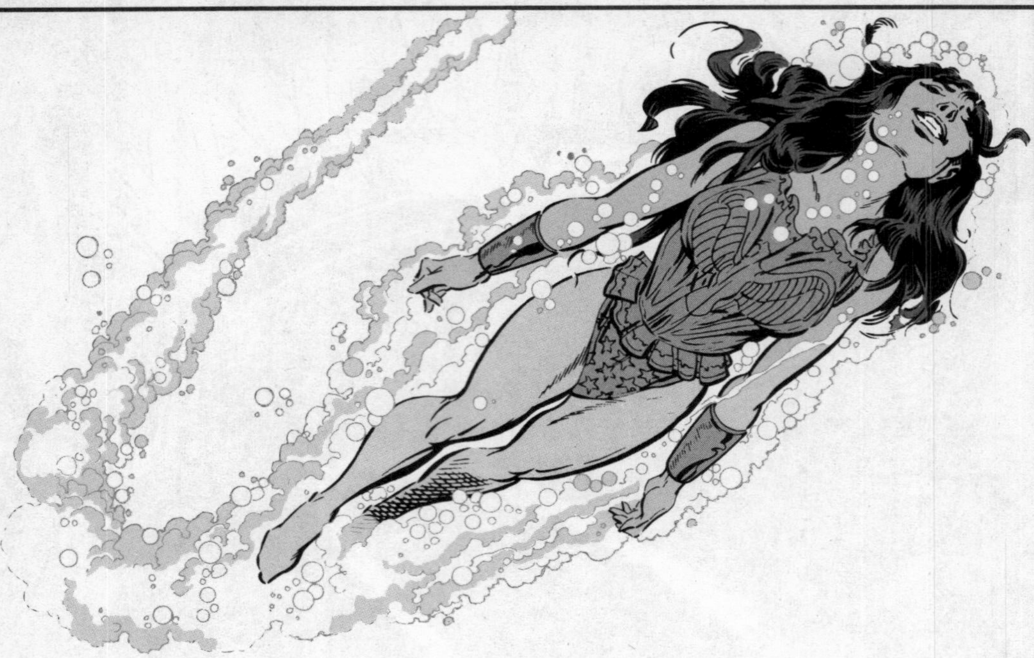

WONDER WOMAN

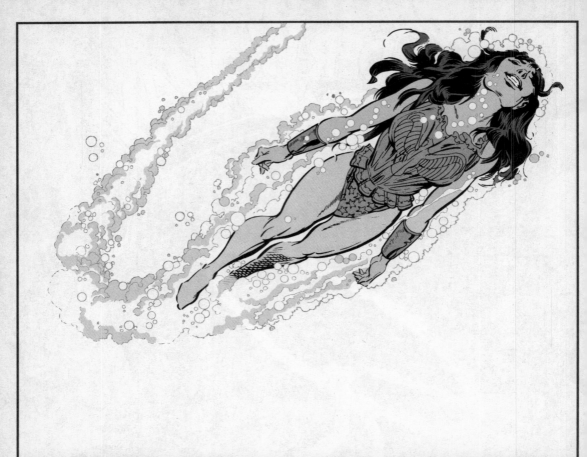

CHAPTER SIX

-- AND HERE'S A RECAP OF OUR ONGOING TOP STORY:

THE STRANGE ATTACK ON LORD HERMES, SELF-PROCLAIMED GOD FROM MT. OLYMPUS, AND A VIDEO CREW IN BOSTON'S COMBAT ZONE.

THERE ON A ERRAND OF MERCY, TO HEAL THE DYING FATHER OF A FAITHFUL WORSHIPPER NAMED EURY, LORD HERMES HOPED TO PROVE HIS GODLY CLAIM.

BUT SOMETHING SEEMS TO HAVE GONE HORRIBLY WRONG.

ANALYSTS ARE NOW STUDYING THE LAST LIVE TRANSMISSIONS TO ASCERTAIN WHETHER IT'S ALL SOME ELABORATE HOAX. SOME CAMERA TRICKERY.

IF IT ISN'T A HOAX, THEN IT APPEARS THAT THE WOMAN EURY HAD SET A TRAP FOR HERMES.

"AND THAT SHE, SOMEHOW, ALLEGEDLY TURNED THE SOUND MAN, BILLY CURLEY, INTO A STATUE, AND THEN DEMOLISHED IT.

"AFTER THAT, THE CAMERA LOST THE PICTURE. THE FATE OF CAMERAMAN OMAR RAMOS IS STILL UNKNOWN."

"HEY, RICHTER! OVER HERE! I THINK I FOUND SOMETHING!"

"WHAT?"

IT'S THE VIDEO CAMERA!

HMM. STILL ON. PROBABLY STILL TRANSMITTING. THEY SAY THAT HERMES GUY CAN DO THAT.

WONDER WHAT THEY WERE SHOOTING HERE?

GOT ME. I HAVEN'T BEEN LISTENING TO THE NEWS OR...

HEY!

SOMETHING MOVING. OVER THERE.

KEEP AWAY FROM ME! KEEP AWAY!

"WHOA! THAT GUY'S SCARED TO DEATH!"

NOW, TAKE IT EASY, MISTER. WE'RE THE POLICE. WE'RE NOT GONNA HURT YOU.

C'MON. JUST TELL US YOUR NAME, OKAY?

P-POLICE? OH MY GOD... BILLY... THAT WITCH... KILLED BILLY.

H-HE TOLD ME... THAT B-BUILDING... ALL WRONG...

"HE'S STRUNG OUT. MUST BE ON SOMETHING..."

NO! DON'T YOU GET IT? THAT OLD BUILDING!

YESTERDAY, THIS WAS AN EMPTY LOT!

BENEATH THE FOUNDATIONS OF THE MYSTERIOUS BUILDING, THE VIOLATED EARTH RUMBLES WITH THE SOUNDS OF DEEP, PONDEROUS BREATHING-- GIANT, CLOGGED BELLOWS STRAINING WITH EVERY EXERTION.

AND BETWEEN EACH MANACLED GUST THUNDERS THE TRIUMPHANT LAUGH OF PHOBOS, GOD OF TERROR!

THEN YOU *DO* RECOGNIZE HIM, OLYMPIAN? DESPITE HOW THE MILLENNIA OF TORTURED IM-PRISONMENT HAS CORRUPTED HIM?

YOU DO REMEMBER *IXION*, THE FIRST AND GREATEST MASS MURDERER EVER TO WALK THIS EARTH. THE ONE *YOU* IMPRISONED EONS AGO!

THE ONE WHO WILL *DESTROY* YOU!

HHHERRR... MMEEESSSS...

COMBAT ZONE

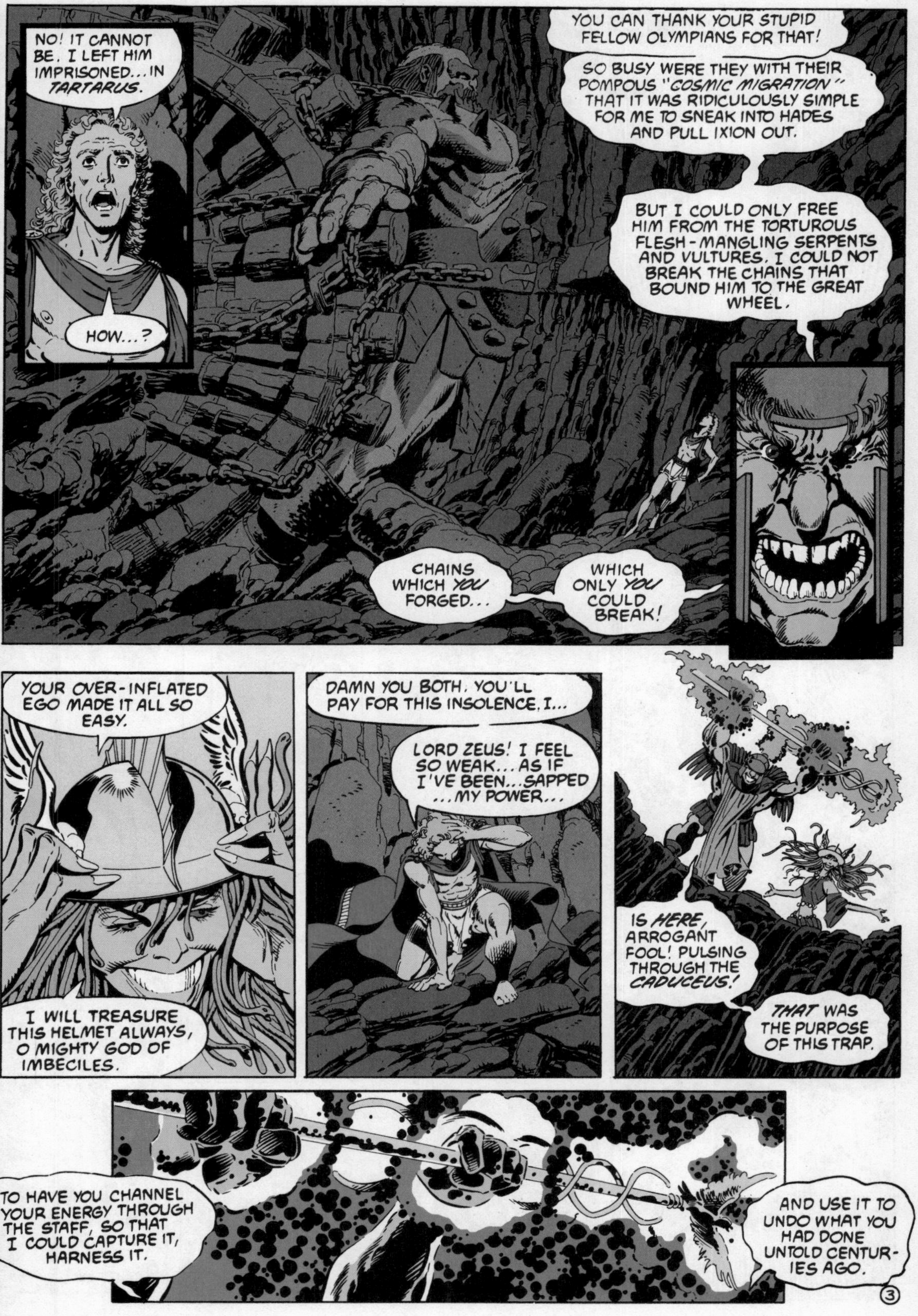
NO! IT CANNOT BE. I LEFT HIM IMPRISONED... IN TARTARUS.
HOW...?
YOU CAN THANK YOUR STUPID FELLOW OLYMPIANS FOR THAT!
SO BUSY WERE THEY WITH THEIR POMPOUS "COSMIC MIGRATION" THAT IT WAS RIDICULOUSLY SIMPLE FOR ME TO SNEAK INTO HADES AND PULL IXION OUT.
BUT I COULD ONLY FREE HIM FROM THE TORTUROUS FLESH-MANGLING SERPENTS AND VULTURES. I COULD NOT BREAK THE CHAINS THAT BOUND HIM TO THE GREAT WHEEL.
CHAINS WHICH YOU FORGED...
WHICH ONLY YOU COULD BREAK!
YOUR OVER-INFLATED EGO MADE IT ALL SO EASY.
I WILL TREASURE THIS HELMET ALWAYS, O MIGHTY GOD OF IMBECILES.
DAMN YOU BOTH. YOU'LL PAY FOR THIS INSOLENCE. I...
LORD ZEUS! I FEEL SO WEAK... AS IF I'VE BEEN... SAPPED ...MY POWER...
IS HERE, ARROGANT FOOL! PULSING THROUGH THE CADUCEUS!
THAT WAS THE PURPOSE OF THIS TRAP.
TO HAVE YOU CHANNEL YOUR ENERGY THROUGH THE STAFF, SO THAT I COULD CAPTURE IT, HARNESS IT.
AND USE IT TO UNDO WHAT YOU HAD DONE UNTOLD CENTURIES AGO.
3

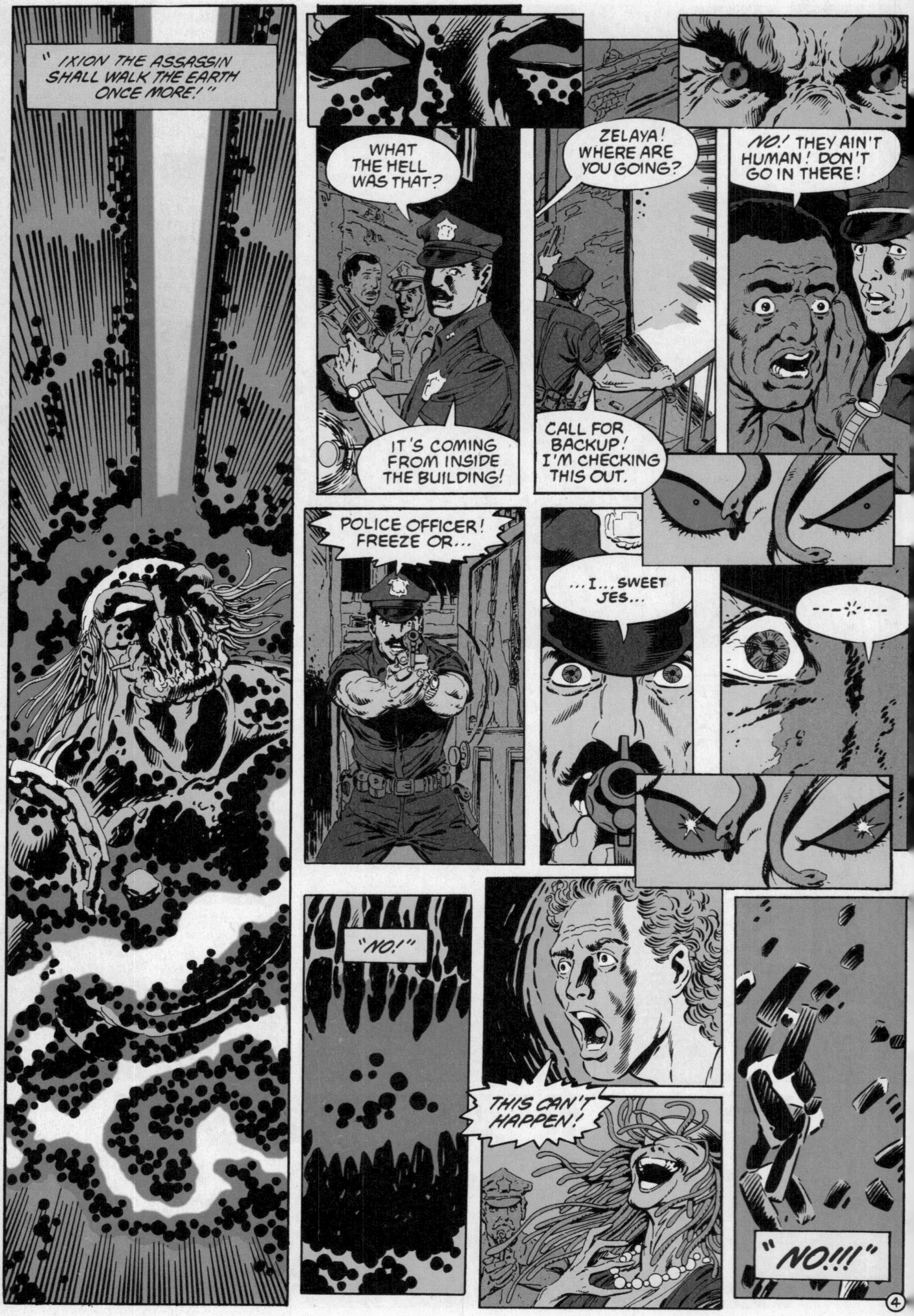
"IXION THE ASSASSIN SHALL WALK THE EARTH ONCE MORE!"
WHAT THE HELL WAS THAT?
IT'S COMING FROM INSIDE THE BUILDING!
ZELAYA! WHERE ARE YOU GOING?
CALL FOR BACKUP! I'M CHECKING THIS OUT.
NO! THEY AIN'T HUMAN! DON'T GO IN THERE!
POLICE OFFICER! FREEZE OR...
...I... SWEET JES...
"NO!"
THIS CAN'T HAPPEN!
"NO!!!"
4

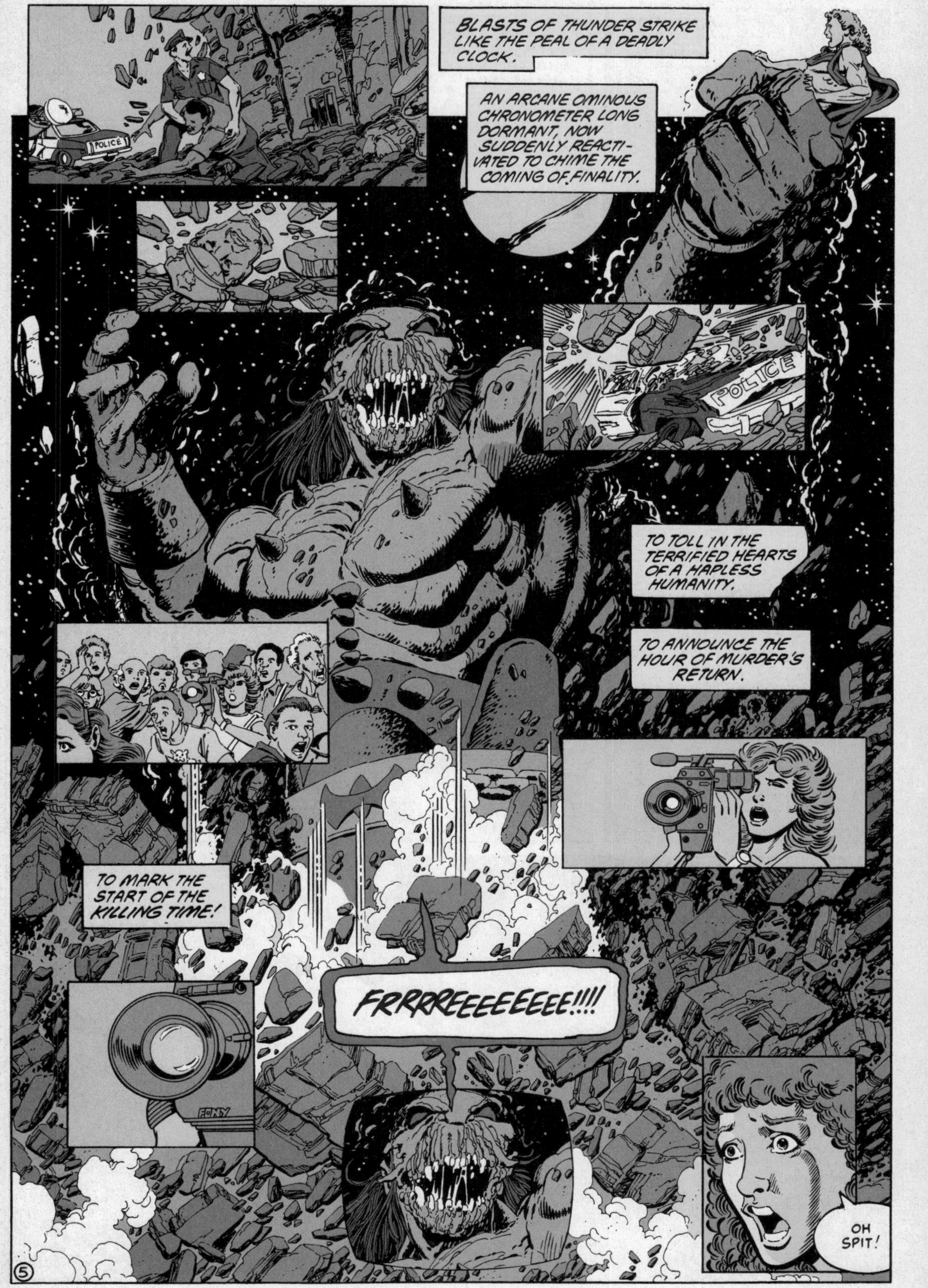
BLASTS OF THUNDER STRIKE LIKE THE PEAL OF A DEADLY CLOCK.
AN ARCANE OMINOUS CHRONOMETER LONG DORMANT, NOW SUDDENLY REACTI-VATED TO CHIME THE COMING OF FINALITY.
POLICE
POLICE
TO TOLL IN THE TERRIFIED HEARTS OF A HAPLESS HUMANITY.
TO ANNOUNCE THE HOUR OF MURDER'S RETURN.
TO MARK THE START OF THE KILLING TIME!
FRRRREEEEEEEEE!!!!
OH SPIT!
5

MOM! *MOM!* TURN ON YOUR TV! QUICK!

IT'S HERMES!

VANESSA, PLEASE! I TOLD YOU I DON'T WANT TO HEAR ANY MORE ABOUT *LORD* HERMES.

BUT, MOM...

VANESSA, CAN'T YOU SEE I'VE GOT COMPANY?

JULIA, MAYBE YOU SHOULD HEAR HER OUT. SHE SEEMS QUITE DISTRESSED.

SHE'S *ALWAYS* DISTRESSED! THAT'S WHAT 13-YEAR OLDS ARE GOOD AT.

VANESSA'S *MY* DAUGHTER, MR. WESTLAKE. I'LL THANK YOU NOT TO INTERFERE.

YES, I-I SEE.

MOTHER! HERMES IS A FRIEND OF DIANA'S!

HE'S IN DEEP TROUBLE!

YOUNG LADY, GIVE ME BACK THAT REMOTE CONTROL! *NOW!*

NO! YOU GOTTA SEE THIS!

LOOK! PLEASE!

HUH? WHO... WHAT THE HECK IS *THAT?*

OH MY LORD. IT'S HIM!

YOU KNOW THAT... THING?

H-HE ONCE TRIED TO KILL ME... KILL US ALL.

IT'S ARES' INSANE SON PHOBOS!

TREMBLE, PUNY MORTALS! TREMBLE WITH TERROR! FOR ON THIS NIGHT YOU ALL WILL *DIE!*

BEHOLD THE HELPLESS HERMES, THE OLYMPIAN FOOL WHO DARED FLAUNT HIS POWER AT YOU!

YOU THOUGHT *HE* WAS POWERFUL? NOW YOU SHALL TASTE *TRUE* GODLY POWER.

YOUR UNWORTHY THROATS WILL *CHOKE* ON IT!

THIS IS LT. PLACIDE OF THE BOSTON POLICE. RELEASE YOUR HOSTAGE AND SURRENDER OR WE COMMENCE SHOOTING. YOU HAVE 30 SECONDS.

LIEUTENANT, ARE YOU CRAZY? TAKE THOSE SUCKERS DOWN!

CAP'N, WE GOTTA GIVE 'EM A CHANCE TO LET GO OF THAT HERMES GUY. GOD OR NO GOD, HE'S STILL A HOSTAGE.

BESIDES, WE GOT 'EM SURROUNDED. THEY AIN'T GETTIN' THROUGH THIS BLOCKADE.

FIFTEEN SECONDS...

TEN...

SUDDENLY...

GREETINGS, MORTALS. IT'S SO WONDERFUL TO SEE THAT THE CENTURIES HAVE NOT LESSENED YOUR PENCHANT FOR FOOLHARDINESS.

WHA...!?

IT'S THAT GORGON DAME! THE ONE WHO TURNED THAT TV GUY TO STONE!

CLOSE YOUR EYES! DON'T LOOK AT HER!

BUT, FOR CAPTAIN JAMES SMITH THE WARNING COMES TOO LATE.

FAREWELL, IMPUDENT ONE. I ENJOYED SHARING YOUR GLANCE.

HA HA HA HA HA HA HA HA HA

QUICK! GET THE CAP'N OUTTA HERE! HURRY!

:OOOMPH: WE'RE TRYING, LIEUTENANT. BUT HE'S SOLID ROCK! WE CAN'T BUDGE HIM!

LT. PLACIDE!

"THE GIANT MONSTER'S COMING TOWARD US!"

DIIIIIIII-EEEEEE. DIIIIIIII-EEEEEE.

IXION. YOUR QUARREL IS WITH ME! LEAVE THOSE MORTALS ALONE!

I CHALLENGE YOU I DEFY YOU! KILL ME IF YOU CAN!

DAMN YOU, IXION, LISTEN TO ME!!

HERMES' CRIES ARE FUTILE AS THE HIDEOUS GARGANTUA QUICKENS HIS STRIDE.

LIEUTENANT, WE CAN'T STOP HIM!

HE'S GONNA STOMP US!

BUG OUT! EVERYBODY!

WE CAN'T HELP THE CAP'N NOW!

RUN!

NO!

WITH A DEAFENING, EARTH-SHAKING CRASH, WHAT WAS ONCE FLESH AND BLOOD IS PULVERIZED INTO DUST

IXION'S TRIUMPHANT HOWL STAMPEDES THROUGH EVERY STREET OF THE TERRIFIED CITY.

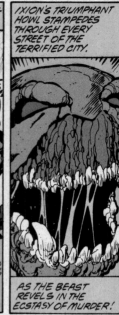

AS THE BEAST REVELS IN THE ECSTASY OF MURDER!

OH MAN, BRIAN. ARE YOU GETTING THIS?

I'M ZOOMING IN FOR A CLOSE UP!

"CAN YOU SEE IT, BRIAN? YOU CAN JUST MAKE OUT HIS WEDDING RING!"

"PAT, GET OUT OF THERE! CAN YOU HEAR ME? THIS IS YOUR PRODUCER SPEAKING. LEAVE THE CAMERA RUNNING AND GET THE HELL AWAY FROM THERE!"

IT'S NO GOOD. SHE MUST HAVE HER HEADPHONES OFF. PAT! PAT!

"WHAT IN THE WORLD...?"

"HELLO MY PRETTY. MY NAME IS EURYALE. WHAT IS YOURS?"

FASCINATING INSTRUMENT A VIDEO CAMERA. MAY I SEE IT?

YES, QUITE FASCINATING.

NOW, DULLARD, A BIG SMILE!

"OH, YOU CALL THAT A SMILE?"

8

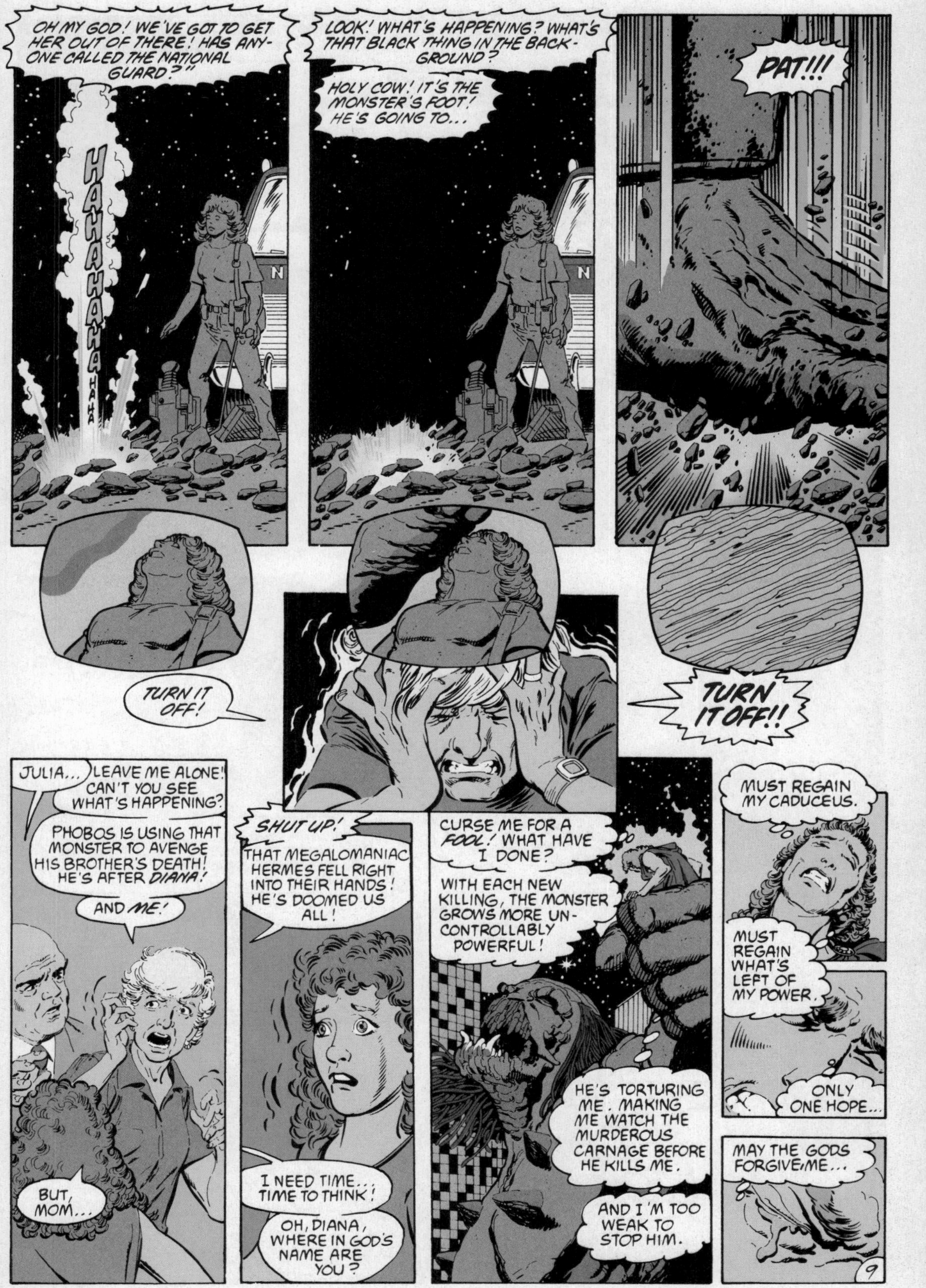
OH MY GOD! WE'VE GOT TO GET HER OUT OF THERE! HAS ANYONE CALLED THE NATIONAL GUARD?"
HAHAHAHAHAHAHA
LOOK! WHAT'S HAPPENING? WHAT'S THAT BLACK THING IN THE BACKGROUND?
HOLY COW! IT'S THE MONSTER'S FOOT! HE'S GOING TO...
PAT!!!
TURN IT OFF!
TURN IT OFF!!
JULIA...
LEAVE ME ALONE! CAN'T YOU SEE WHAT'S HAPPENING?
PHOBOS IS USING THAT MONSTER TO AVENGE HIS BROTHER'S DEATH! HE'S AFTER DIANA!
AND ME!
BUT, MOM...
SHUT UP!
THAT MEGALOMANIAC HERMES FELL RIGHT INTO THEIR HANDS! HE'S DOOMED US ALL!
I NEED TIME... TIME TO THINK!
OH, DIANA, WHERE IN GOD'S NAME ARE YOU?
CURSE ME FOR A FOOL! WHAT HAVE I DONE?
WITH EACH NEW KILLING, THE MONSTER GROWS MORE UNCONTROLLABLY POWERFUL!
HE'S TORTURING ME. MAKING ME WATCH THE MURDEROUS CARNAGE BEFORE HE KILLS ME.
AND I'M TOO WEAK TO STOP HIM.
MUST REGAIN MY CADUCEUS.
MUST REGAIN WHAT'S LEFT OF MY POWER.
ONLY ONE HOPE...
MAY THE GODS FORGIVE ME...
9

THE BEAUTIFUL WOODLANDS OF NEW HAMPSHIRE, WHERE LORD HERMES FIRST TOOK MORTAL FORM SO THAT HE MIGHT MORE READILY WALK AMID THE JOYS OF NATURE UNDETECTED.

WHERE, AS A SIGN OF THE GOD'S FAVOR, HE HAD ERECTED HIS GREAT TEMPLE. A REFUGE FROM CURIOUS EYES. A SANCTUARY.

AND FOR AN AMAZON PRINCESS, A PLACE FOR PRAYER.

SOFT LIPS CHANT OUT TO THE CRYSTAL MOON.

AN ELEGANT SILHOUETTE BATHES IN ITS GLOW.

THE RITES OF THE NEREIDS ARE FULFILLED.

AH, YES! THANK YOU, PANOPEA! I NEEDED THIS!

THESE PAST DAYS HAVE BEEN SO FULL OF CONFUSION AND CONFLICT, I FEARED MY MIND WOULD BURST FROM THE STRAIN.

BUT *HERE!* HERE I CAN IMMERSE MYSELF IN THE WELLS OF SIMPLICITY.

HERE, EVERYTHING IS CLEAR.

AWAY FROM THE CLAMOR OF THE WORLD ABOVE, DIANA LUXURIATES IN THE PLEASURES OF THE FLUID TRANQUILITY.

GLEEFULLY REMINDED THAT THERE IS STILL SOME PURITY LEFT ON THIS WORLD.

UNTIL, SADLY, EVEN THE GENTLE LAMB OF PEACE ROARS OUT LIKE A LION.

156

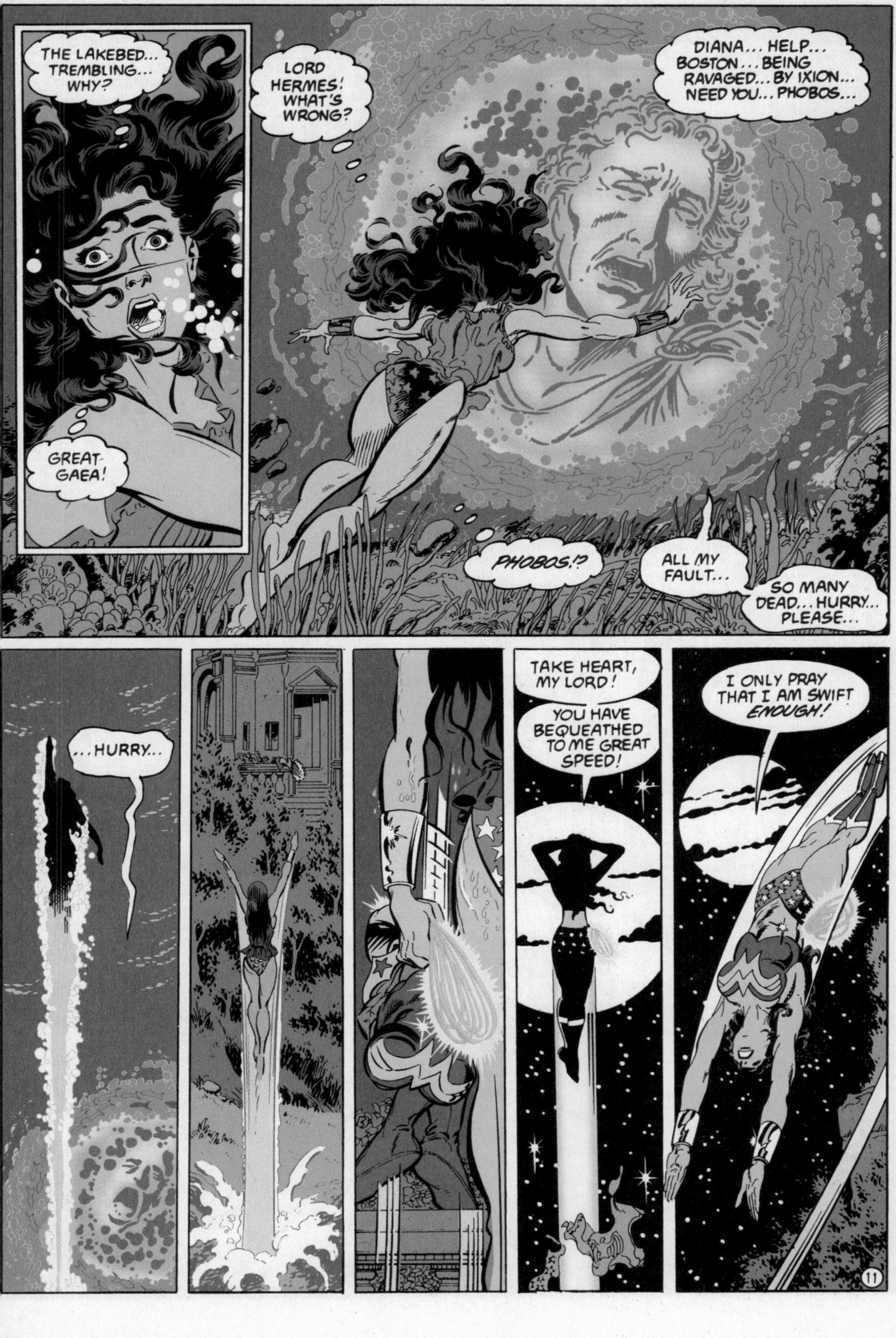
THE LAKEBED... TREMBLING... WHY?
GREAT GAEA!
LORD HERMES! WHAT'S WRONG?
DIANA... HELP... BOSTON... BEING RAVAGED... BY IXION... NEED YOU... PHOBOS...
PHOBOS!?
ALL MY FAULT...
SO MANY DEAD... HURRY... PLEASE...
...HURRY...
TAKE HEART, MY LORD!
YOU HAVE BEQUEATHED TO ME GREAT SPEED!
I ONLY PRAY THAT I AM SWIFT ENOUGH!
11

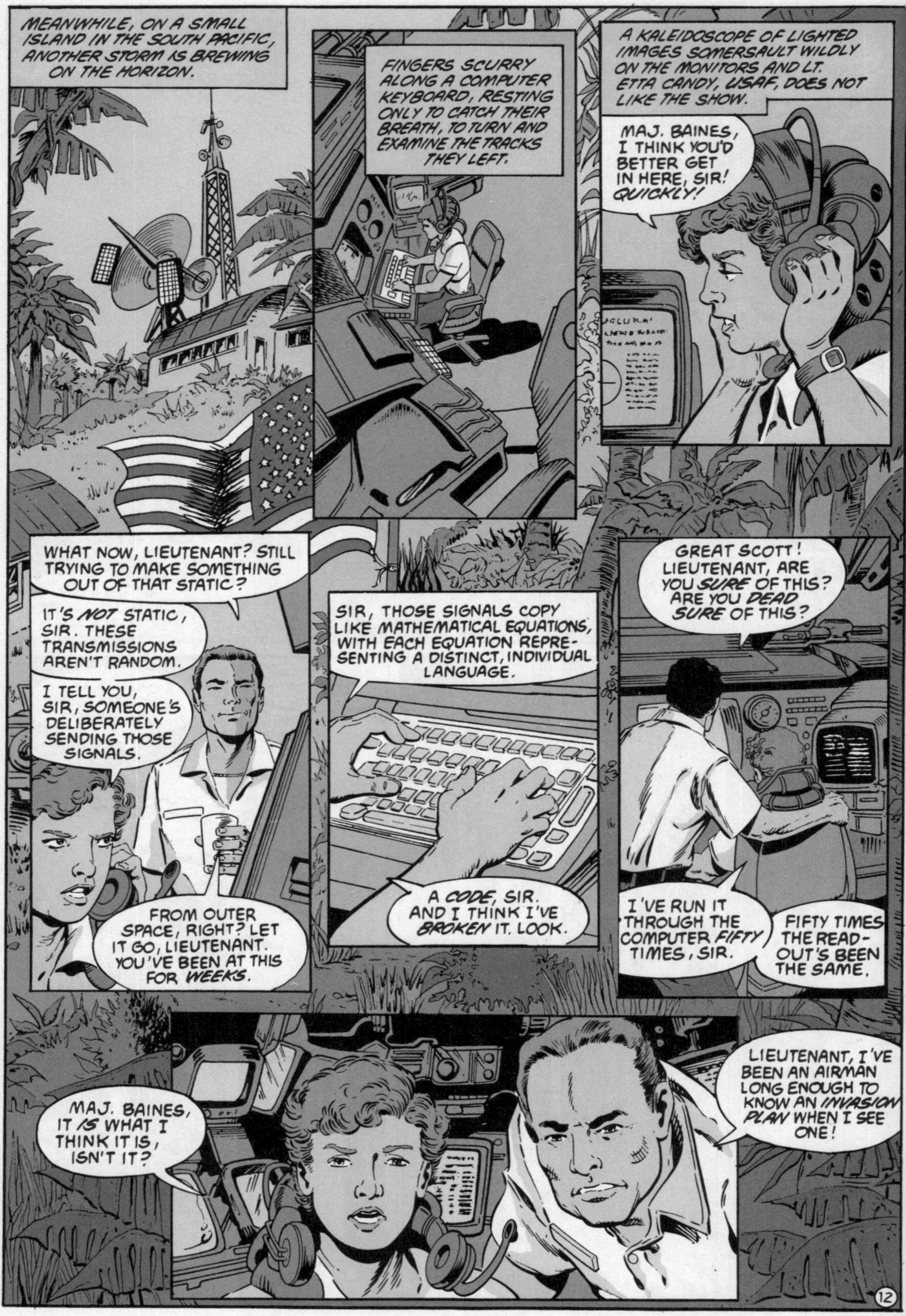
MEANWHILE, ON A SMALL ISLAND IN THE SOUTH PACIFIC, ANOTHER STORM IS BREWING ON THE HORIZON.
FINGERS SCURRY ALONG A COMPUTER KEYBOARD, RESTING ONLY TO CATCH THEIR BREATH, TO TURN AND EXAMINE THE TRACKS THEY LEFT.
A KALEIDOSCOPE OF LIGHTED IMAGES SOMERSAULT WILDLY ON THE MONITORS AND LT. ETTA CANDY, USAF, DOES NOT LIKE THE SHOW.
MAJ. BAINES, I THINK YOU'D BETTER GET IN HERE, SIR! QUICKLY!
WHAT NOW, LIEUTENANT? STILL TRYING TO MAKE SOMETHING OUT OF THAT STATIC?
IT'S NOT STATIC, SIR. THESE TRANSMISSIONS AREN'T RANDOM.
I TELL YOU, SIR, SOMEONE'S DELIBERATELY SENDING THOSE SIGNALS.
FROM OUTER SPACE, RIGHT? LET IT GO, LIEUTENANT. YOU'VE BEEN AT THIS FOR WEEKS.
SIR, THOSE SIGNALS COPY LIKE MATHEMATICAL EQUATIONS, WITH EACH EQUATION REPRESENTING A DISTINCT, INDIVIDUAL LANGUAGE.
A CODE, SIR. AND I THINK I'VE BROKEN IT. LOOK.
GREAT SCOTT! LIEUTENANT, ARE YOU SURE OF THIS? ARE YOU DEAD SURE OF THIS?
I'VE RUN IT THROUGH THE COMPUTER FIFTY TIMES, SIR.
FIFTY TIMES THE READ-OUT'S BEEN THE SAME.
MAJ. BAINES, IT IS WHAT I THINK IT IS, ISN'T IT?
LIEUTENANT, I'VE BEEN AN AIRMAN LONG ENOUGH TO KNOW AN INVASION PLAN WHEN I SEE ONE!
12

FRANTIC EYES BULGE FROM BEHIND THE CONTORTED MASK OF TERROR!

JOINED BY A TEEMING PARADE OF OTHER MASKS, EACH MORE TWISTED THAN THE LAST.

TRANSFORMING THE STREETS OF BOSTON INTO AN OBSCENE MARDI GRAS.

SCAMPERING THROUGH SHATTERED PAVEMENT LIKE SCATTERED ANTS, DESPERATELY SEEKING REFUGE.

REFUGE FROM THE TERROR. REFUGE FROM THE KILLING.

UNMINDFUL, OR PERHAPS TOO MINDFUL, OF THOSE TRAGIC SOULS NOW PART OF THAT TRAMPLED PAVEMENT.

WHILE PERCHED ABOVE THEM IS TERROR HIMSELF, HIS LAUGHTER SHREDDING THE NIGHT SKY TO PIECES.

YES! YES! RUN, YOU FOOLS! CRUSH EACH OTHER!

TRUST NO ONE! EVERYONE IS YOUR ENEMY! RUN! RUN!!

PHOBOS!

ENOUGH!

WITH THE POUNDING CRASH OF BONE AGAINST BONE, TERROR'S LAUGHTER IS ABRUPTLY SILENCED!

YOU! UNTIE ME, YOU WRETCHED WOMAN!

NO, LORD PHOBOS. I KNOW YOUR DREADFUL TOXIN IS BASED ON DECEIT...ON LIES.

WHILE BOUND BY HESTIA'S LASSO OF TRUTH, YOU SHALL SPEW YOUR VENOM NO LONGER!

FOOL! THAT WILL ONLY LESSEN THE PANIC! THAT WILL NOT STOP THE KILLING!

AS YOU MURDERED MY BROTHER DEIMOS, SO TOO SHALL MILLIONS DIE!

YOU CAN THANK HERMES FOR THAT!

13

SINCE ITS RESTORATION IN 1833, THE U.S.S. FRIGATE *CONSTITUTION* HAS STOOD AS A MONUMENT TO THE CREATION OF A COUNTRY.

A SYMBOL OF LIBERTY.

BUT IN THE HANDS OF A MADDENED REFUGEE FROM HELL, THE HISTORIC LANDMARK IS JUST ANOTHER INSTRUMENT OF DEATH!

THE HELPLESS GOD FROM OLYMPUS CAN MERELY LOOK ON WITH ANGUISH AND GUILT.

SUDDENLY, HOPE STREAKS THROUGH THE SKY LIKE A STAR-SPANGLED COMET.

DIANA!

THANK THE FATES!

AND IN ONE DEFT MOVEMENT, THE WAR VESSEL KNOWN AS "OLD IRONSIDES" IS FREED FROM THE GRASP OF MAMMOTH FINGERS.

WWOO---MMMAAANNN--PRREE-PARRRE--TO--DIIIIEE!!

DIANA, NO! FIND MY CADUCEUS! IT'S OUR ONLY CHANCE!

I DON'T KNOW WHERE TO LOOK!

AND MORE MAY PERISH WHILE I SEARCH!

14

I HAVE TO ATTACK!

BUT THIS TIME, THE ENRAGED BEHEMOTH IS READY!

DIIIIEEE!!!

OOMPH!

GODS FORGIVE ME, I TELEGRAPHED THAT CHARGE LIKE A TYRO!

BARELY REGAINED MY SENSES IN TIME TO AVOID CRASHING INTO THAT BUILDING.

IT'S TOO CROWDED HERE. IF I'M TO GAIN AN ADVANTAGE, I HAVE TO GET THE BEAST INTO OPEN GROUND.

MUST CATCH HIM BY SURPRISE!

A VOLCANO OF PAIN AND SHOCK ERUPTS FROM IXION'S SCARRED THROAT AS HE SUDDENLY FINDS HIMSELF HOISTED UPWARD...

NOW!

HIS FINGERS SNAP OPEN, RELEASING THE GOD OF MESSENGERS...

WHO DROPS LIKE ONE DEAD INTO THE FOAMY BRINE.

THE BOSTON CROWD STARES INTO THE SMOKING SKY AS THEIR MURDEROUS OPPRESSOR IS ROCKETED AWAY FROM THEIR CITY.

AND THE WAILS OF TORMENT SURRENDER TO THE HAILS OF JOY.

15

WITH AMAZON MUSCLES STRAINING, PRINCESS DIANA REACHES THE CLOSEST OPEN BATTLEFIELD SHE CAN THINK OF...

AND, WITH A MIGHTY HEAVE, THRUSTS IXION INTO THE RED CLAY OF GAYHEAD CLIFFS IN MARTHA'S VINEYARD.

GREAT GAEA! HE'S NOT MOVING! DID I THROW HIM TOO HARD?

I DIDN'T WANT TO KILL HIM!

DIIIEEE!!

HE WAS FAKING!

ALMOST CAUGHT ME OFF GUARD.

BUT I SHAN'T LET THAT HAPPEN TO ME AGAIN!

AAAARRRRHH!!

NOOO!!! YOUUU...WWILLL... NNOTT...TAKE...MMEEE... BAAACK!!!

III...KILLL... YOOOJU...ORRR... YOUUU--HAVVE-- TOOO--KILLL-- MEEE!!!

KILLL--MEEEE!!!

16

WHILE BACK IN BOSTON, IN WHAT HAS LITERALLY BECOME THE COMBAT ZONE...

FIRE, MEN! KEEP FIRING!

BLOW THAT SUCKER APART!!

EURYALE! CURSE YOU, WENCH, WHERE ARE YOU!?

I NEED YOU! EURYALE!

I AM HERE, DARK TOAD. HOW CAN YOU EXPECT ONE TO HEAR ANYTHING AMID THIS BOOMING CACOPHONY?

MOTHER CETO! WHO HAS ROPED YOU?

WHO DO YOU THINK!? UNTIE ME! WE MUST FIND THAT ACCURSED AMAZON AND I WILL PERSONALLY TORTURE HER BEYOND DEATH!

CAN'T WAIT UNTIL AFTER I'VE FINISHED PLAYING WITH THESE HUMANS? IT'S BEEN AGES SINCE I'VE ENJOYED MYSELF SO.

NO! THE AMAZON FIRST!

UNTIE ME!!

OH, VERY WELL. NOW, CEASE SQUIRMING WHILE...

EH? I CAN'T UNDO THE KNOT!

THEN CUT IT, DAMN YOU!

IT WON'T CLEAVE. ONLY A GOD CAN UNBIND THIS MAGIC TIE!

WAIT! HERMES! WHAT HAS BECOME OF HERMES?

NO!

THE CADUCEUS!

NOOOOOOOO!

17

EURYALE! SHE'S DEAD, PHOBOS. BY THE ONLY MEANS OF DESTROYING A GORGON.

DECAPITATION.

HOLD YOUR FIRE, MORTALS. LORD HERMES IS IN CONTROL NOW.

YOU UNDERESTIMATED ME, FETID VIPER. WHEN IXION RELEASED ME, I STILL HAD ENOUGH POWER TO INFILTRATE THE CATACOMBS OF THIS CITY'S SEWER SYSTEM.

AND WAITED FOR MY CHANCE TO RETRIEVE THIS.

THE STAFF THAT WILL KILL YOU EVEN MORE HORRIBLY THAN THE GORGON, IF YOU DO NOT TELL ME WHAT I WANT TO KNOW.

WELL?

GAYHEAD CLIFFS.

AAARRRGGHH!!

IXION, I CAN FEEL YOUR STRENGTH EBBING. YOU ARE NO MATCH AGAINST ME.

I BESEECH YOU TO SURRENDER.

NOO... KILL... OR... BEEE... KILLED...

SO... LOOONG... AGO... WAASS... KIIINGG... MUU--MANNN... ETERRR--NI--TY... OF... PAAIIINN... TORRR--TURRRE...

... UNTILLL... ONLY... MONSSS--TERRR... RREE--MAAINNED...

WON'T... G-GO... BAAACK... KILLLL... OR... DIEEE...

"YOU HAVE DONE WELL, MY BEAUTIFUL ONE!"

LORD HERMES!

YES, DIANA. AND THIS SPINELESS WRETCH HAS SHOWN ME THE WAY TO METE OUT THE PROPER PENALTY TO THAT HOMICIDAL GROTESQUERY.

18

IXION! PREPARE TO RETURN TO THE INFERNO!

THESE SERPENTS SHALL FORM YOUR *NEW* CHAINS...

...WHICH NO MAN OR GOD SHALL EVER BREAK!

NOOOOOO!!...NO MORE!...KILL... ME...NOWW!!...NOOWW

NO, YOUR PAIN AND TORMENT ARE BUT *BEGINNING!*

LASHED ONCE AGAIN UPON THE GREAT WHEEL, YOUR SCREAMS WILL RESOUND FOR ALL *ETERNITY.*

BUT, MY LORD, TARTARUS HAS BEEN ABSORBED IN THE COSMIC MIGRATION.

WHERE WILL THE GREAT WHEEL BE PLACED?

YES, OLYMPIAN. TELL THE AMAZON *WHERE* IXION WILL BE IMPRISONED. TELL THE PATHETIC FOOL THAT ALL HER SISTERHOOD'S SACRIFICES HAVE BEEN FOR *NOTHING!*

"THAT THE ASSASSIN MUST BE PLACED BENEATH HER BELOVED PARADISE ISLAND..."

"MAKING OF IT A FORTRESS ONCE MORE!"

NO. DEAR GAEA, NO.

I'M SORRY, PRINCESS BUT IT IS ONLY UNTIL THE NEW OLYMPUS IS FORMED.

BUT... HOW LONG? WE'VE MADE SO MANY *PLANS.*

YOU FREED IXION! TH-THERE *MUST* BE SOME ALTERNATIVE!

PLEASE, DIANA, DO NOT BE ANGRY. REMEMBER THAT EVEN WE GODS ARE NOT INFALLIBLE.

YES, LORD HERMES. NEITHER ARE WE AMAZONS.

BUT FOR CENTURIES YOU HAVE TOLD US TO SUFFER FOR *OUR* SINS.

NOW YOU TELL US TO SUFFER FOR *YOURS.*

FORGIVE ME, LORD HERMES, BUT THAT IS *NOT* FAIR.

SUDDENLY, THE SHADE OF NIGHT RATTLES WITH THE ROAR OF JETS.

PACER TO SQUAD LEADER. I HAVE TARGET ON SCOPES. WILL FIRE ON COMMAND. OVER.

HOLD YOUR FIRE, PACER. THE TARGET SEEMS TO BE SECURED DOWN THERE. OVER.

19

BUT THEN, ABRUPTLY, THE IMPOSSIBLE HAPPENS.

KIIILLL!!! KIIILLL!!!

PLEEEEASSSE...

LORD HERMES, HE'S BROKEN FREE! HE'S HEADING TOWARD THOSE JETS!

WE MUST STOP...

NO, DIANA!

WHAT!?

YOU PRAYED FOR AN ALTERNATIVE, PRINCESS.

THE FATES HAVE PROVIDED YOU WITH ONE.

LOOK OUT! HE'S ATTACKING!

FIRE!!

AS IXION'S SCREAMS FILL THE NIGHT, DIANA IS A STATUE.

THOUGH EVERY FIBER OF HER BEING BEGS HER TO INTERCEDE, STILL SHE DOES NOT MOVE.

FOR THE SCREAMS ARE OF RELIEF, ALMOST GRATITUDE, AND THE THUNDER IS BUT THE TOLLING OF THE GREAT CLOCK.

MARKING THE END OF THE KILLING TIME.

CHIMING THE DEATH KNELL FOR EARTH'S FIRST MURDERER

IXION, ONCE KING, NOW NOT EVEN MAN...

...AFTER CENTURIES OF HELL...

...HAS, AT LAST, PAID HIS FINAL PENANCE.

"AND SO BOSTON'S NIGHT OF TERROR IS OVER. THE GIANT CREATURE CRUMBLED INTO DUST SOON AFTER THESE PICTURES WERE TAKEN. ALREADY THE TIDE IS DRAGGING THE REMAINS INTO THE SEA.

"AS IF TRYING FUTILELY TO WASH AWAY THE NIGHTMARISH MEMORIES."

IN THE CITY, THE GRISLY JOB OF CARTING OFF THE DEAD CONTINUES. WITNESSES DESCRIBED THE SCENE AS THE REFUSE FROM A SLAUGHTERHOUSE. DEATHS ARE ESTIMATED IN THE HUNDREDS.

ONLY WONDER WOMAN'S EXPULSION OF THE MONSTER PREVENTED MORE DISASTER.

AT LEAST WE CAN BE GRATEFUL FOR THAT.

AN APB IS OUT TO FIND THE MAN WHO CALLED HIMSELF LORD HERMES, LAST SEEN CARRYING OFF THE ALLEGED MASTERMIND OF THIS TERRIBLE, HORRIBLE INCIDENT.

MOM, DO YOU THINK DIANA'S OKAY?

I'M FINE, NESSIE. IN BODY AT LEAST.

DIANA! YOU CAME BACK! WHERE'S HERMES?

I DON'T REALLY KNOW... I...

BABY, CAN I SPEAK WITH DIANA ALONE FOR A MOMENT?

HUH? OH, SURE, UM... I'LL BE UPSTAIRS.

JULIA, I'M SORRY. I SHOULD NEVER HAVE PLACED YOU IN SUCH A CONFRONTATIONAL POSITION AGAINST HERMES...

DIANA...

SWEETIE, YOU DON'T HAVE TO...

YES, I DO.

I KNEW HE WAS WRONG, YET I LET MY REVERENCE FOR HIM CLOUD MY JUDGMENT.

THOUGH MY EVERY INSTINCT TOLD ME YOU WERE RIGHT, I COULDN'T GO AGAINST THE WILL OF MY GOD.

CONSIDERING HOW OBDURATELY I ADVOCATED MY STANCE, I CAN'T SAY I BLAMED YOU.

JULIA, PLEASE, IF I'VE MADE YOU ANGRY...

NO, SWEETIE, IT WASN'T YOU. IN A WAY IT WASN'T EVEN HERMES.

IT WAS SOMETHING ELSE, WHICH UNFORTUNATELY EXACERBATED AN ALREADY TENSE SITUATION.

I GUESS NONE OF YOU AMAZONS, BEING BLESSED WITH AN EVERLASTING NONAGE, HAVE EVER EXPERIENCED MENOPAUSE.

(21)

MENOPAUSE. I'VE *READ* ABOUT THAT.

SO HAVE I. BUT IT'S DIFFERENT TO GO *THROUGH* IT.

IT'S LIKE THE FLIP SIDE OF PUBERTY, AN INESCAPABLE PART OF GROWING OLDER. ONE OF THE STRANGE PERKS TO BEING A WOMAN.

A *MORTAL* WOMAN ANYWAY.

DIANA, I'M THE ONE WHO'S SORRY FOR MY SUDDEN, CHURLISHNESS TOWARD YOU AND HERMES.

I'M AFRAID YOU WERE CAUGHT IN THE AFTERBURN OF A NASTY HOT FLASH.

YOU'D THINK THAT A WOMAN OF MY EDUCATIONAL BACKGROUND COULD HAVE AT LEAST *SURMISED* WHAT WAS MAKING ME SO DARN...WELL... CRANKY.

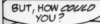

BUT, HOW *COULD* YOU?

SINCE MEETING ME, YOUR LIFE HAS BEEN A MAELSTROM -- AN EXISTENCE WHICH WOULD HAVE QUASHED THE SPIRIT OF A LESSER BEING.

AFTER ALL THAT HAS HAPPENED MAYBE I *SHOULD* LEAVE...

YOU DO AND I'LL HOGTIE YOU WITH YOUR OWN LASSO!

I'M NOT MAKING THE SAME MISTAKE TWICE.

"BUT, JULIA, AFTER LAST NIGHT, THINGS ARE GOING TO GET *MUCH ROUGHER.*"

"THEN WE'LL WEATHER IT *TOGETHER.* AS WE ALWAYS HAVE."

"NOW THEN, IS HERMES ALL RIGHT?"

"I SUPPOSE SO. HE WENT TO DISPOSE OF PHOBOS."

"BUT, HE SHOULD HAVE RETURNED BY NOW. I PRAY NOTHING *ELSE* HAS GONE WRONG."

"DIANA, HE'S GOING TO NEED TIME. HE'S PROBABLY SUFFERING FROM GREAT SHAME AND GUILT ABOUT WHAT HAPPENED LAST NIGHT."

"AND I *ADDED* TO HIS MISERY. DEAR ATHENA, I SHOULD NOT HAVE SCOLDED HIM SO. I-I WAS JUST SO UPSET."

"YOU SCOLDED HERMES? THAT MUST HAVE DEVASTATED HIM."

"HE LOOKED AS IF I HAD PLUNGED A DAGGER INTO HIS HEART."

"I CAN IMAGINE. I SEE HOW HE LOOKS AT YOU."

"NO! OUR RELATIONSHIP IS NOT LIKE THAT AT ALL."

"ARE YOU SURE HERMES KNOWS THAT?"

"HE MUST! H-HE'S A GOD."

"YES, SWEETHEART, BUT REMEMBER:

"EVEN A GOD CAN BE ALL TOO HUMAN."

Preliminary art for an unused T-shirt design.

GALLERY

Left: Wonder Woman art from a
JLA POSTCARD set by Pérez.
Color by Tom Smith.

Right: This art was created by Pérez specifically
for the 50th Anniversary celebration
of Wonder Woman in 1990.
Color by Tom Smith.

Five years before Pérez launched a new series starring the Amazing Amazon,
he illustrated this pinup for WONDER WOMAN (first series) #300. Color by Tom Smith.

This pinup by Pérez was the opening image of the WONDER WOMAN GALLERY (1996). Color by Tatjana Wood.

Pérez supplied this cover image for WONDER WOMAN #120, celebrating the tenth year of her relaunched series.

Pérez illustrated the "Wonder Woman: Avatar of Truth" art originally seen in the VS. System trading card game (Upper Deck Entertainment).

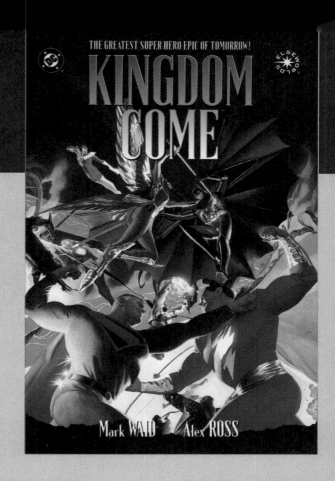